Laurence Donovan

The Official Florida Bicentennial Commemorative Book is published by
Florida Bicentennial Commemorative Journal, Inc., a subsidiary of Worth
International Communications Corporation, 1800 North 20th Avenue, Post
Office Box 2226, Hollywood, Florida 33022, under the exclusive authori-
zation granted by the Bicentennial Commission of Florida.

BORN OF THE SUN

Editors: Joan E. Gill
Beth R. Read

The Official Florida Bicentennial Commemorative Book

BORN OF THE SUN

Indian effigy of Florida panther.

VALIDATION

Major manuscripts have been approved for publication by Dr. Charlton W. Tebeau, acknowledged dean of Florida historians. Dr. Tebeau is the author of *History of Florida.* The Editors wish to thank him for his efforts and additions, and for his ability to appreciate the difference between materials written for academicians and those written for a popular readership.

The Editors also acknowledge the time spent by Dr. Samuel Proctor who read the major manuscripts but is not responsible for the content of the book. We thank him for his scholarly comments many of which it was impossible to incorporate because of the nature of the book.

An effort has been made to reach an agreement on facts that can be substantiated; however, numerous areas are open to differing interpretations even among the experts.

Occasionally literary license has been used to spark an interest in the Florida heritage. The camera eye and impressions of many artists and writers have broadened the scope of the book.

In compiling *Born of the Sun,* it became evident that history and folklore are inseparably bound together in the Florida experience.

BORN OF THE SUN

I think continually of those who were truly great.
Who, from the womb, remembered the soul's history
Through corridors of light where the hours are suns,
Endless and singing. . .

The names of those who in their lives fought for life,
Who wore at their hearts the fire's centre.
Born of the sun, they travelled a short while toward the sun
And left the vivid air signed with their honour.

–Stephen Spender

7

A SPECIAL PLACE TO CELEBRATE

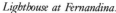

Solar Flares

Old Spanish Coin

Lighthouse at Fernandina.

We glided through the open drawbridge at Marathon and headed for the open sea, leaving behind the incomparable Florida Keys and a dazzling setting sun. As our ketch coasted on the evening breeze, I recalled the intrepid explorers who had sailed these Florida waters centuries before: men like Ponce de León, whose frail, high-pooped caravel arrived in 1513, and Hernando de Soto, who landed on the Florida West Coast seeking treasure.

Suddenly, the eerie wail of a distant whistle ended my reverie. The low-lying shore had almost vanished in the dusk and a railroad train seemed to creep across the watery horizon, smoke belching from its stack, passenger cars cheerily aglow. That was the spring of 1934.

A year later, the Flager railway that had helped open the Florida frontier was gone from the Keys, wiped out by a hurricane that took more than 400 lives. But in my memory, that odd vision of the Florida iron horse survives, a sobering reminder that much of the Sunshine State still remains a frontier—and a vulnerable one. Whether my grandchildren and yours will enjoy that frontier depends upon how swiftly man acts to preserve it. And Florida must be preserved. This great state has been my family's winter home for more than 50 years; and each time I return, after travels that often take me to far-away places, I am struck by the uniqueness of Florida. No place on earth is quite the same, and *Born of the Sun* captures it all.

I was thirteen when I first stepped back into Florida history. The year was 1915 and my parents had taken me to St. Augustine, oldest continuous European settlement in the United States. I prowled through the Castillo de San Marcos and imagined myself commanding the cannon of the great fortress against the New World enemies of Spain. Later, I toured the historic city in a horse-drawn surrey and thrilled at the sight of a man wrestling an alligator.

Alligators were plentiful then, but over the years hunters decimated them. Now vigorous enforcement of wildlife protection laws has helped Florida 'gators stage a comeback. Other threatened species in Florida, protected by law, also are beginning to thrive again—the American bald eagle, the brown pelican, and numerous wading birds once hunted nearly to extinction for their plumes.

Other measures will not only protect threatened species, but land and water resources as well, including vital sub-surface fresh water, environmentally endangered areas and land needed for recreation. These

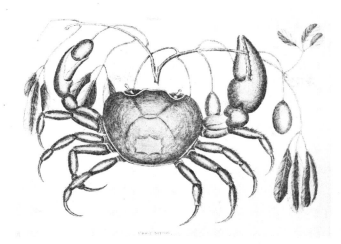

Land crab drawn by
Mark Catesby in the 1730s.

Sun shines through coconut palms now
on the endangered list.

measures will help ensure the survival of areas like the Big Cypress, the sprawling Everglades, and Payne's Prairie.

I know from experience, both personal and professional, how priceless—and how fragile—the ecological balance of Florida is, and how vitally important it is to maintain it. For years, the National Geographic Society has supported conservation, ecological research, and other research projects basic to our understanding of the Earth. Many of these projects focused on Florida. I watched the development of Fairchild Tropical Garden by the late David Fairchild, my uncle and Coconut Grove neighbor. I joined this great botanist and plant explorer in his travels many years ago as he sought exotic plant specimens for his now-famous botanical paradise—a most spectacular sight on Biscayne Bay. The Society helped in studies by the University of Miami of Gulf Stream zoo-plankton, coral reefs, shrimp, squid, and pelagic fishes, and also supported research at other universities in the state including the University of Florida, Florida State University, and the University of South Florida.

Florida to me is more than research projects: it is home. From our house overlooking Biscayne Bay, I have long watched Florida wrestle with the problems of progress. I have seen fish die as pollution tainted the waters of the bay. Before my family even came to the Grove, the roseate spoonbill clattered its beak as it foraged on coral flats where our house was to be built. We don't hear the spoonbill in the Grove anymore—it has been pushed out. But these beautiful birds are safe now in several sanctuaries around the state.

I can celebrate the survival of the spoonbills, and more. Antipollution laws are cleaning up the bay and anglers again catch fish a stone's throw from our home. And while I expect never to hear the spoonbill's clatter from my backyard, another erstwhile native has returned to our neighborhood: the land crab. These strange and comical creatures once swarmed over local roads, sometimes causing auto accidents; then they,too seemed to disappear. Now they're back, perhaps a nuisance to our lawns, but a welcome sign, I believe, that the balance of nature is being restored.

That's something for each of us to celebrate. I invite all thoughtful Americans to put *Born of the Sun* at the top of their Bicentennial reading lists—it's an exciting story.

–MELVILLE BELL GROSVENOR, LL.D., Sc.D., Litt.D.
EDITOR-IN-CHIEF AND CHAIRMAN OF THE BOARD
NATIONAL GEOGRAPHIC SOCIETY

Florida Panther

Limes, Capsicum, Mammy.

Artistry of early Floridians is revealed by carved wooden masks unearthed at Key Marco.

A REGION APART / A LAND IN TRUST

Weeden Island Ceremonial Vessel found in the Bush Mound, Okaloosa County, dates from 1000 A.D. and probably was used to hold the ashes of a chief or religious leader. Artifacts with similar style and paints have been found in Central and South America and Mexico.

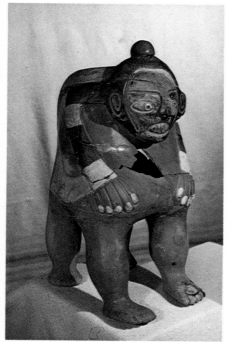

Florida was one of the first of the lands discovered in the New World. John Cabot is said to have sighted the Cape of Florida in 1497. Ponce de León claimed Florida for Spain in 1513 and named the new land more than one hundred years before the Pilgrims arrived at Plymouth Rock. The first permanent and oldest continuous European settlement was established in St. Augustine in 1565 and a short-lived community at Pensacola was established in 1559. There are many firsts for Florida. Florida, however, was not one of the first to join the United States. It was foreign territory until 1821 and its delayed allegiance to the stars and stripes is obvious by the record of five national flags to which it has pledged allegiance. It remained a territory until 1845 when it became the twenty-seventh state of the Union.

Born of the Sun is not a history book. It is a book that takes a look at what Florida is like and what it meant to be a Floridian at significant times in the past, what it means today, and what it may mean in the future. *Born of the Sun* holds a mirror to the complexities and uniqueness and the commonalities that are bound together in the word symbols, Florida and Floridians.

When the decision was made to compile the book according to the American Revolution Bicentennial Administration themes of Heritage, Festival, and Horizons, the editors departed from tradition. A changed focal length led to the discovery that Florida history could best be viewed as a flowing pageant of ideas and happenings in which the past, present, and future are alive with human interest. Impressions of artists and writers are interwoven to tell the living Florida experience.

In a search for facts and flavor, the editors have gone to scholars and folklorists, to archivists and private collectors, for written and graphic materials. Journeys around the state and beyond produced a combination of talent. The distinguished list of contributors includes best-selling authors as well as scholars whose work has never seen popular publication. All

Wood engraving of a March day in St. Augustine during the 1880s.

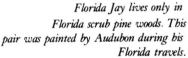

Florida Jay lives only in Florida scrub pine woods. This pair was painted by Audubon during his Florida travels.

liked the idea of writing, in this instance, for a broad audience, sharing their years of study and experience and their interpretations of their favorite subjects with other Floridians, young and old. Some of the writers contacted each other, exchanging ideas and dovetailing chapters. Others sustained a continuing conversation with the editors as the book progressed.

The search for unusual and appropriate illustrations to be used as an integral part of the whole story of the Florida experience led into Florida archives, national archives, British archives, public and private collections, small and large. Treasures were found in the most surprising places. Remarkably, the extensive heritage of Florida is just now being discovered.

Old theories are being challenged by new evidence. New concepts are being advanced. Did the early peoples and cultures of Florida come across the waters from Central and South America, rather than down the continent from the Midwest? Did the introduction of corn into Florida and then into the Midwest follow this route? Founding father Benjamin Franklin was an early researcher into the mysteries of the Gulf Stream, and Paul Revere emerges as engraver of the map of Florida by Bernard Romans. Does the myth of Pocahontas have its origins in Florida? What is it about the "land of flowers" that inspires artistic creativity, as it did for Coleridge and Stephen Foster, Frederic Delius, LeMoyne, Audubon, Catesby, St. Gaudens, Marjorie Kinnan Rawlings, and Ernest Hemingway? What is it about Florida that makes it a region apart and a land that must be held in trust?

The reader will find *Born of the Sun* filled with information and entertainment, flavored with the unexpected because the Florida heritage is a rich mixture of interwoven fact and lore.

Enjoy *Born of the Sun*. It is full of surprises.

—JOAN E. GILL
—BETH R. READ

Mr. SAMUEL ADAMS.

The Honble. JOHN HANCOCK. Efqr.

1776 IN FLORIDA

During the feverish days of battles and debate when the founding fathers framed and approved the Declaration of Independence, Floridians were flying the British flag and sending and receiving packets and greetings from the Crown.

Far removed from the thunderous tumult to the northeast, unaware or unmoved by the violations of freedoms and the curbs on trade, the leaders, merchants and others in the region of St. Augustine and Pensacola continued on about their business and pleasure. They worried about their crops, about the Indians, and about their shipments, but worried little about their rights. In the public square in St. Augustine, they hung Sam Adams and John Hancock in effigy and drank to the health of King George III. They celebrated their role as a sanctuary for loyalists and St. Augustine remained a peaceful city that today is recognized as the oldest continuing settlement in the United States.

The year 1776 was not a time when Floridians were angry. They did not feel that they had been overtaxed. Protest seemed inappropriate and rioting against British authority was treason. St. Augustine, the capital of East Florida, was a somewhat comfortable community in which to live and work, one of the small pockets of culture and comfort in the vast wilderness of Colonial America. Pensacola was being expanded and developed as the capital of West Florida according to a British town plan. The main concern of the people of Florida for many years had been one of allegiance, as the territory was busily bought, sold, and traded amongst the various nations maneuvering for strength in the New World.

When the Revolution was over, the Floridas again changed hands, and allegiance. The Spanish flag once more flew above the small settlements. British loyalists moved out and new Spanish colonists arrived at a time when the old colonies to the north were trying a new independence. It was the middle of the next century before Floridians would become part of the United States.

—J.E.G. / B.R.R.

FLORIDIANS TOAST KING GEORGE III

GEORGE the III KING of GREAT BRITAIN.&

July 4, 1776: earnest delegates of the Second Continental Congress adopted the Declaration of Independence in Philadelphia, denounced the tyrannical rule of George III and Parliament, and signified the birth of a new republic with celebrations and bonfires.

July 20, 1776: The news reached Florida, coming down by packet boat. There were no celebrations and bonfires except the burning in effigy of Sam Adams. Floridians accepted the authority of Parliament; they prayed for and toasted the health of George III probably with more fervor after 1776 than ever.

There were thirty British colonies in the Western Hemisphere, including Canada, the two Floridas, and the British West Indies. The royal colonies of East and West Florida joined those who upheld British authority and institutions. The loyalty of Florida had been apparent long before 1776. Stamps had been sold and controversial customs duties collected without violence during the past 10 years; had the shipment of tea for Florida not been stopped in Charleston, it doubtless would have been sold without protest; and Floridians had refused to send delegates to any Stamp Act Congress or Continental Congress.

To understand why they did not join the rebellion, look closely at the Floridians of 1776 to see who they were and where they lived. There were, of course, two Floridas: St. Augustine was the capital of British East Florida with a western boundary at the Apalachicola River. Pensacola was the capital of British West Florida, its western limits extended to the Mississippi River and its territory included the communities of Baton Rouge and Natchez. These Floridas contained a mixed population of widely varying religions, colors, and languages.

For the most part, English-speaking whites comprised the upper class. They had emigrated from Georgia, South Carolina, England, and Scotland. Whether on the St. Marys River bordering Georgia, in the capitals at St. Augustine and Pensacola, or in remote Natchez, the Scottish burr and tartan plaid were close at hand. For a variety of reasons, primarily economic, numerous McIntoshs, Grants, Campbells, and McGillivrays served as governors, merchants, ministers, indentured servants, and Indian traders. Acquiring thousands of acres, ambitious Englishmen and Ameri-

British redcoats seem right and proper in the streets of St. Augustine as British Florida of 1776 is recreated for 1976.

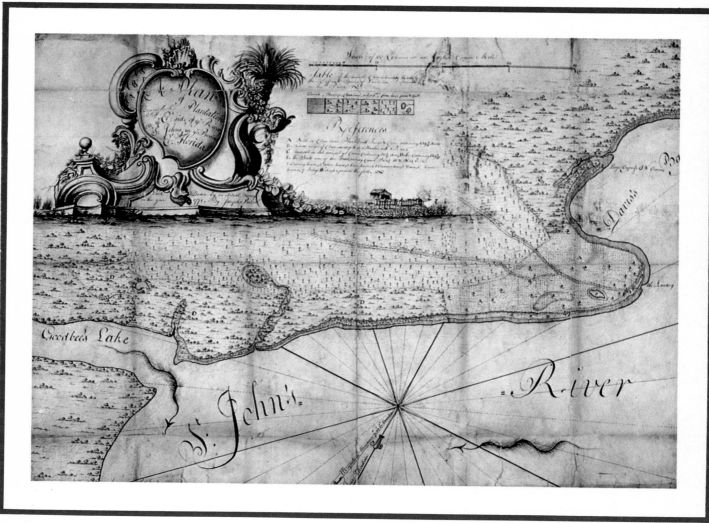

Old British map dated 1771 details the St.
Johns River valley, the scene of early settlement
and trade.

Casa Sanchez
St. Augustine

cans also moved into Florida. Scion of a distinguished South Carolina family, John Moultrie settled by the Matanzas River below St. Augustine and built a plantation house, Bella Vista, which, along with assorted outbuildings, readily accommodated his family and his many slaves. As a matter of fact, Bella Vista has one hundred rooms!

White Catholics, probably as numerous as Protestants, were concentrated in two areas. Almost one thousand Minorcans lived at New Smyrna, which was seventy miles south of St. Augustine in East Florida's most populous community outside the capital. Still dressing in their colorful Mediterranean clothes, these poor "Minorcans," in fact, came from Greece and Sicily as well as Minorca. Greek, Sicilian, Catalan, English, and a unique pidgin language might be heard in the rice and indigo fields and palmetto thatched huts of New Smyrna. Father Pedro Camps, the conscientious Catholic priest from Minorca, ministered to his parishioners for whom the American dream was yet to be realized. West Florida Catholics were Frenchmen. Living near Mobile, Lake Pontchartrain, and Natchez, they formerly had been part of French Louisiana. They remained on their lands after 1763 and were joined by new French immigrants brought into West Florida by British promoters. The French language, church, creole architecture, and style of cooking persisted in British West Florida.

It is easy to overlook the fact that whites comprised only a minority of the population. The Floridas were like Georgia and South Carolina; Blacks almost equalled or outnumbered whites. Blacks tilled rice and indigo fields, felled trees, cut barrel staves, constructed houses, served as blacksmiths, butchers, and in a variety of trades. Rarely a ship called at St. Augustine or Pensacola that did not have some, and often a large number of, Black crewmen aboard. Largely due to Black slave labor, the Floridas enjoyed a measure of prosperity in 1776. Blacks worked on plantations along the St. Johns and St. Marys Rivers in East Florida and on the Escambia and Mississippi Rivers in West Florida; they stayed in St. Augustine and Pensacola in the same houses as the whites or in cabins outside town; and they lived in Indian villages and in separate communities either as slaves or as free "black Indians."

British soldier.

Another group of Floridians were red, and they too probably outnumbered whites in 1776. Like the Blacks, the Indians or Native Americans were scattered throughout Florida. Lower Creeks and Seminoles (a name that had come into use only a few years before the Revolution) were concentrated in the Gainesville and Tallahassee areas. Several hundred lived close by St. Augustine. Lower Creeks and Choctaws made up the major tribes in West Florida. These Indians were farmers and lived in permanent villages, although hunting parties ranged many miles for deerskins which they brought to trading posts on the St. Johns River and to warehouses at Pensacola and Mobile. Indians dressed in either the European or the native fashion. Some lived in cabins hardly distinguishable from those of white frontiersmen, and many adopted coats, linen shirts, saddles—and vices—of the whites. Often mixed-bloods, chiefs spoke not only English but several Indian languages, and they perhaps owned slaves to till their fields. In some instances Indian chiefs were more literate than the newly-arrived British immigrants. Floridians in 1776 did not have to read in the Old Testament about the Tower of Babel: it was right at hand. One might hear snatches of Greek, Sicilian, Catalan, Spanish, Fanti, Fulani, Mandingo, Gaelic, French, German, Muskogee, Choctaw, Hitchiti, in addition to assorted English dialects.

As was typical for almost any frontier community, women were scarce in British Florida. Some of them ran shops, taverns, and inns, and served as midwives and domestic servants. Widows usually had the chance to remarry immediately. Mary Peavett's second husband had barely been laid to rest in St. Augustine before she took on another half her age. Soldiers, Indian traders, and civil officials frequently were not married or did not bring their wives to Florida. High ranking officers, and in one instance the governor, imported mistresses or someone else's wife into Florida. Hundreds of sailors called annually at the ports of St. Augustine and Pensacola, and mariners spent part of their shore leave in local brothels.

The confusion of languages in Florida in 1776 sounded like the Biblical Tower of Babel. Escher woodcut, Tower of Babel, shows construction of the building at a standstill because black and white workers, lacking a common language, are unable to understand each other.

When the Revolution broke out, Floridians were branded as "Tories." A number of reasons explain this loyalty. The two new frontier provinces had been under British rule for only twelve years. Monies raised by the Stamp Act and other types of taxation by Parliament had been spent generously in the Floridas. Powerful in other colonies, representative government was weak or non-existent in the Floridas. With large Black and Indian populations and an exposed coastline, the white ruling class in Florida wanted and needed military and naval protection from the mother country. In sharp contrast to Boston and New York, redcoats were

*Florida has often been referred to as the Garden
of Eden, a paradise, an idyllic place on earth.
This myth began hundreds of years ago and
recently believers reinforced it. Now it is
suggested that not only was the Garden of Eden
in north Florida but also Noah's Ark was built
in Wakulla County. After all, where else in
the world grows a gopherwood forest?*

*The Garden of Eden, seen through the eyes of
Currier and Ives, has a different look to those
who claim its location along the banks of the
Apalachicola River. The Torreya or gopherwood tree, mentioned in the Bible, grows here
for all who care to come and see. Although
others may claim another part of Florida for
their Garden of Eden, the Torreya that grows
here grows nowhere else in the world.*

welcomed at Pensacola and St. Augustine. Soldiers, civil authorities, Anglican clergymen, and even merchants were paid directly or indirectly by Britain and it was to their advantage not to break away from the mother country.

Three times before the end of 1778 American Whigs invaded East Florida but never reached St. Augustine. After 1779 when she entered the war, Spain began to take over all of West Florida. Baton Rouge was captured in 1779. Pensacola fell in May, 1781 in the largest battle ever fought in Florida. But for long periods during the Revolutionary War—almost ten years for those living near St. Augustine—Floridians went about their usual tasks. They continued to export rice, indigo, naval stores, barrel staves, deerskins, and oranges cut up and preserved in kegs of West Indian rum. Merchants and artisans did a thriving business attending to the needs of soldiers, sailors enjoying shore leave, and Tory refugees, and owners of inns, public houses, billiard parlors, and skittle alleys prospered.

Pensacola and St. Augustine residents might visit the market and purchase hot bread, freshly slaughtered meat, a variety of fish, vegetables, cakes, and pastries. Rushing about town on an errand one might brush against a newly-arrived angry loyalist refugee, an Indian, or even a pig or cow. With fish rotting on the beach at low tide, butcher's abattoirs located just outside town, privies scattered about, and horses a primary means of communication, there was reason for thanks when a springtime breeze wafted the scent of orange blossoms through a window with wooden shutters open wide.

The British Floridas were at once a Garden of Eden and raw, brutal frontier colonies. Proportionally soldiers were probably more numerous in the Floridas than in any other British American colony. The army—and civilians and sailors as well—had its full share of cutthroats, thieves, and degenerates. For breaches of discipline soldiers were lashed to a cannon and suffered fifty to five hundred lashes. After building their coffins, more serious offenders were shot.

Minorcans, French, and British indentured servants and Black slaves endured a harsh life. Backbreaking labor in clearing fields and cutting timber, ruthless overseers and masters, primitive shelter, diseases, and wartime dislocations all contributed to a high death rate. Yet even the most oppressed field hand or depraved soldier might look up and see the sun shining through live oaks draped with Spanish moss, watch a great blue heron or brown pelican gracefully fly by, hear the roar and thrashings of hundreds of alligators in the distance, and in the early morning discover deer bounding through a savannah still dotted with patches of fog.

Pensacola and St. Augustine, farther removed from the frontier, offered a more pleasant life. Bath houses, billiard parlors, plays staged by officers in the garrison, shops vending hardware, clothing, tobacco, silverware, and books, and even bawdy houses made life more bearable. One could count on the Scots to turn out in force whenever the Saint Andrews Society organized a dinner or party. After a hard day, off-duty soldiers, sailors, and artisans might drop by a tavern and, while gossiping and reading an imported newspaper, down a tankard or two of Jamaica rum, beer, or cider. Balls put on by the governor and merchants, promenades alongside the bay, and formal debates in the council chamber helped bridge the gap between St. Augustine and London. Even at some of the new country homes, like Lt. Governor Moultrie's imposing Bella Vista outside St. Augustine, one might stand by the formal garden, close his eyes, almost hear the foxes and hounds in the distance, and imagine himself an English squire.

After the outbreak of the Revolution the military character of the Floridas became even more pronounced. English soldiers with heavy Brown Bess muskets, red woolen coats, and freshly tarred black gaiters, kilted Scotsmen, bitter Tory refugees organized into provincial units, German mercenaries, armed Black slaves, and painted Indians with new muskets and knives grew more numerous. Along with hundreds of sailors ashore, they discouraged any Floridian who might be tempted to speak up for George Washington and the Continental Congress. American Whigs never succeeded in liberating the Floridas. Spain captured all of West Florida by 1781, but only secured East Florida through the 1783 peace settlement. Upon hearing about the forthcoming cession of the provinces, East Floridians were aghast because they had truly won the war and lost the peace. They had no choice, however, but to leave or subject themselves to Spanish rule.

Although British rule in Florida was short lived, one cannot so easily dismiss the British regime. Part of the British Florida mixed population—Minorcans, Englishmen, Scots, Blacks, and Frenchmen——remained. They and their descendants would later play an important role in the economic, political, and social life of Florida. The blood of Tories and their offspring was shed on both sides in the Seminole wars. In time, Revolutionary Tories and their progeny accommodated themselves to republicanism. Along with the numerous Americans who arrived in Florida after 1821, they helped stamp the characteristics and traditions of modern Florida.

—J. LEITCH WRIGHT

The Mysterious Map of Paul Revere

Paul Revere was a remarkable man with a Florida connection. In Boston he recorded events like the famous Bloody Massacre; he was well-known for his midnight ride, heralded as a marvelous engraver, gold- and silver-smith of Colonial days, the creator of great domes, and a maker of bells that still ring out in New England steeples.

But how many Floridians or Americans know that Paul Revere engraved the maps for Bernard Roman's *Concise Natural History of East and West Florida in* 1775? Interestingly enough, Romans himself referred to the production of the enormous maps in 1775 as "a struggle with 'the art and mystery' of printing from copper plates," according to Clarence S. Brigham who wrote about the Paul Revere engravings. Romans might have had a kind of vision because during July, 1975, it appeared that a new mystery relates to these maps: some of which have disappeared from the Public Record Office in London, with nary a clue. One complete copy is said to be safe at the Library of Congress but elsewhere there remain only partial pieces of this large work.

Of course, Paul Revere, as a Mason was at home with the mysteries.

Bloody Massacre.

17

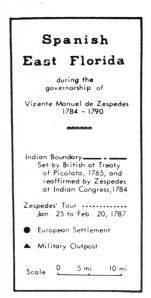

Spanish East Florida

during the
governorship of

Vizente Manuel de Zespedes
1784 - 1790

Indian Boundary———·——
Set by British at Treaty
of Picolata, 1765, and
reaffirmed by Zespedes
at Indian Congress,1784

Zespedes' Tour ············
Jan. 25 to Feb. 20, 1787

● European Settlement

▲ Military Outpost

Scale 0   5 mi   10 mi

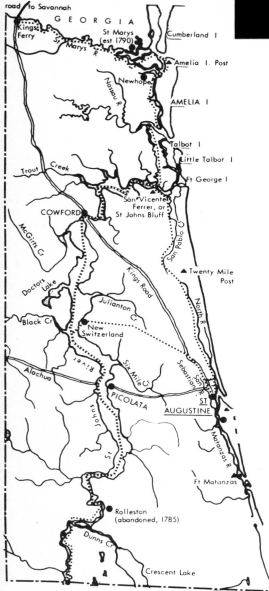

FLORIDIANS TOAST A SPANISH KING

THE 1789 SAINT AUGUSTINE CELEBRATION

Famous mild Florida winter weather graced Saint Augustine on the afternoon of December 2, 1789, when the stage was set for local observance of Charles IV's ascent to the Spanish throne. Doorways and balconies throughout the town were brightened with hangings, flags, flowers and greenery, or whatever the inhabitants could contrive in the way of decoration. The first event took place in front of the government buildings, the combination of residences, offices, storerooms, stables and lesser buildings enclosed in a large block between the rear defense line of the town and the plaza. The governor's residence faced one end of the oblong "Plaza de Armas" extending three blocks east to the wharf on the Matanzas river. Wooden balconies of the residence were draped with yards of scarlet silks. Outside the residence, against the wall facing the plaza, stood a canopy of crimson damask with plain satin drapes at the side and white taffeta curtains across the front. The canopy rested on a small carpeted platform with steps descending toward the plaza. Within this throne-like enclosure rested the portraits of Charles IV and his Italian-born queen, Maria Louisa of Parma. The honor of standing guard beside the royal portraits was assigned to the grenadiers, élite corps of the Third Battalion of Cuba.

Stationed at the four corners of the plaza were pickets of infantrymen. A small artillery squad occupied the side of the plaza toward the river, near the buildings serving as guard house, butchering area and farmers' market. In the center of the plaza, carpenters had erected a large square platform, with thick rugs spread over the floor and the steps along one side. The balustrades on the other three sides were decorated with ornamental tapestries.

About the middle of the afternoon, top-ranking military officers, leading officials of the finance and supply division, and a few prominent citizens assembled before the governor's residence. All were on horseback. Promptly at four o'clock Governor Zéspedes appeared, sword at his side, mounted on a horse with richly ornamented trappings. The governor was

Charles IV, the King of Spain, was toasted by the colonists in St. Augustine when he ascended to the throne. In the painting, he is pictured with the Royal family in a formal portrait by Goya.

wearing the bright red uniform of the Havana regiment, decorated with the gold emblems signifying his rank as brigadier of the royal armies of Spain. Accompanied by the waiting escort, the governor first paraded around the tree-bordered *Plaza de Armas*, returning to the official buildings in time to greet Lieutenant Zéspedes as he rode through the gates on a gaily caparisoned steed, accompanied by Colonel Morales and Captain Saavedra, the two officers acting as *reyes de armas* for this occasion. Now the escorting band formed a double file as the procession marched down the center toward the local parish church, located in the upper floor of a building on the south side of the plaza. Leading the procession were the first and second adjutants of the military staff, followed by the governor and his son who was bearing the royal ensign, and behind them came the *reyes de armas*. At the doors of the church building, the entire group dismounted and accompanied the royal ensign into the body of the church where it was consecrated in a brief ceremony.

The religious service was in charge of the vicar and ecclesiastical judge, Father Thomas Hassett, an Irish priest trained in Salamanca, who had administered two Negro schools in Philadelphia during the American Revolution before coming to Saint Augustine in 1784. He was assisted by other priests in the community: assistant presbyter Father Miguel O'Reilly, Irish troop chaplain who was a veteran of service in the Caribbean islands; Father Francisco Traconis, Havana-born hospital chaplain and primary school teacher; and Father Pedro Camps, frail and dedicated Minorcan missionary who had accompanied his countrymen to the New Smyrna colony in 1768.

When the religious ceremony was over, the men in the procession again mounted their horses for the short ride from the church to the platform in the center of the plaza. By this time the crowd of onlookers had grown to sizable proportions. The governor and his son and the *reyes de armas* alighted by the steps leading up to the platform. The assembly was called to order by

Old St. Augustine

"Architecturally, it is a storehouse of interesting detail. Historically, it makes us aware of our ties with Europe and gives us a sense of the continuity of our living history.

It was an established town fifty-five years before the Pilgrims landed on Plymouth Rock and forty-two years before the English settled Jamestown. By the time of the American Revolution it was 210 years old." —CORNELIUS VANDERBILT, JR.
The Living Past of America

The Last Conqueror

Pedro Menéndez de Avilés, the founder, in 1545, of St. Augustine, was undoubtedly the last *conquistador*, the last conqueror. By the time he was grown, from a boyhood spent fighting French pirates in the Bay of Biscay, the Spanish empire in the New World had all been discovered, conquered, and rapidly bureaucratized under the rigid rules imposed by the King. The Casa de Contratación, or Chamber of Commerce, controlled all industry with a mass of red tape in the hands of officials. There was no more room for swash-buckling, nothing left to be taken over and governed, except that still mythical shape of Florida north of the Caribbean.

Florida was known, after the expedition of Hernando de Soto, to contain no gold but that taken from Spanish shipwrecks, no jewels but some collections of fresh water pearls in Apalachee, and an unending series of hostile Indian villages. Spanish ships and people were ravaged by the Indians, and the French had established forts on the Atlantic coast, even in Florida. The King of Spain knew that something must be done to make Florida a true outpost of Spain. He needed a man who in daring and courage would be the equal of Cortez and Balboa and all those other *Conquistadors* of the great days of the conquests. The king found him in the prison of the Casa de Contratación in Seville, under charges of smuggling. He was Pedro Menéndez. Immediately released and set up as Captain General of a fleet and Adelantado, he was sent to drive the French out of Florida from their new Fort Caroline on the St. Johns River. He was sent to make Florida safe—safe for the treasure fleets that sailed up the coast and home to Spain, and safe for officials, soldiers, and colonists.

The story of Menéndez storming Fort Caroline and killing all the Frenchmen, especially their leader, Ribault, and the others who had escaped from the fort, is well-known. What has been forgotten is that he became the first Governor of Florida to be captured by the charm of the long strange flat land, and to love it. —M.S.D.

the sonorous intonation of the *reyes de armas* who announced: "Silence, hear, listen, attention!" At this moment, Lieutenant Zéspedes raised the royal ensign and led the crowd in three cheers for "Castile!" while the portraits of the new monarchs were unveiled. Simultaneously the air was shaken by the discharge of the field pieces mounted at the end of the plaza, salutes from government and private ships in the harbor, the roll of drums by the infantrymen, pealing of church bells, and a triple salvo from the artillery in the Castillo de San Marcos. In the midst of this joyous din, Governor Zéspedes flung into the crowd the silver medals commemorating the great occasion.

While the wave of excitement continued, the leading officials descended the steps from the platform, mounted their horses and took their places for a grand parade around the town. The procession line lengthened with the addition of a contingent of dragoons and the four infantry pickets previously posted at the corners of the plaza. Marching in time to a band playing martial music, the parade headed down Saint George Street to the barracks located at the southern end of the residential district. Halting at the Saint Francis barracks, for a second time they shouted *vivas* for the new monarchs to the accompaniment of artillery fire. From this point, the parade turned toward the river, followed Marine Street back toward the plaza, then continued along San Carlos Street to the Castillo de San Marcos. On the grassy embankments outside, to the sound of cannon in the fortress, the acclamations of the king resounded for the third and final time. Again in motion, the procession passed beside the old line of fortification extending from the Castillo to the drawbridge and city gates, and returned along Hornabeque Street to the governor's residence. At the conclusion of the parade, the royal standard was placed between the royal portraits under the canopy outside the official buildings.

By this time, night was approaching and the general mood of merrymaking prevailed throughout the town. At dusk, bonfires were lighted in the plaza, their flames flickering through the border of orange trees; and candles appeared in the windows of the houses. During the evening, specially talented clerks from the finance and supply department performed a dance around the bonfires, imitating the rhythmic Indian

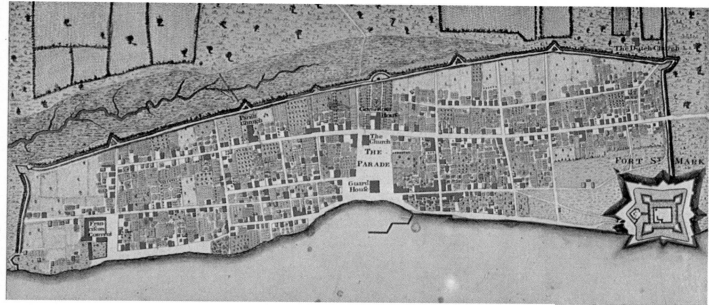

dances observed during Indian congresses held in the same plaza. The large platform in the center of the plaza became a theatrical stage in the evening, when the Havana regiment presented the opening night performance of *Amigo, Amante y Leal*.

The title indicates the three-pronged problem facing the protagonist, Don Félix, caught in the midst of conflicting obligations to his closest friend, his lady love, and his overlord, the Prince of Parma. His initial bold action is to hand over his sweetheart to the unrestrainable desires of the reckless prince, solely in order to serve him with loyalty. The plot becomes almost insuperably entangled thereafter, requiring a few improbable twists to reach a solution. Emotional tension reaches a climax in the third act when Don Félix appears with a sword, begging his friend to kill him. Almost immediately his sweetheart, Aurora, comes on stage with dagger upraised, threatening suicide. In a swift denouement, the prince relinquishes his claims for Aurora, unwilling that Don Félix should suffer for his unreasonable indications of loyalty. Somehow Aurora survives her various encounters with her honor unblemished, and her mind undisillusioned by the wavering behavior of her principal admirer.

The moral was clearly apparent to the Saint Augustine audience in 1789; loyalty to a superior officer was more important than personal inclination toward any woman. *Amigo, Amante y Leal* proved to be an enjoyable play, with prettily embroidered phrases of the best baroque tradition in the lengthy speeches, as well as rapid interchanges of metrical dialogue. Interest was maintained with a liberal sprinkling of jokes, a servant—as usual—providing the comic relief. The production was such an outstanding success that repeat performances were scheduled for the two subsequent evenings.

Besides attending the productions staged in the plaza, the soldiers and townspeople were all gathering in private parties. The most outstanding social event of the evening was the open house at the governor's residence, where Lieutenant Zéspedes acted as host to leading Saint Augustine military officers, government officials and private families. Shortly after the end of the parade, guests assembled for *refresco*, with famous Spanish wines served to the gentlemen, and punch, tea, coffee, or

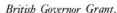

21

Love Story

A strange story has come from the Menéndez expedition around the South Florida coast. Told in the narrative, *Pedro Meneéndez de Avilés* by his chronicler-brother-in-law, Solis de Meras, it is the story of an Indian woman who truly seems to have fallen in love with the great Adelantado. She was the sister-wife of the Calusa chief, Carlos (the Indian chiefs of Florida had the almost Egyptian habit of keeping power in one family), when Carlos tried to give her to Menéndez for a wife—her brother was at his elbow—and he wanted to be faithful. Carlos insisted. It was clear he was enormously impressed with the great Adelantado. He probably also realized the Indians could no longer fight off the increasing Spanish horde and thought if his sister had a child by Menéndez it would bind them together.

Menéndez evaded the issue by sending Carlos' sister to Havana to be baptized and educated in the language and the Faith. When he visited Havana, she tried to get into his bedroom, even slept on the mat before his door. It was no use. Menéndez was not to be seduced. The sister was returned to Carlos, not at all about to bear Menéndez a child.

The result was that Carlos rebelled and was killed by Spanish soldiers, as was the son who took his place. All the tribes of South Florida rose up, burning and rioting. They escaped Menéndez' vengeance by retreating to the Everglades and for two hundred years Spain had no control over that whole end of the peninsula. Despite the brief founding of another mission of the Miami river, Spanish power never was established along those southern, hostile and invincible coasts.　　　　　—M.S.D.

Proclamation piece distributed at the St. Augustine celebration of 1789.

chocolate for the ladies. Musicians arrived later to provide entertainment for listeners and dancers in a form of social entertainment called a *sarao*, a Portuguese term akin to the French *soirée*. Dancing customarily opened with a formal minuet, with elegant steps familiar to élite society throughout the continent and European colonies. But as the evening grew cooler and spirits gayer, the violin was replaced by the guitar and livelier *contredances* occupied the floor. Forming squares, lines or circles, couples glided and whirled and bowed in a swift succession of figures until the approach of dawn. Late in the evening, an elaborate supper was served, probably featuring ham, cold turkey, olives, dates, figs, oranges and decorated cakes. The midnight buffet, called by the French word *ambigú*, was adopted by Spanish society in the later eighteenth century when so many French customs became fashionable among the upper classes.

The spirit of revelry was even more animated in humbler Saint Augustine residences, where guests followed the intricate regional dances of southern Spain, Minorca, and the Canary Islands. But dance partners were not available for all the men in Saint Augustine, a town with a high military population temporarily increased by the lingering Havana regiment. All the wine ships were overflowing, as well as the convenient tavern opposite the gate to Saint Francis barracks. Boisterous groups of soldiers joined in singing popular songs, improvising a few solo lyrics, while their comrades played cards or dice in the background.

Only a brief period of repose was accorded the officialdom of Saint Augustine who managed to dance until dawn on the morning of December 3, 1789. At 9 o'clock in the morning, the governor and his coterie plus a representation of local residents were all present in the parish church for high mass chanted by Father Hassett. At the conclusion of the service, all joined in singing the "Te Deum," to give solemn thanks to God for the advent of a new and glorious reign. By afternoon, they were all ready for a siesta in preparation for a continuation of the festivities. The evenings of December 3 and 4, the plaza was again bright with the light of bonfires providing illumination for the second and third performances of *Amigo, Amante y*

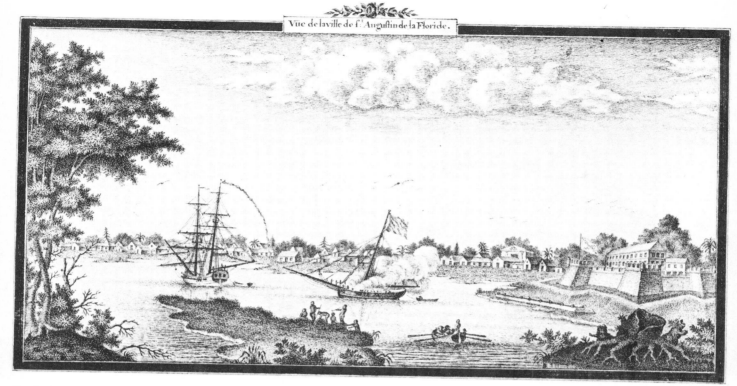

Vûe de laville de f. Augustin de la Floride.

St. Augustine

Leal. Parties again took place in homes with candle-lit windows, and for two more nights there was wine and punch, supper and dancing till dawn at the governor's residence. Governor Zéspedes, now in his seventieth year, was undoubtedly relieved to have his son assume the responsibilities of host for this social marathon.

The three day period of public rejoicing concluded on the evening of December 4, culminating with a triumphal float drawn through town by six horses. This magnificently decorated construction was the work of the local carpenter's guild, a group with a large representation from the Minorcan population. It was large enough to carry all guild members, who sported red cockades in their broad hats and carried flaming torches in their hands. At every street corner they paused to give cheers for the new rulers, with echoing cheers from the little groups of observers.

By the morning of December 5, participants in these festivities were relieved to lapse into a less eventful pattern of existence. The following week, Governor Zéspedes finally got around to sending notarized reports of the celebration to the king and colonial secretary, enclosing with each letter three of the commemorative medals. It may be difficult to determine the permanent results of this tremendous celebration of the local community of Saint Augustine. Adherence to the Spanish monarchy brought them scant physical comfort or security. Before the American flag was raised over the Castillo de San Marcos on July 10, 1821, the people endured many months without salary or local subsidy. Meanwhile they combatted Indian raids, pirate incursions, and the more serious revolutions and invasions along the Georgia border. In spite of these many vicissitudes, the Spanish officers and their successors, as well as the diversified townspeople and their descendants, maintained their unwavering loyalty to the Spanish crown, so enthusiastically displayed in December of 1789.

—HELEN HORNBECK TANNER

Hand wrought details like this doorknocker still attest to the Spanish background and special European flavor of the Old City.

23

The tradition of planting goes far back into history and native Floridians of different eras have long harvested food from land and sea. The famous artist LeMoyne first depicted Indian communities in Florida which predated by many years Cuscowilla.

CUSCOWILLA: 1776

A Seminole Village in 1776

Led by their famed chief, Cowkeeper, the Oconee Creeks probably fled to Florida from Georgia to escape the raids of Cherokee Indians. Although there is little information before 1776, it is certain the Cuscowilla had been established by 1750 just south of Payne's Prairie near present day Micanopy. The area around the prairie had been the home of Timucuan Indians, who, like the Creeks, were farmers. Good soils for farming and the herds of cattle left by the Timucuans attracted the Creeks to Alachua.

In Florida, Cowkeeper and his people remained staunch allies of the British and continued to deal with British traders following the Revolutionary War when Spain again ruled Florida.

After Cowkeeper's death in the late 1770s Chief Payne, for whom Payne's Prairie is named, became chief of the Alachua "Seminoles," as they were then called. When American troops under Colonel Newnan attacked the Alachua settlement in 1812, Payne was killed. Chief Micanopy, who became head chief shortly after Payne's death, moved the settlement south to Lake and Sumter counties to avoid further bloodshed.

The former site of Cuscowilla was visited in 1822 by William H. Simons, a South Carolinean, who reported that the "intended town of Micconope is situated on an elevated spot, on the northwestern border of Cuscowilla Lake, near to the site of the ancient Tuskawilla town, mentioned by Bartram. A few wild plum trees, and corn hills, mark the spot where rude forefathers of the wigwam once dwelt."

The best description of Cuscowilla, or of any Indian village in Florida at the time of the Revolutionary War, is provided by the naturalist William Bartram in his book, *Travels through North and South Carolina, Georgia, East and West Florida*, originally published in 1791. Bartram visited the village sometime in 1776–77. The descriptions of the town and the nearby Alachua Savannah, Payne's Prairie, which follow are quoted from his narrative. They add a colorful dimension to our appreciation of northern Florida 200 years ago.

—JERALD T. MILANICH

"The town stands on the most pleasant situation that could be well imagined or desired, in an inland country; upon a high swelling ridge of sand hills, within three or four hundred yards of a large and beautiful lake, the circular shore of which continually washes a sandy beach, under a moderately high sloping bank, terminated on one side by extensive forests, consisting of Orange groves, overtopped with grand Magnolias, Palms, Poplar, Tilia, Live Oaks, and others already noticed; and, the opposite point of the crescent, gradually retires with hommocky projecting points, indenting the grassy marshes, and lastly terminates in infinite green plains and meadows, united with the skies and waters of the lake. Such a natural landscape, such a rural scene, is not to be imitated by the united ingenuity and labour of man. At present the ground betwixt the town and the lake is adorned by an open grove of very tall Pine trees, which standing at a considerable distance from each other, admit a delightful prospect of the sparkling waters. The lake abounds with various excellent fish and wild fowl; there are incredible numbers of the latter, especially in the winter season, when they arrive here from the north to winter. . . .

"They plant but little here about the town; only a small garden plot at each habitation, consisting of a little Corn, Beans, Tobacco, Citruls, &c. Their plantation, which supplies them with the chief of their vegetable provisions, . . . lies on the rich prolific lands bordering on the great Alachua savanna, about two miles distance. This plantation is one common enclosure, and is worked and tended by the whole community; yet every family has its particular part, according to its own appointment, marked off when planted; and this portion receives the common labour and assistance until ripe, when each family gathers and deposits in its granary its own proper share, setting apart a small gift or contribution for the public granary, which stands in the centre of the plantation.

"The youth, under the supervisal of some of their ancient people, are daily stationed in the fields, and are continually whooping and hallooing, to chase away crows, jackdaws, black-birds, and such predatory animals; and the lads are armed with bows and arrows, and being trained up to it from their early youth, are sure at a mark, and in the course of the day load themselves with squirrels, birds, &c. The men in turn patrole the corn fields at night, to protect their provisions from the depredations of night rovers, as bears, raccoons, and deer; the two former being immoderately fond of young corn, when the grain is filled with a rich milk, as sweet and nourishing as cream; and the deer are as fond of the Potatoe vines.

"We were welcomed to the town, and conducted by the young men and maidens to the chief's house, which stood on an eminence, and was distinguished from the rest by its superior magnitude, a large flag being hoisted on a high staff at one corner. We immediately alighted: the chief, who is called the Cowkeeper, attended by several ancient men, came to us, and in a very free and sociable manner, shook our hands, or rather arms, (a form of salutation peculiar to the American Indians) saying at the same time, 'You are come.' We followed him to an apartment prepared for the reception of their guests.

"The town of Cuscowilla, which is the capital of the Alachua tribe, contains about thirty habitations, each of which consists of two houses nearly the same size, about thirty feet in length, twelve feet wide, and about the same in height. The door is placed midway on one side or in the front. This house is divided equally, across, into two apartments, one of which is the cook room and common hall, and the other the lodging room. The other house is nearly of the same dimensions, standing about twenty yards from the dwelling house, its end fronting the door. The building is two stories high, and constructed in a different manner. It is divided transversely, as the other, but the end next the dwelling house is open on three sides, supported by posts or pillars. It has an open loft or platform, the ascent to which is by a portable stair or ladder: this is a pleasant, cool, airy situation, and here the master or chief of the family retires to repose in the hot seasons, and receives his guests or visitors. The other half of this building is closed on all sides by notched logs; the lowest or ground part is a potatoe house, and the upper story over it a granary for corn and other provisions.

"Their houses are constructed of a kind of frame. In the first place, strong corner pillars are fixed in the ground, with others somewhat less, ranging on a line between; these are strengthened by cross pieces of timber, and the whole with the roof is covered close with the bark of the Cypress tree. The dwelling stands near the middle of a square yard, encompassed by a low bank, formed with the earth taken out of the yard, which is always carefully swept. Their towns are clean, the inhabitants being particular in laying their filth at a proper distance from their dwellings, which undoubtedly contributes to the healthiness of their habitations.

"The extensive Alachua savanna is a level green plain, above fifteen miles over, fifty miles in circumference, and scarcely a tree or bush of any kind to be seen on it. It is encircled with high, sloping hills, covered with waving forests and fragrant Orange groves, rising from an exuberantly fertile soil. The towering magnolia grandiflora and transcendent Palm, stand conspicuous amongst them. At the same time are seen innumerable droves of cattle; the lordly bull, lowing cow, and sleek capricious heifer. The hills and groves re-echo their cheerful, social voices. Herds of sprightly deer, squadrons of the beautiful fleet Siminole horse, flocks of turkeys, civilized communities of the sonorous watchful crane, mix together, appearing happy and contented in the enjoyment of peace, till disturbed and affrighted by the warrior man.

"Behold yonder, coming upon them through the darkened groves, sneakingly and unawares, the naked red warrior, invading the Elysian fields and green plains of Alachua. At the terrible appearance of the painted, fearless, uncontrolled, and free Siminole, the peaceful innocent nations are at once thrown into disorder and dismay. See the different tribes and bands, how they draw towards each other! as it were deliberating upon the general good. Suddenly they speed off with their young in the centre; but the roebuck fears him not: here he lays himself down, bathes and flounces in the cool flood. The red warrior, whose plumed head flashes lightning, whoops in vein; his proud ambitious horse strains and pants; the earth glides from under his feet, his flowing mane whistles in the wind, as he comes up full of vain hopes. The bounding roe views his rapid approaches, rises up, lifts aloft his antlered head, erects the white flag, and fetching a shrill whistle, says to his fleet, and free associates, 'follow'; he bounds off, and in a few minutes distances his foe a mile; suddenly he stops, turns about, and laughing says 'how vain! go chase meteors in the azure plains above, or hunt butterflies in the fields about your towns.'"

William Bartram

Chief Micanopy, in robes befitting a chieftain, sits for his portrait by artist George Catlin, famous for his nineteenth century paintings of American Indians.

A TREATY SIGNING, 1765

On November 18, 1765, the four small guns on top of Fort Picolata on the St. Johns River scattered the birds as a salute sounded for the small river schooner tied up to the bank beside massed Indian canoes. British governor Grant of St. Augustine and other officers and guests landed and strolled to their seats under the green arbor of branches set to shade them. The ranks of red-coated British soldiers lining the clearing presented arms smartly with their bayonetted muskets as the guns continued to bang salutes. Indian drums and rattles marked the advance of the Indian chiefs from the river bank, tall painted red men of the Florida tribes, feathers and emblemed deerskins fluttering to their stamping ceremonial dancing march.

It was a great day for the British in Florida *circa* 1763 and for the Indians. It was a day of great pomp and military ceremony: the British king, through his representative Governor Grant of St. Augustine, was about to sign with the assembled Indian chiefs a new treaty. In it the British King promised to leave the Indians free on their lands so long as the Indians acknowledged his sovereignty and relinquished all claim to the special lands the British meant to occupy from the west bank of the St. Johns to the Atlantic Ocean.

Two men, a father and son from the American colony of Pennsylvania far to the north, happened to be traveling in the Carolinas and Georgia and arrived at St. Augustine in time to be invited by Governor

English poet, Samuel Taylor Coleridge, is reputed to have been reading Bartram's descriptions of Florida springs and rivers when he fell into a drug-enduced sleep. While he slept, he dreamed and had a vision and composed a long poem as the scenes flashed through his mind. He awoke and started to write down the poem, but was interrupted. When he returned, he could remember only the hauntingly beautiful fragment known as Kubla Khan.

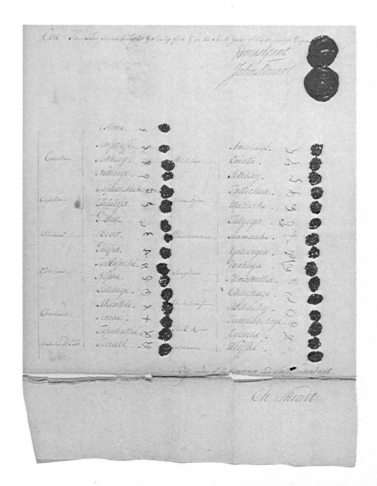

Treaty in Public Record Office, London, shows wax seals and marks of Florida Indian chieftains along with signatures of British officials.

26

Grant to be his guests at the small square fort at Picolata, to witness the treaty ceremony. The father, however, lay at some distance hidden by bushes in the deep shade of the trees, miserably ill and vomiting, feverish with malaria he had contracted as they rode horseback south from the Carolinas. He was John Bartram, the internationally recognized Royal Botanist from Philadelphia, friend of the great scientists of Europe like Linnaeus, Catesby, Callison, and Dillenius, and one of the founding members of the American Philosophical Society of Philadelphia, set up in 1743 by Benjamin Franklin. For the first time a distinguished botanist was studying and writing about the native plant material of the Carolinas, Georgia, and Florida only so recently opened by the British.

But it was young "Billy," his son, who wrote the journal paragraph briefly describing the day at Picolata. He wrote with a vividness and appreciation which starts up from the page as something so different from his father's matter-of-fact botanical notations that it catches the attention of every reader. Even if that were all that Billy Bartram had ever written, it would be outstanding.

In planning the expedition, John Bartram had decided to take his son William, known as "Billy," along with him, in hopes the experience would change him from a careless and happy-go-lucky youth who as yet had occupied himself with nothing of importance, and perhaps give him a new sense of purpose. Fortunately for us all, the expedition did everything for Billy that his erudite father had hoped. Because of what he had seen and experienced, when Billy returned he studied everything of botany, zoology, mineralogy and any other scientific writings he could find in the libraries of Philadelphia gentlemen.

No longer as "Billy" but as William Bartram, combining, as has been written of him, "the mind of a scientist with the soul of a poet," he made another journey through the Carolinas, Georgia, and Florida that lasted for four years, from 1773 to 1777. In 1791 he published the book that told about everything he did and saw and studied: trees, plants, birds, rivers, towns, lakes, weather, people, alligators, fish—everything—but in particular his close observations of the Indians, their villages, tribes, customs, beliefs. It is one of the greatest of American nature classics and just about the most important book ever to be written about Florida.

The book created a great stir in England. The poet Wordsworth read it with delight and his sister Dorothy passed it on to their friend, the poet Coleridge. Coleridge was reading Bartram when he slept and dreamed the dream of rivers running underground in caverns "measureless to man." When he woke, he set down the dream in his great unfinished poem, "Kubla Khan." It was Bartram's description of the rivers and springs and natural fountains of Florida, of forests and open places and the Indians that is reflected in the poems of Wordsworth and, especially, Coleridge. Much of the philosophy of the French writers, Rousseau and Chateaubriand, also reflects a fascination with the wild lands and people of Florida. It all began with William Bartram at Picolata.

—MARJORY STONEMAN DOUGLAS

KUBLA KHAN
Or, A Vision in a Dream

In Xanadu did Kubla Khan
A stately pleasure-dome decree:
Where Alph, the sacred river, ran
Through caverns measureless to man
    Down to a sunless sea.
So twice five miles of fertile ground
With walls and towers were girdled round:
And there were gardens bright with sinuous rills,
Where blossomed many an incense-bearing tree;
And here were forests ancient as the hills,
Enfolding sunny spots of greenery.
But oh! that deep romantic chasm which slanted
Down the green hill athwart a cedarn cover!
A savage place! as holy and enchanted
As e'er beneath a waning moon was haunted
By woman wailing for her demon-lover!
And from this chasm, with ceaseless turmoil seething,
As if this earth in fast thick pants were breathing,
A mighty fountain momently was forced:
Amid whose swift half-intermitted burst
Huge fragments vaulted like rebounding hail,
Or chaffy grain beneath the thresher's flail:
And 'mid these dancing rocks at once and ever
It flung up momently the sacred river.
Five miles meandering with a mazy motion
Through wood and dale the sacred river ran,
Then reached the caverns measureless to man,
And sank in tumult to a lifeless ocean:
And 'mid this tumult Kubla heard from far
Ancestral voices prophesying war!
    The shadow of the dome of pleasure
    Floated midway on the waves;
    Where was heard the mingled measure
    From the fountain and the caves.
It was a miracle of rare device,
A sunny pleasure-dome with caves of ice!

    A damsel with a dulcimer
    In a vision once I saw:
    It was an Abyssinian maid,
    And on her dulcimer she played,
    Singing of Mount Abora.
    Could I revive within me
    Her symphony and song,
    To such a deep delight 'twould win me,
That with music loud and long,
I would build that dome in air,
That sunny dome! those caves of ice!
And all who heard should see them there,
And all should cry, Beware! Beware!
His flashing eyes, his floating hair!
Weave a circle round him thrice,
And close your eyes with holy dread,
For he on honey-dew hath fed,
And drunk the milk of Paradise.

—SAMUEL TAYLOR COLERIDGE

Map dated 1564.

CUBAN MIAMI: 1743

Freedom Tower.

Long overlooked, the first short-lived Cuban community in Miami was settled on the river banks. This site is close to the Freedom Tower where some two hundred years later thousands of Cuban refugees were greeted as they entered Miami. The Spanish heritage and the Latin American ties are deeply rooted in Florida history—past, present and future.

Florida property titles can often be traced back to their original Spanish owners through Spanish land grants.

REDISCOVERED: SANTA MARIA DE LORETO

On July 13, 1743, two Italian Jesuits, Fathers Guiseppe Saverio Alagna and Jose Maria Monaco arrived in South Florida. Their mission was commissioned by the Spanish authorities in Havana to work among the two hundred or so Indians who spent one season of each year fishing on the Miami River and in Biscayne Bay. The two priests came with sailors and soldiers. They set to work, with the Indians, building a fort on the north side of the Miami River.

The small settlement at the mouth of the river was named Santa Maria de Loreto, after the ancient pilgrimage center in Italy. It emerges as the Cuban Miami of 1743. The fort was a triangular wooden structure surrounded by a ditch, an embankment, and a stockade. In each corner was a mortar to dominate the Indian village, the river, and the path that led inland. The flag of Spain was raised over the finished fort on August 8. A month later Father Alagna went back to Havana with their report, leaving Father Monaco at Santa Maria with a squad of soldiers.

The missionaries were optimistic, but their plans called for a military commitment and considerable expense: they wanted Cuban families sent to start a settlement, a garrison of 25 soldiers, and two ships. The bureaucrats were more practical. Few souls were to be gained, especially in view of the hostile attitude of the local Indians. The new settlement needed protection against raids by the English from Carolina and Georgia and their Creek and Seminole allies. The Governor in Havana ordered the recall of the mission and the destruction of the fort—to keep it from the English—even before he forwarded the Jesuit report to Spain.

In Spain the Council of the Indies agreed that it was not God's will to preserve Santa Maria de Loreto. So there was no permanent Cuban settlement of Miami until more than two hundred years later. Even the early Spanish name of the settlement was forgotten until the Jesuit report with its map was recently discovered in the archives in Seville.

—WILLIAM C. STURTEVANT

THE RIGHT TO BE WRONG

The Huguenots of the French settlement at Fort Caroline were not the first to seek the right to be wrong in the New World—or the last. Leif Erickson led a band of Vikings seeking freedom and opportunity to the New England coast five hundred years earlier and spent a winter there. The Huguenots were, however, the first to give up their lives on American soil defending that right. They never had a chance to show what they might have done. A Spanish force, asserting its claim, destroyed the Huguenots and their settlement in 1565.

Along Florida shores, and inland too, battles have been waged. Fighting and massacres persisted as peoples from all over the world fought for flags, honor, money, and territory. Then there are those who fled from tyranny, and were destroyed. But the blood they left upon the sands of Florida at Fort Caroline and Matanzas became the seeds from which a towering tree of individual freedom of opinion and expression has grown in the New World. To the protection of its branches and its shade, millions of others have come, people who were "wrong" in their own lands because they did not agree with established authority, whether religious or political. They have found here a freedom of worship, political belief, and equality of opportunity which exists to the same degree nowhere else in the world.

A half century after the death of Fort Caroline, a group of dissenters, "wrong" in the eyes of the Established Church of England, scrambled ashore in Massachusetts. Strangely enough, once they had secured their own freedom of belief in the New World, these Dissenters became as intolerant as those they had fled. The very stubbornness of the Puritans of Massachusetts caused others to leave the colony. They, in turn, set up new centers where they could be "right," seeking always for the goal of every thinking man: the discovery of truth for himself.

A country loses its greatness, its freedom, yes even its right to exist, when it starts shackling its people and its centers of learning with demands that they conform to rules of thought or teaching set down by a governmental, or even a self-appointed, body. People must dare to be

The father of our country was not the first or last to be considered wrong when he took a firm stand against the British in military or verbal battles.

On the St. Johns River, Fort Caroline was built by the French Huguenots in the sixteenth century. The site in present-day Jacksonville reminds Floridians of the French connection and the diversity of nations which sought to plant their flags in Florida.

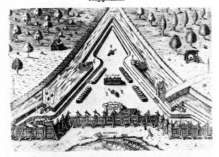

Fort Caroline

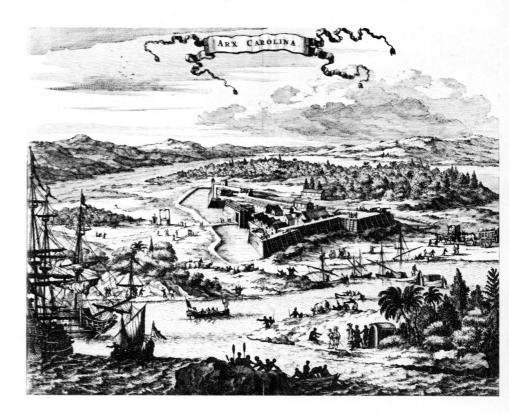

Union ranks marching in Fernandina brought Civil War close to Floridians.

"wrong," as was Pharaoh Amenhetep IV thirty-five hundred years ago when he substituted the worship of one god for the many deities of the Egyptian Pantheon; as was Socrates when he "corrupted" the youth of Athens with ideas of truth and beauty; as was Galileo when he saw a universe revealed in his telescope; as were the Huguenots who died upon Florida sands. The challenge is to speak out and act in defense of the right to seek truth wherever it may be found.

America is free today because a whole nation decided to be "wrong" in the eyes of George III of England and because others of the "wrong" from all over the world flocked to help. During that terrible winter at Valley Forge, George Washington was considered wrong by many members of the Continental Congress, sitting in Yorktown because Philadelphia and New York were in British hands. A concerted movement—the so-called Conway Cabal—was under foot to demote Washington and place Horatio Gates, the hero of Saratoga, in his position as Commander-in-Chief.

Washington, however, had powerful help. A Frenchman, Lafayette, inspired the world to cheer the starving Americans. A German peasant's son, "Baron" de Kalb, whipped a starving "rag, tag and bobtail" outfit into an army—reputedly with a single English word, "Goddam." A Jewish banker, Haym Salomon, was the financial genius of the Revolution. And Polish Count Casimir Pulaski helped add the dash and verve of cavalry to the American forces.

The United States became free when the wrong proved themselves to be right. It has remained free because strong men have dared lead its people to greatness. If our nation is ever destroyed, it will be because those who fought to prove themselves right in some things, grew intolerant and rigid in their rightness, forgot their own precious heritage, and denied to others—the right to be wrong.

—FRANK SLAUGHTER

COMMUNITY AND HUMAN DIGNITY

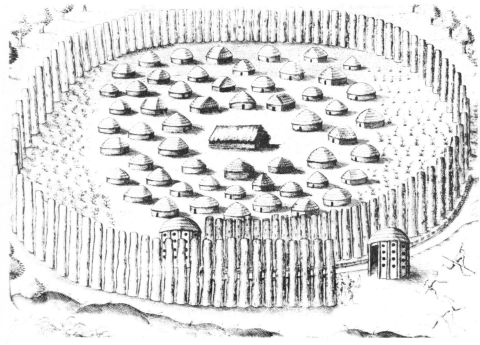

DeBry engraving based on LeMoyne drawing of Indian community in the 1560s.

Cleaning up birds after oil spill off St. Petersburg.

Porch sitting, Florida-style.

When Europeans first stepped on Florida shores, they were surprised by the unexpected living patterns of the native Americans. They reported that strange peoples and cultures had evolved across the ocean. Some respected the native Americans that they encountered, and honored the land and its resources as a trust. Those who could understand human values and rights only in Old World terms neither accepted nor honored the spirit of the peoples and ways they found in the New World.

Community and human dignity in Florida waxed and waned as flag after national flag was raised over the sunbathed land. Living patterns changed time and again, as different manners and customs were introduced into old and new settlements. Although Florida was one of the first regions discovered of the New World, it was also one of the last frontiers. The frontier has colored all of Florida history and the ways in which people have gathered in groups within its borders.

A new way of living together was born on the North American continent in 1776 as the United States of America was formed. As a territory, Florida joined the new community in 1821. The hope of that experiment was, and remains, that within its structures and its boundaries lies the possibility of community and human dignity for all.

It is appropriate in the Bicentennial year that Floridians celebrate the experiment in living together that was born 200 years ago; it functions still, and contains the hope and the means for continuing their search for community and human dignity. Yet even as they celebrate, Floridians are taking a new look at their social structures, their needs, and their relationship to each other and to the land.
—J.E.G./B.R.R.

*Weeden Island Indian effigy has human form.
It probably was used in religious ceremony
and buried with a dead priest or leader.*

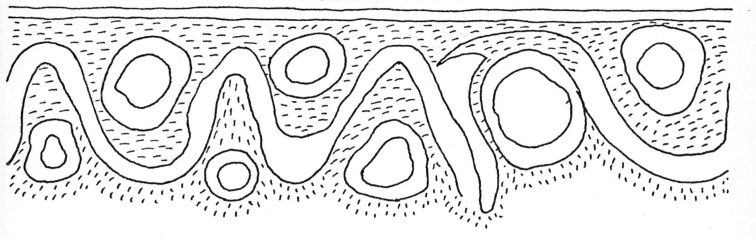

DIGGING UP THE PAST

Thousands and thousands of places in Florida are marked by the activities
of prehistoric Indians. Large and small, patches of stained earth or huge
mounds of shell or dirt, each of these places, or "sites," is a unique record.
Found in all parts of Florida these sites record man's continuing efforts to
adapt to nature and to change nature to fit his needs.

Every society has specific styles for everything that it makes or
uses. Each set or pattern of styles, whether in automobiles, skirt length,
pants or loin cloths, pottery decoration or arrowheads, reflects a set or
pattern distinctive of a culture, a society, at a particular time. Precise
scientific methods of excavation and recording can reveal which things
truly belong together and so were left by a single culture, because a lower
layer of material is always older than one on top of it.

A great deal about ancient Florida has been learned by the type of
investigation used by scientists, the police, and Sherlock Holmes. All are
detectives in a sense. A fingerprint pattern distinguishes every individual,
and every culture has its own distinguishing set of styles.

By the end of the ice age, some 10,000 years ago, there were
people, Indians, all over the New World. They may have come here from
Asia much earlier. In most of North America, east of the great deserts, a
special kind of spear point has been found that is associated with the
remains of the great animals of the end of the ice age, the Mammoth,
Mastodon, Giant Buffalo and others. In the far west, the points have been
found right in the skeletons. The evidence in Florida is not this good, but
the same kind of spear point has been found and the skeletons of the
animals. The circumstantial evidence indicates that man was here and
lived by hunting the great animals.

Over thousands of years, the climate and the environment
changed. The great animals disappeared. Forests replaced grasslands, and
man learned to develop a new way of life. What kind of life? In sites where
the bones of forest animals like the deer are uncovered, new kinds of flint
points are found and a new invention—the throwing stick. Designed to

Stemmed knives and an arrow
or spear point from Weeden Island.

33

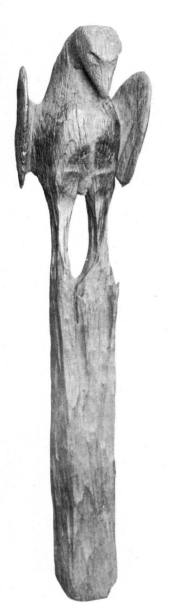

Carved wooden eagle is from the region of Lake Okeechobee. Dating from shortly after the time of Christ, the carving was first shaped by fire and then scraped with gouges made from shark's teeth.

fell game, the throwing stick was used to hurl heavy darts tipped with the new points. The art of hunting progressed in Florida as the spearlike weapons were wielded by bronzed natives pursuing prey.

At this time, about 5000–6000 B.C., some brave soul—or a hungry person—or a curious person with a gourmet's love of variety—made another discovery. He tasted and liked shellfish. He spread the word, "You can *eat* shellfish." This was very important because at last, here miraculously, was a steady harvest that could not get away like running animals or swimming fish. With this discovery, the Florida Indians were able to settle down. Community began.

The great shell mounds of the state began to rise, especially in the valley of the St. Johns River. Some of these piles of shells, the debris of many meals, were still growing when the Spaniards arrived. At the very bottom, are found the points, spear-thrower parts, deer bones, and other remains of the oldest, Archaic, culture. As "the dig" is read from the bottom up on a cleanly cut face into one of these mounds, layer after layer, pottery is introduced, decoration is added, styles change, tools and spear points change, layer after layer for thousands of years. This way of life, an economic system based on hunting and shellfish, was still the dominant life style in the St. Johns valley and the Everglades in the sixteenth and seventeenth centuries.

Florida Indians eventually participated in a great revolution, one that most people all over the world participate in sooner or later. This revolution was the introduction of cultivated plants, of an economy based on farming instead of on hunting and gathering. No longer must the Indians depend on unaided nature for food. No longer would the old people and the babies die of hunger when the deer or rabbits were gone, or a flood washed out the shellfish bars. Now nature could feed people by producing food, ever more and more, through plants and gardens.

The earliest evidence of this revolution in Florida is found near Lake Okeechobee. Here, along with ditches dug in huge circles to drain the wet savannah, and later, with long ridges built up to provide garden plots above the wet soil, the pollen from corn has been found. Radioactive carbon dating of charcoal from cooking fires reveals that corn was being grown here by at least 500 B.C., and possibly even 500 years earlier. The culture, the patterns of living at the site, did change, of course. At the time of the birth of Christ the people in Florida held elaborate ceremonial rites. For these ceremonies they built large mounds and excavated ponds. In the ponds they built wooden platforms for their dead and carved large wooden figures of birds and animals which were used as parts of the platform.

While excavating this site, something new was uncovered: lime! It was burned from shells in the village near the mounds and close to the platforms. This discovery led archeological detectives to look for other evidence, to ask questions and find answers. What was the lime used for? The only thing lime is used for by Indians anywhere, except for mortar or plaster, is in preparing corn to be eaten as food. Earlier scientist-detectives thought this technique was limited to Middle America—until it was found here in Florida.

This seems reasonable; Florida Indians could have been in contact with that area, but the long ridges and circular ditches are a South American idea. The corn could have come from either area, although it developed from a wild grass in Mexico. So, the detectives looked South again for clues. Some intensive work by a linguist demonstrated that the major language spoken in Florida in historic times was not really related to other North American Indian languages, but to one spoken in the Orinoco River delta in South America.

Putting all of these clues together with stratigraphy, artifact styles and their changes, and Carbon-14 dates, it seems probable that the language reached Florida first with the people who were some of the earliest shell-heap dwellers along the St. Johns. Like other early Caribbean and South American people, they tended to use sea shells for tools even when they lived inland. The corn, and the lime technique for preparing it, may have come next, but probably not until some other ideas about pottery making and decorating came across the Caribbean into the St. Johns, too. The earthworks were really only needed in the savannah country around Lake Okeechobee, and, it is suspected, came with or just after the corn and lime. Traffic across the Caribbean seems to have been pretty heavy for a few thousand years.

By the time the people around Lake Okeechobee built their mounds and platforms, 500 or 1000 years after they started to farm, the agricultural revolution reached north Florida, particularly the northwest coast. Strangely, developments here seem to stem from the midwestern United States rather than from Southern Florida. With the appearance of mounds in the north, the population multiplied tremendously; thousands of people were living in areas where there might have been only a dozen a few years earlier. In the mounds, the bodies of a few people are found and unusual objects like pan pipes bound in copper, copper ear ornaments, pipes with the bowl in the center of a flat base with one end acting as the stem, and pottery from far off places or in unusual forms completely unlike those which were used as cook pots. All of these things, in mounds, are far commoner to the north in the Ohio-Illinois area, along with a culture called "Hopewell."

North or south, the bodies of the people in the mounds can only be a very few people out of the total in their societies. Were those buried in mounds very special people? Probably so—leaders of some kind whose pipes, copper ornaments and unusual pots are supposed to be marks of their high status. Most early people buried their leaders with actual possessions and symbolic items as well.

But why a population increase? Only good, effective agriculture could do it. More pieces of the puzzle are put together by making an analogy with recent primitive people. The high status individuals must be not only social leaders, but priests—priests of a religion connected with crop fertility! Where had this come from? South America? The Caribbean? Only the elaborate things buried with the priests, had come down to Florida from the North. Hence the religion and the agriculture here must have come to Florida from the north. And the styles of everyday pottery and tools are ones with very old roots in northern Florida.

The case files grow. The best case that can be built now, which accounts for all the evidence to date, suggests that the ideas about how to grow, store, and prepare corn came into South Florida first. With the corn came religious ideas, reflected in most American Indian legends. The corn, the storage and preparation methods, and the religious ideas spread,

Ceremonial vessel used by Florida Indians is incised with ancient symbol of the swastika often used in the Orient and the Americas. In modern times the design, reversed, was used in Germany as a symbol of the Nazi party and the Third Reich.

Bowl and incising pattern from Safety Harbor.

Points found at Lake Kanapaha near Gainesville are from the Archaic period of 7000–2000 B.C. and are presumed to be for darts used with the atlatl or throwing stick. The name "Kanapaha" is from the Timucua words for "palmetto leaves" and "house" and refers to their dwellings.

eventually reaching the Midwestern corn belt, then as today the region where corn productivity was the highest. There, in "Hopewell" culture, the religion developed complexity in the populous and rich societies. Complicated symbols, badges of office and social status, were created. This system then spread back south until it reached northern Florida where, as a system, it was more effective than anything the people there had earlier.

In the Lake Okeechobee area, the ideas from the Midwest had little effect on daily life. The people continued with the corn fields on raised ridges, adapted to their special situation, which had served them for a very long time and which continued to serve them until the archaeological record ends in the seventeenth century A.D. Once agriculture reached northern Florida, especially the panhandle, societies there became the largest and most complex in the state, and continued to change, with increasing speed, in the direction of even greater size and complexity.

The first mounds in the north, with the "Hopewell" ideas, were built by people using old southern styles in pottery making. First, it was decorated with checker designs or simple lines, both stamped on four-legged vessels. Quickly this stamping developed into very complex designs, with elaborate curvilinear designs. These local ideas appear in the debris left by large villages, near the corn gardens and the mounds where the priests were buried.

In this northern part of the state, the residents continued to increase in numbers, and, as always happens, their social structures become more complex. Whenever people come together in larger numbers, more rules for behavior are made, and between classes of people more differences appear. Very shortly, instead of small mounds growing a bit in size as each priest passed on and was buried with his religious insignia, huge burial mounds are found which were built in *one* ceremony. In them are many bodies and far more objects, all placed during the ceremony. The complicated and check stamped pottery continued to be used, in everyday life and in ceremonies. A new kind of pottery appears, too, used in villages and mounds. It has new shapes and new decoration, with attractive patterns placed on the vessels with paint, incised lines, punctuated dots, and impressions of fish nets. All of these styles, new to Florida, had been developing for centuries out in the Mississippi Valley. Certainly, some of the new ideas about ceremonies came from there too.

Floridians have to improve things. For ceremonial purposes, to be used in their temples and to be buried with their great men, they developed special varieties of both their own stamped ware and the new "Weeden Island" styles. Ceremonial vessels are shaped like birds, animals,

Incising, or markings, on pieces of pottery called "sherds" tell when the pottery was made because people at one time and place used the same type of markings. Sherds, along with various animal bones and shells, are common in Indian middens because middens were garbage dumps for villages.

and people. Other forms are odd and unusual in other ways. Some, whether simple forms or effigies, are decorated with holes cut into them in patterns so that they could not hold anything.

Each burial mound, now the product of a single ceremony, was, really, a fossilized ceremony. Another clue, aside from the obvious evidence for careful planning and execution, is that in these mounds, none of the layers of earth, from top to a bottom as much as thirty feet below, was ever exposed to the rain with its washing and flattening effect. In the Southeast, this means building in a few days or a few weeks.

What prompted these ceremonies? What were they like? First, probably, a great man, a priest and leader, died. In a procession from a temple, sometimes on a flat topped pyramid, a "temple mound," his body was taken on a litter to the place where the funeral ceremony was to be held. In the procession were his wives, relatives, lesser officials, and many other people. During the ceremony, some of these people were sacrificed so that they might continue to serve the leader in the afterworld. Often the bodies or bones of earlier leaders were brought with him, too. So were all of the sacred vessels and ornaments used in the temple.

As the ceremony proceeded, his body was put in a grave, a layer of dirt added, the people sacrificed put into other graves, layers of special earth brought in, and the sacred vessels and other bones or bodies put in place. Layer by layer, grave by grave, body by body, the ceremony continued, the mound grew and finally was completed. The sequence, in rather precise detail, has been observed in several Florida mounds and similar funeral ceremonies were held by the historic Natchez Indians in Louisiana.

This northern Florida variant of the "Weeden Island" culture combines elements from many points in the past and many different cultures. Local pottery, pottery from the west, new ideas, platform or temple mounds, burial in mounds of a few great priest-chiefs, all show up in single communities at one point in time and space, a characteristic of an increase in complexity of all societies.

The Weeden Island pottery, of western origin, was used all down the coast of peninsular Florida. Often the stamped pottery is found with it. But, it is found only in burial mounds, mounds of the old style with the burial, each generation, of a chief or priest and a few sacred vessels. On the Florida west coast these mounds continued to be built all the way into the historic period, long after they were given up in northern Florida.

The pottery used in villages for everyday occupations, all over peninsular Florida, varies only slightly from place to place and from time to time. Everyday pots were simple open bowls, rarely decorated at all.

Stylized Weeden Island duck could have no useful purpose because of its many holes. It probably was a symbol used in a religious ceremony. Most artifacts are found in pieces like the sherds at the top of the page and must be put together like this duck, if all the pieces can be found.

38

Social patterns in most of the state remained simple, and were very different from the increasingly complex societies of northern Florida. The use of the special "Hopewell" objects, the Weeden Island pottery styles, the stamped pottery, and other later features all appeared along the St. Johns, following each other in the same succession in which they appeared elsewhere. As with the rest of the peninsula, everyday life seems not to have been affected at all. Only the frills for a few leaders changed. Otherwise, people stayed home and ate clams.

Far to the north, a culture called Mississippian had been developing since about 1000 A.D. Over most of midwestern and then southern United States, huge cities developed, each part of what might be termed an empire. In each of these cities, there were large flat-topped earthen pyramids, each with a temple on top, much like the stone pyramids of Central America. These regularly laid out cities, with tens of thousands of inhabitants, great pyramids, plazas, and manufacturing areas, may well be regarded as civilizations. Each empire, each state of which they were a part might have many cities, towns, villages, and farms. All of this tremendous growth could not have been caused and supported just by corn farming. Corn farming had been around, and used, for a thousand years. The new feature probably was the introduction of a kind of mechanized farming—use of the heavy hoe in large furrowed fields instead of the earlier small gardens with digging sticks for farming tools.

Just before de Soto came along, two of these great empires swept over northern Florida, replacing the old cultures with their stamped and Weeden Island pottery. The new societies differed in only very minor ways, although they did maintain their distinctiveness. Now, in northern Florida, there were two great states, each with great cities, flat-topped mounds, and many trade connections with each other and the north. The western society, called Pensacola, used shell mixed with pottery clay and is related to a huge metropolis in Alabama called Moundville. The eastern state, much like the western, except that the people used sand in the old style to mix with pottery clay, is called Fort Walton. Sand or shell, east or west, a new way of life was present.

As might be expected, this affected peninsular Florida little. Some temple mounds were built, but not the cities. A few new ornaments appear with burials, and they and Mississippian pots appear in burial mounds, often the same ones that had been growing for a thousand years or more. One culture, around Tampa Bay, is particularly interesting. This Safety Harbor culture is representative of the society and the people encountered by Hernando de Soto when he landed in 1540. The people did build temple mounds, but not cities. They did use, ceremonially, some ideas about pottery shapes and decoration, and some ornaments, which came to them from west of the Mississippi River, the area occupied today by western Louisiana and eastern Texas. This contact, and its social effect, is not understood at all.

With the advent of Hernando de Soto and his journey across the southeast, the story of Florida prehistory ends. From the moment the first white man stepped ashore, the story changes, and the interaction between the Indian and the European cultures begins a whole new historical tale.

—WILLIAM H. SEARS

"The skull was black when they brought it to me. It was black from the irons and acids and mineral replacements of iceage gravels. It was polished and worn and gleaming from the alterations of unnumbered years. It had made strange journeys after the death of its occupant; it had moved with glacial slowness in the beds of rivers; it had been tumbled by floods and, becoming an object of grisly beauty, had been picked up and passed from hand to hand by men the individual had never seen in life.

Finally it was brought to me.

It was my duty to tell them about the skull.

It was my professional duty to clothe these bones once more with the faint essence of a personality, to speak of a man or a woman, young or old, as the bones might tell the story. It was my task to read the racial features in a forgotten face, stare deep into the hollow sockets through which had once passed in endless procession the days and seasons and the shed tears of long ago."

—LOREN EISELEY
The Night Country

Weeden Island Plain effigy vessel. Original of this copy is from a mound at Aspalaga Landing on the Apalachicola River.

39

Massacre of the Whites by the Indians and Blacks in Florida.

The above is intended to represent the horrid Massacre of the Whites in Florida, in December 1835, and January, February, March and April 1836, when near Four Hundred (including women and children) fell victims to the barbarity of the Negroes and Indians.

Conflict inevitably arises when two groups of people want to use the same lands. This conflict is seen in different ways by each group. Early drawings show how conflict over the land in Florida was seen from eyes of the white colonists and from eyes of the Indians.

HUNTING INDIANS IN FLORIDA WITH BLOOD HOUNDS.

WHERE HAVE ALL THE INDIANS GONE?

*Painted Florida warrior was drawn by artist
LeMoyne who came to Florida with French
Huguenots in the 1500s.*

Florida was the home of more than one hundred thousand Indians when
Christopher Columbus first sailed to the New World. They were descendants of nomadic Indian hunters who had entered the state in search of
game at least ten thousand years earlier. But today there are no living
descendants of these first Floridians. European diseases, warfare, and
enslavement completely destroyed the aboriginal Indian people during the
two hundred years after the founding of St. Augustine in 1565. By 1720
North Florida was deserted. When the Spanish withdrew to Cuba in 1763
they took the few remaining Indians and mestizos who had been living in St.
Augustine and in South Florida with them.

Interior Florida was not uninhabited for long. After the Indians in
northern Florida had abandoned their traditional lands, other Indian
groups from Georgia and Alabama moved southward, into the deserted
areas of Tallahassee and later Alachua County. These Indians were the
ancestors of the Seminole and Miccosukee peoples who today live in South
Florida.

Village life for the Indians in Florida at the time the Europeans
came—their houses and community plans, their food and tools and
pottery—were as varied as the Florida environment. Coastal villages were
not like those inland; in the northern hardwood forests, the people lived in
ways that were different from those who lived in the savannahs of the Lake
Okeechobee Basin. Many of the aboriginal groups, however, had religious
beliefs and ceremonies and military and civil political organizations that
were very much alike. These patterns of living were changed during the
colonial period when the Indian cultures were forced to adjust to the ideas
and lifestyles that were brought by the Europeans.

Numerous visits by Spanish sailors are documented for the Florida
coasts from 1502 to 1528 and earlier ones probably occurred. These
explorations, however, including those by Juan Ponce de León, were little
more than attempts to find out what the land was like and to contact the

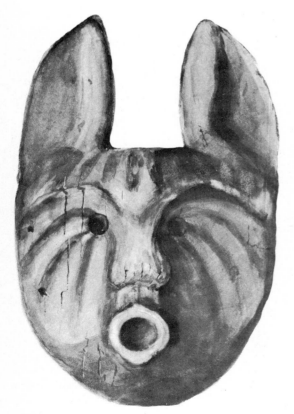

Carved and painted wooden masks and deer head unearthed at Key Marco. Deer head was probably used as a lure in hunting.

Indians in hopes of finding gold ores or precious stones. With the overland expedition undertaken by Pánfilo de Narváez from Tampa Bay in 1528 and that of Hernando de Soto, also from Tampa Bay, in 1539, the nature of Spanish attempts at exploration changed. Narváez had 350 men; de Soto had 600. For the first time relatively large numbers of Europeans came into contact with the even larger numbers of Indians who lived in the more populous inland portions of the state. Diseases, to which the Europeans had built up resistances, were spread among Indians who had no immunities to these illnesses. Measles and even the common cold cut a killing swath through the native populations of northern Florida.

Most heavily hit were the Tocobaga Indians, living around Tampa Bay, the various western Timucuan tribes in the forests from Ocala northward and the Apalachee who inhabited present-day Leon and Jefferson Counties. These three groups, along with the Calusa Indians of southwestern Florida, represented the most complex Indian cultures in the state. By the time the French built Ft. Caroline in 1562 the aboriginal Indians had lost at least 25 percent of their populations.

With the Spanish take-over of Florida, minor garrisons of soldiers were established among the Tocobaga, the Calusa near Estero Bay, and the Tequesta in Dade County. Although these garrisons were withdrawn in less than two years, the brief but intense contact resulted in more deaths from disease. As St. Augustine became the primary Florida settlement, the living patterns of the eastern Timucuan tribes in that area were disrupted, a sequence already begun by the French. Later, intense Spanish missionary efforts in east Florida, beginning in 1595, north Florida around 1606, and northwest Florida by 1635 led to further cultural changes. Throughout the seventeenth century the Spanish priests reported almost matter-of-factly the numerous "pestilences" which struck the mission Indians.

Ranches and farms were built in northern Florida to feed the Spanish population of St. Augustine. Spanish soldiers and officials coerced the Indians to serve as laborers, often promising them trade goods which never seemed to arrive from St. Augustine. A Timucuan chief writing in 1656 complained that he and his people were promised axes, hoes, and clothes "and all we get is sweat and labor." Maltreatment of the Indians led to several rebellions which were quickly subdued by the Spanish who burned the stored food supplies and corn fields, forcing the warriors to return home and take up hunting and gathering of wild foods.

The Indians were caught between the Franciscan priests who wished to Christianize them and the Spanish governor and military who saw them as a labor pool which could help support the population of St. Augustine. Bickering between the priests and the military, each trying to gain the upper hand in dealing with the Indians, only hastened the end of the Indian way of life.

Spanish quarreling continued until more than twenty North Florida Timucuan and Apalachee missions were destroyed by English soldiers and slavers from the Carolina colonies, aided by Indian allies. Begun in 1702 and completed several years later, the destruction of the missions was the final blow for the north Florida Indians. By 1710 most of

"I do my best to keep a little feeling of the jungle around my old stone building and its adjoining bit of hammock, for I have a theory that it is a good plan, if you want to have a carefree time in your garden. . .to have some place where ideas of order and neatness are not allowed to crowd out completely the sense of freedom which must have characterized the environment of primitive man. . . ."

—DAVID FAIRCHILD
The World Grows Round My Door

Calusas

"These Indians occupy a very rocky and a very marshy country. They have no product of mines, or thing that we have in this part of the world. The men go naked, and the women in a shawl made of kind of palm-leaf, split and woven. They are subjects of Carlos, and pay him tribute of all the things I have before mentioned, food and roots, the skins of deer, and other articles."

—HERNANDO D'ESCALANTE FONTANEDA,
circa 1575

Apalachee

"Their food is maize and fish; and there is a very great deal that they eat; but their usual food is fish. They make bread from a certain root, such as I have described before as growing in swamps; and they have much fruit of many different kinds, which to mention would be endless."

—HERNANDO D'ESCALANTE FONTANEDA,
circa 1575

The Vanished Mission Trail

The Franciscan Mission Trail in California is well marked and visitors can marvel along the Camino Real at the early stone structures, often topped by red Spanish thigh-molded tiles. But the Florida mission trail which predates the California chain has vanished. Not only did the British sack and burn the mission buildings but nature finished off the job. The buildings were made of wood with roofs that were sometimes thatched, so they simply rotted away.

Map of missions along the Old Spanish Road in Florida

The Missions of La Florida
At the Time of Bishop Calderón's Visitation
1674-1675
Scale in Miles

Drawing of military button found at Ft. Pierce.

them had either moved westward out of Florida or to the immediate area of St. Augustine where they were forced to live like "gypsies, here today, and gone tomorrow." Their traditional subsistence, religious, and governmental patterns had broken down, and they ceased to exist as ethnically distinct groups.

The more southerly Indians—the Tocobaga, Calusa, Tequesta, and others—also slowly declined in population. In an attempt to escape raids by the Georgia and Alabama Indians who sought their wealth and hunting grounds, they moved southward. By 1743 less than 200 remained, clustered along Biscayne Bay. In two hundred years several thousand Europeans had effectively decimated Florida of its native peoples. Archaeological excavations and the many documents left by the French and Spanish in their efforts to colonize the state are the only evidence we have of this destruction and the attempts by the Indians to evolve new ways of living that would allow them to survive.

Florida Indians can be divided into two major groups—northern farmers and southern hunters and gatherers. The Apalachee, Timucua (actually divided into at least fourteen tribes), Tocobaga, and other smaller tribes in northern Florida cultivated corn, squash, beans, tobacco, and other minor crops to supplement the wild plants and animals, especially deer, turtles, turkeys, and fish, which formed the major portion of their diet. The Tequesta, Ais, Jaega, and other southern Indians lived as semi-nomads, relying entirely on wild foods; they grew no crops. One of the greatest puzzles regarding the Florida aborigines is whether or not the

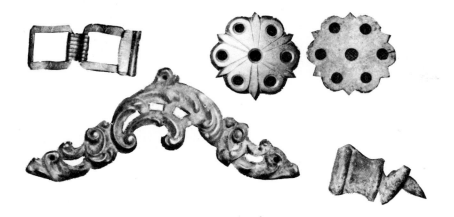

Calusa, who evolved a complex political state in southwestern Florida, were non-horticultural as stated by the Spanish, or if they grew squash, maize, and tubers at inland locations and traded them to the coastal towns. Most likely the complex Calusa culture could not have existed without some farming; recent archaeological discoveries show that maize and squash cultivation were indeed present previous to European contact in the Lake Okeechobee Basin and on the Collier County coast.

The tribal organization of the Calusa and the northern farming tribes was similar to that of the Creeks, Cherokee, and other Southeast peoples. Tribes were composed of five to twenty or more villages. Each village had its own civil chiefs who also were responsible for religious and ceremonial activities. The chief of the most important village also served as the tribal chief. Tribal religious structures, council houses or temples, were often placed at the main village. At times the temples and the house of the tribal chief were placed atop large earthen platforms. In addition to the head chiefs, there were many assistant chiefs, various counselors, and priests. A similar hierarchy of military chiefs existed alongside the civil chiefs, but functioned only in times of war.

The tribal name usually was the same as that of the main town. The tribal chief also took this name. For instance, among the Potano, a Timucuan tribe in Alachua County, the main village and the head chief also shared the name Potano. Names of other villages often coincided with the names of assistant tribal chiefs selected from those villages.

As the Indian population declined and because it was easier to deal with the Indians at the village level, the Spanish worked to consolidate the Indians into fewer villages with larger populations. The traditional political hierarchies began to break down. Village chiefs became more autonomous, and the priests took advantage of this by working to install a chief who was friendly to the Spanish or, better yet, already converted to Christianity. This made the conversion of the villagers easier because they usually followed the lead of their chief.

The Spanish priests brought tools, ceramics, clothing, and other goods to the Indians along with new foods. Cattle, pigs, and horses were introduced. A variety of new cultivated crops, including peaches, figs, oranges, wheat, and watermelons, probably increased the importance of domesticated foods in the Indian diet, allowing villagers to spend less time

"No one, I suppose, would believe that an archaeologist is a man who knows where last year's lace valentines have gone, or that from the surface of rubbish heaps the thin and ghostly essence of things human keeps rising through the centuries until the plaintive murmur of dead men and women may take precedence at times over the living voice. A man who has once looked with the archaeological eye will never see quite normally. He will be wounded by what other men call trifles. It is possible to refine the sense of time until an old shoe in the bunch of grass or a pile of nineteenth-century beer bottles in an abandoned mining town tolls in one's head like a hall clock. This is the price one pays for learning to read time from surfaces other than an illuminated dial. It is the melancholy secret of the artifact, the humanly touched thing."

—LOREN EISELEY
The Night Country

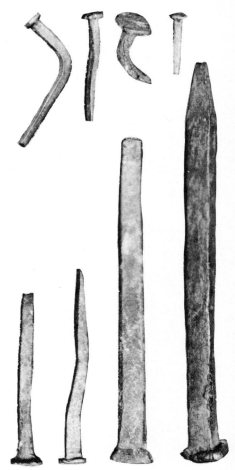

Wooden club carved by mission Indians is from marsh muck at site of mission village, San Juan del Puerto, on Ft. George Island.

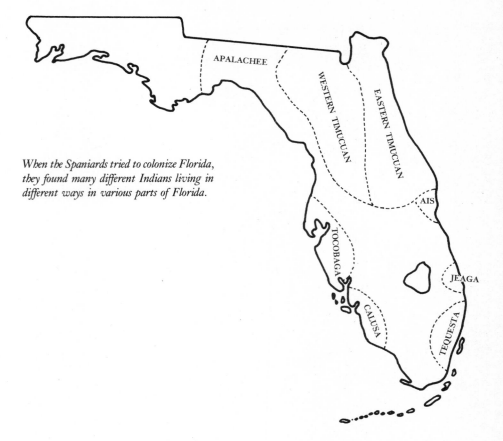

When the Spaniards tried to colonize Florida, they found many different Indians living in different ways in various parts of Florida.

APALACHEE

WESTERN TIMUCUAN

EASTERN TIMUCUAN

AIS

TOCOBAGA

JEAGA

CALUSA

TEQUESTA

Rimmed pot is from a trash pit at the site of an old Spanish mission in Jefferson County, San Joseph de Ocuya.

in search of seasonally available wild foods. The use of hoes and, perhaps, more intensive methods of farming led to more rapid soil exhaustion, causing villages to be moved more frequently. Culture changes accelerated as traditional habits and customs were abandoned.

The priests hastened these changes by attaching high status and importance to Spanish traits and by exhorting the Indians to give up their traditional beliefs and practices which were seen as pagan or the "work of the Devil." A Franciscan confessional book printed in 1613 illustrates these attempts to alter traditional views, beliefs, and practices. Questions recommended to be asked of the Indians during confession include: Before you go hunting, have you first made a prayer using tobacco? Have you made the ceremony of rain? Have you made some sorcerer use arts of the Devil to look for something lost? When some relative died, have you cut your hair?

Under the influence of the priests, it took only a few generations for traditional ways to be lost. The interment of individuals in burial mounds disappeared soon after the establishment of the mission system. Flint knapping faded away at about the time that the villages began to cluster around St. Augustine and Spanish metal tools became more available. Some traditional skills endured because they were encouraged by the Spaniards. Aboriginal pottery was made in St. Augustine right up to 1763. Vessels, copies of Spanish plates, pitchers, and bowls, were needed by the townspeople because the ships bringing crockery from Spain did not always arrive.

Attempts were made to teach the Spanish language to the mission Indians. By 1615 some Timucuans could read and write in Spanish; others were taught to write their own language using the Spanish alphabet. In

46

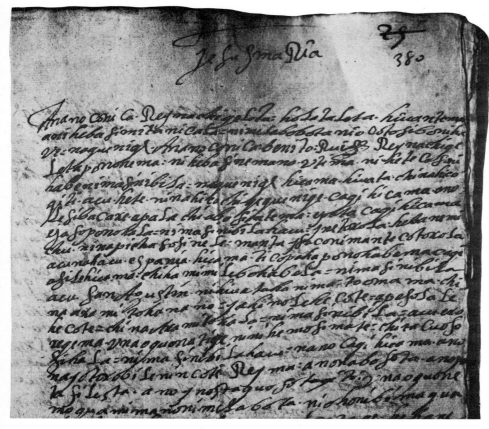

Portion of original letter in Timucuan Indian language written in 1656 by chief of Spanish mission village on the Aucilla River to Governor Diego de Rebolledo of Florida. Following salutation, "Jesus Maria," letter begins: "Señor Governor who represents the King, we come to speak to you: have mercy on us; we beg you to hear us." Outlining alleged mistreatment of the Indians by Spanish soldiers, the letter probably was written at the urging of Franciscan priests who wished to lay the blame for a recent Indian rebellion at the feet of the soldiers. The letter was ultimately passed on to St. Augustine and then to Seville, Spain, where it was found in the twentieth century.

1686 the king of Spain issued an edict requiring priests "using the most subtle methods they dispose" to teach Spanish to all of the Florida Indians. After the 1730s, census data no longer listed the Indians in St. Augustine by tribal or linguistic affiliation. The north Florida languages most likely became extinct several decades before 1763.

Despite the efforts of the priests to preserve the aboriginal populations by making them docile, Christian, and Hispanic, the cruel but effective raids by the English crushed the mission system and caused the final destruction of the north Florida aborigines. In 1710, the Englishman Thomas Nairne, himself a leader of raids into Florida, wrote:

> There remains not now so much as one village with ten houses in it in all Florida that is subject to the Spaniards; nor have they any houses or cattle left, but such as they can protect by the guns of their castle of St. Augustine. . . .

The first quarter of the eighteenth century was a tempestuous time in Florida history. Events elsewhere in the Southeast eventually led to the Florida of the Revolutionary War period, a Florida held by the British and by a Seminole Indian population rapidly establishing itself in the northern two-thirds of the state. England, controlling the colonies from the Carolinas north, sought to force Spanish withdrawal from Florida, and continually encouraged Indian raids against the Spanish.

In 1715 many of the Creek Indians and their allies in Georgia and South Carolina declared war on the English. To escape English retaliation, certain of the tribes moved southward either to St. Augustine or to the

Old woodcut shows Indian Village in the Everglades.

47

Sam Jones

Osceola, Alligator, Wild Cat, and Tiger Tail have gone down in history as the Indian heroes of the Seminole War of 1835–42. That may be because they were either captured or surrendered and peacefully took their followers to Arkansas Territory. For it was the white man who wrote the history, and kind words were reserved for those who did the white man's bidding. There were no kind words for Sam Jones, an obstinate Miccosukee medicine man whose steel-gutted fortitude helped to keep up the Indians' spirit in a never-surrender determination.

Little is known about the real Sam Jones, whose Indian name was Arpeika, except that he was in his seventies at the beginning of the war, that he was ferocious looking, and that his influence on his followers was enormous. Unlike other Indian leaders, Jones refused to meet with the white man to discuss peace. His peace plan was simple and well known: If the white men would go away and leave the Indians alone there would be no war.

Jones refused to talk about surrender or about leaving Florida, and he ordered followers put to death who showed signs of weakening. Incensed after hearing that Colonel Harney had hanged five Indians and strung up the dead body of his friend Chekika, he ordered white captives burned alive by igniting resinous pine splinters stuck into their bodies. Although cruel, this stopped Army hangings.

The old Indian leader became known as Sam Jones-Be-Damned and the "great rascal" of the Seminole War. The Army was ordered to bring in Jones by "fair means or foul." Never captured, Jones died peacefully in Big Cypress Swamp, far into his nineties. When he was dying word went out far and wide, and "every Indian in Florida" was present at the time of his death, according to Josie Billie, a descendant of Sam Jones' followers. It wasn't that the Indians loved Sam Jones so much. They feared him; none dared to ignore the call when he was dying.

"Sam Jones, he man of four souls," said Billie. "He fighting man. He man to be feared." But had there been no Sam Jones, there might be no Indians in Florida today.

—NIXON SMILEY

Flint-Chattahoochee-Apalachicola area. The Spanish saw an opportunity to ally themselves with the retreating Creeks against the English. Representatives from St. Augustine were sent to the Creeks to urge them to move down into Florida. The efforts were partially successful as portions of the old province of Apalachee were reoccupied by Creeks.

During the 1720s and 1730s raids by the English on the Spanish and raids by the Cherokee on the Georgia Creeks led to further population shifts into northern Florida. The English advances into Florida, especially the raids by General Oglethorpe on St. Augustine in 1740 and 1742, did much to weaken the Spanish hold. By 1750 it was the Creeks rather than the Spanish who controlled northern Florida. Eventually Spain was forced to trade the Florida colony to Great Britain in exchange for Cuba, which recently had been captured by the British.

During the subsequent British period, numerous treaties were signed between the Creeks and the new government of Florida. The various Florida tribes saw that it was to their advantage to deal with the British apart from their northern relatives, and the Seminole began to emerge as a separate people. Because the Creeks in Florida had left their villages in Georgia and Alabama, and because they were somewhat nomadic in their hunting trips in Florida, the Spanish had often referred to them as *cimarrones*, meaning wild ones or runaways. Eventually the Creeks and British corrupted this word into Seminole, the name the Indians bear today.

Following the Revolutionary War when Spain regained Florida, Seminole villages stretched down the state from north of Tallahassee to west of Lake Okeechobee. The three main areas of settlement were on

SORROWS OF THE SEMINOLES—BANISHED FROM FLORIDA.

Lake Mikasuki in Leon County, at Tallahassee, and just south of Payne's Prairie in Alachua County. Cuscowilla, on the edge of Payne's Prairie, was founded by the famed chief, Cowkeeper. He was succeeded by Chief Payne and then by Micanopy, both of whom have left their names to modern landmarks.

The First Seminole War, begun when Andrew Jackson marched into Spanish Florida, forced some of the more northern Seminoles down into the central portion of the state. It was the Treaty of Moultrie Creek, however, signed in 1823 between the Seminoles and the new United States territory of Florida, that moved the Seminoles into Central Florida. The treaty set up a reservation extending from Ocala to Lake Okeechobee. After the treaty went into effect and northern Florida was once again deserted, white settlers began moving onto the rich farm lands. Homesteads and towns, like Micanopy, sprang up and the important agricultural tradition of Florida was established.

The refusal of some Seminole to be moved westward from the reservation to Indian Territory in Oklahoma led to the Second Seminole War (1835–1842). Using guerrilla-like tactics, the 1500 Seminole warriors were able to create a military stand-off with the United States troops, which numbered as many as 9000 men. Eventually, however, all of the Seminole except for a core of about 300 were removed to Oklahoma. Those who resisted the removal escaped by hiding in the almost impenetrable Everglades. The more than 2500 Miccosukee, who take their name from Lake Mikasuki where their ancestors once lived, and Seminole who live in South Florida today are the descendants of those 300 Indians.

—JERALD T. MILANICH

Billy Bowlegs III and friend outside church in Dania.

49

FREEBOOTERS
AND FILIBUSTERERS

Gregor McGregor, after fighting with Napoleon and Simón Bolívar, joined the American revolution, captured Fernandina Island, and flew the Green Cross of Florida over the island for three months.

British-owned Florida was in ferment after the outbreak of the American Revolution. Not only were the Colonies to the north at war with England, but so were the Spanish in the south and in the west. While the British may have controlled St. Augustine and Pensacola, their authority over the Indian-occupied countryside was tenuous at best. Still, Florida became a refuge for thousands of Tories who preferred King George III to such "despicable" characters as John Hancock and Samuel Adams, whose effigies were hanged and burned in the public square at St. Augustine. The refugee stream was swelled enormously after the British defeat at Yorktown. But, having lost the war, Britain no longer needed or wanted Florida, a military and an economic liability, and, after twenty years of occupancy, in 1783 returned the wilderness to Spain.

With the refugee stream, during and after the Revolution, came countless rascals—traitors, masters of intrigue, deserters, outlaws, murderers, thieves, opportunists, and deadbeats. A few were lovable rascals, like Captain John (Don Juan) McQueen, confidant of George Washington during the Revolution. Not so lovable were a host of others: Daniel McGirt, turncoat and outlaw; William Augustus Bowles, British agent and despoiler; Gregor McGregor, adventurer and opportunist; William Panton, Indian trader and paid British agent; Zephaniah Kingsley, profane slave trader, and John Houstoun McIntosh, who, with the encouragement of Thomas Jefferson and James Madison, sought to seize Florida and turn it over to the United States.

Early in the rebellion, Daniel McGirt, a Carolinian, fled the Revolutionary army and joined the British East Florida Rangers as a lieutenant-colonel. He quickly displayed his talents in leading torch raids through the south Georgia countryside. The Rangers returned with 1,800 cattle and horses from a single raid. Unemployed by the end of the war, McGirt turned to banditry, preying on the British and the Americans, and later on the Spanish. The British captured him, but before McGirt could be brought to trial the Spanish arrived to take possession of Florida, and he was sent to Havana for trial. The rascal must have had charm, because the Spanish released him on his promise to stay out of Florida. Soon back in his old haunts, he was again captured. Instead of hanging him, the Spanish packed him off to Nassau where he entered the employment of the Bahamian governor, Lord Dunmore, as a spy and planner of intrigue.

Better known than McGirt was William Panton, organizer of the Indian trading firm of Panton, Leslie & Company. A Scot, Panton was loyal to no one except himself, but he would do anything for a buck. His firm was kicked out of the northern Colonies because his activities among the Indians were suspect. Moving to St. Augustine with his partner, John Leslie, Panton organized a trading organization that, by the end of the Revolution, covered much of the Indian territory in the Southeast. Panton's greatest coup was bringing into his firm as a partner Alexander McGillivray, half-Creek, half-Scot leader of an Indian confederation that included 6000 warriors. Financed by Britain, Panton proceeded to arm and incite the Creeks, as well as the 2500 Seminoles in Florida, against the Colonies and later against the Republic. By guile and persuasion, Panton held onto his trade empire after the British surrendered Florida to Spain.

Most arrogant of the rascals was William Bowles, who challenged the king of Spain. Bowles, a native of Maryland, turned his back on the Revolution at thirteen to join the British navy. At fifteen we find him in Florida, an ensign in the British defense forces at Pensacola. But Bowles and trouble were inseparable, and he was soon kicked out of the British navy.

Moving in with the Creeks, Bowles studied their language and customs, and, ingratiating himself with a chief, won the hand of the leader's daughter. Thereafter he conducted himself as Prince William Bowles. After the war, Bowles went to Nassau, where he offered Lord Dunmore a plan that promised to enrich both—the undermining and takeover of the Indian trade controlled by Panton, Leslie & Company. With arrogant disregard for

Changeling William Bowles—American colonist, British navyman, Indian prince, Spanish prisoner.

Panton Leslie Trading Post—a center for political plots and money schemers in Colonial Florida.

Political plotting between Florida and Cuba is easy because they are close, yet separated by water, and have many miles of coastline hard to patrol, as is evident even in this early Spanish map.

the Spanish, Bowles entered Ponce de León Inlet with two ships of armed men and Indian trading supplies. His intention was to take possession of the Panton, Leslie store on the St. Johns River and set up his own trading post. His plans went awry, and Bowles, directing his ships to the Gulf Coast, led his adventurers across Florida to attack the Panton, Leslie store at St. Marks. Captured, he was sent to Havana for trial. On the way, however, a storm wrecked the ship and Bowles escaped. Making his way to Indian territory, Bowles began issuing high-sounding proclamations as a "director of the Muskogee nation." Among his "state papers" was a directive to the king of Spain for the setting up of an independent Indian state in Spanish territory. Bowles condescended to assist the Spanish in setting up the nation, but, should the king decide against his suggestion, he was ready to "make war on your Majesty."

A $4500 reward offered by the Spanish governor of West Florida resulted in Bowles' capture in 1803. Shipped to Havana and locked in Morro Castle, Bowles refused to recognize Spanish jurisdiction or to testify in his defense. When the governor of Cuba offered to visit him and discuss the seriousness of his case, Bowles replied: "I am sunk low indeed, but not so low as to receive a visit from the Governor General of Cuba." To emphasize his arrogance and defiance, Bowles fasted until his death.

In the early 1790s, a new face appeared in St. Augustine, that of Captain John McQueen. Tall and handsome, and imposing with gray appearing in his temples, this suave man-of-the-world moved immediately into the top circles of St. Augustine society. A Philadelphian, McQueen had married the daughter of a wealthy South Carolina planter before the Revolution. As a captain in the Revolutionary navy, McQueen served as special courier between Washington and Lafayette and between the general and American representatives in France, Benjamin Franklin and Thomas Jefferson. After the war, McQueen moved his family to Georgia, where he acquired a plantation near Savannah and began speculating in land. The land boom collapsed, leaving McQueen in debt and unable to pay his taxes. To avoid jail, he turned over his plantation to his wife and fled to Spanish Florida.

Soon buddy-buddy with the Spanish governor, McQueen acquired a grant of land on Fort George Sound, a tributary of the St. Johns, where he built a modest house and started a plantation. While his slaves worked the

Copyright 1876, by Currier & Ives, N.Y.

THE FIRST MEETING OF WASHINGTON AND LAFAYETTE.

cotton and indigo, the imposing Don Juan took over another job, that of Commander of the St. Johns—a job with military and social positions requiring that he maintain a home in St. Augustine. We can see him, his silver hair beginning to match the silver buttons of his scarlet coat, moving among the guests at the governor's dinner parties with the grace of an old cat, and speaking Spanish with a Philadelphia accent. Meanwhile, McQueen was converted to Catholicism. His way of life was costly, though, and money wasn't coming in fast enough to pay off his Georgia debts. The governor offered the Commander of the St. Johns an opportunity that not only promised to enrich him, but the governor also.

Camped in the keys along the Florida Straits was a colony of Bahamians, ready to pounce on wrecked vessels and haul off their cargo to Nassau for sale. These wreckers, mostly New Englanders who fled to the Bahamas during the Revolution, were little more than pirates. The Spanish, however, lacked ships and men to drive them out. So, at the behest of the governor, Commander McQueen organized a fleet and a crew of cutthroats equal to the cutthroats from the Bahamas, and prepared to take over the wrecking in the name of the King of Spain. In order to raise money for the venture, McQueen sold his plantation to John Houstoun McIntosh, a fellow veteran of the Revolution and a planter on the St. Johns. As the day approached for Don Juan McQueen to raise the Spanish colors and sail his fleet out of the St. Augustine harbor, he was stricken by a heart attack and, instead of the governor going to the docks to see his favorite commander off, he led a procession to the cathedral where one of the most extravagant funeral services in St. Augustine history was held.

Long before the colorful Don Juan was laid to rest, John Houstoun McIntosh was engaged in intrigue aimed at undermining Spanish authority and setting up Florida as a ripe plum to be picked by the United States. Jefferson encouraged McIntosh while he was Washington's secretary of

Although he never set foot in Florida Thomas Jefferson's connection is confirmed by his encouragement of political intrigue within its boundaries when he served as Washington's Secretary of State.

Don Juan McQueen, special courier between Washington and Lafayette, came to Florida and was later named Commander of the St. Johns by the Spanish Governor.

53

A *"blackmarket" flourished in Spanish Florida as slave ships landed and traders smuggled slaves across the border into Georgia.*

McQueen-Kingsley house, pride of colonial Florida, still stands on Ft. George Island.

Slave quarters on Kingsley Plantation are made of "tabby," a mixture of oyster shells, lime, sand, and sea water.

state. Spain had opened Florida to settlement by Americans, and Jefferson hoped 100,000 would take advantage of the invitation, thus forming a colony of such unrest that Spain would be happy to part with the territory. The large numbers failed to materialize, but those who did come caused trouble enough. McIntosh, however, was arrested and hauled off to Havana, where he spent two years in Morro Castle while President Washington pulled diplomatic strings to secure his release. Wiser but undismayed, McIntosh returned to Florida and resumed his intrigues.

President Jefferson's purchase of Louisiana Territory from Napoleon in 1803 whetted the appetite of the new republic to gobble Florida, and James Madison, Secretary of State, encouraged the Americans in Spanish Florida to do their patriotic duty. The McQueen house on Fort George Island, now McIntosh's home, became headquarters for the planning of insurrection and take-over.

Congress, during Jefferson's administration, had passed an act outlawing further importation of slaves. The prices for human contraband soared, and Spanish Fernandina became a center for the illegal entry of slaves into the United States. An outraged Congress in 1811 secretly authorized President Madison to annex northeast Florida. Early in 1812, Madison sent General George Mathews to take over military operations in the insurrection he was relying on McIntosh to foster. McIntosh called his "Patriots" to a meeting on the St. Marys River, where a government of the East Florida Republic was formed. McIntosh was elected president.

Joined by a rabble army from the south Georgia pine barrens, organized for the Florida venture, the Patriots marched on Fernandina. Taking it was so easy that Mathews and McIntosh, forgetting Madison's limited objectives, decided to seize all of East Florida, including the citadel at St. Augustine. When Madison received word that the Patriots had St. Augustine under siege, he sent Governor David Mitchell of Georgia to relieve Mathews and apologize to the Spanish governor. Madison, on verge of a new war with Britain, wanted to avoid trouble with Spain. What was left of the Patriots' cutthroats hastened toward the Georgia border, driving cattle, horses, and slaves they captured along the way.

Instead of hanging McIntosh, the Spanish released him on his promise to behave. But, having squandered his fortune on the venture, he was forced to sell the McQueen plantation to Zephaniah Kingsley, a foul-mouthed, cursing Scot slave trader from whom he had borrowed heavily. Kingsley built himself a new home, atop of which was erected a captain's walk so the colorful little man, wearing a big hat and flowing cape, could watch for the arrival in Fort George Sound of his slave ships from Africa. He lived here with his Black wife, Princess Anna Madgegine Jai, daughter of a Senegalese chief, whom he had married in Africa in a tribal ceremony.

Both the McQueen house and the Kingsley house, connected by a covered walk, have survived. Now owned by the state, they are open to the public for a fee. Nearby are the shells of Kingsley's tabby-constructed slave quarters.

Although Kingsley was one of the men in Florida most wanted by the United States before Florida became a possession, after the peninsula was ceded by Spain the former slave trader was appointed by President Monroe in 1821 to serve on a federal commission charged with the re-

sponsibility of bringing the territory into the folds of the Republic. Giving up the illegal trade in slaves, Kingsley began training them as carpenters, masons, wheelwrights, and in other trades, enabling him to sell them at a much higher price than a field hand.

Florida had one final act in the historical farce involving colorful rascals before it was ceded by Spain to the United States. In 1817, Gregor McGregor, a veteran of the Napoleonic wars and Simón Bolívar's revolution in Venezuela, led an army of American adventurers into Fernandina, which surrendered without a shot, and raised the Green Cross of Florida flag. McGregor's aim was to take all of Florida, but he failed to get the assistance from the United States government that he had expected, and, after holding Fernandina for three months, sailed away and left his new republic in the hands of his lieutenants. Two days later, the pirate Luis Aury arrived to raise the flag of the "Republic of Mexico." A U.S. Naval squadron put an end to Aury's reign, but during the short period that the pirates held Fernandina they moved more than a thousand slaves over the Georgia line.

Nearly half a century of international intrigue ended with Andrew Jackson's second invasion of Spanish Florida. Jackson had paid his first visit in 1814, when he marched into Pensacola after his destruction of the Creek nation in the Battle of Horseshoe Bend. From Pensacola he hastened to meet the British in the Battle of New Orleans. Jackson was back in Florida in 1818, punishing the Seminoles for their scalping forays into Georgia and Alabama, and taunting the Spanish for their harboring of alleged spies and trouble-makers. To show his disdain of the weak Spanish authority, Jackson ordered the execution of Alexander Arbuthnot, British agent and trader, and Robert Chrystie Ambrister, Indian agitator. Jackson proved such a disaster to the Spanish that they agreed to cede Florida to the United States, thus ending whatever hopes European powers may have entertained of regaining a military and economic foothold in the area. Jackson's visit also ended the farcical schemes of restless adventurers who for so long had chosen Florida to display their talents as freebooters and filibusterers.

—NIXON SMILEY

The trial of Robert Ambrister is shown in this engraving from a biography of Andrew Jackson published in 1848. Jackson ordered the execution of Britishers Robert Ambrister and Alexander Arbuthnot in defiance of Spanish rule, Spanish courts, and international law.

The incident is typical of Jackson's style of personal military campaigning and diplomacy in Florida in the years just before it was ceded to the United States.

Andrew Jackson, invader of colonial Florida.

55

POLITICS OUT OF THE FRONTIER

A sense of isolation from the mainstream of America, common attitudes about the institutions and values connected with slavery, concerns over the hazards of frontier life and a desire for further development promoted unity among Floridians and helped bind Florida to the South during the first half of the nineteenth century.

When Florida entered the Union in March 1845, paired with Iowa to preserve the precarious balance of free and slave states, the pattern of her political parties was already well established. Although new to the United States as a territory in 1819 or state in 1845, Florida nonetheless was an old region, especially in terms of her political needs.

In 1845, as in 1565, Florida was still a frontier and that fact was the key to her politics. The distances separating the few pockets of settlement—St. Augustine on the Atlantic Ocean, Pensacola on the Gulf of Mexico, and Key West at the southern tip—slowed communication and political unity. The inland hamlets were sparsely arranged along the northern tier of the peninsula and major Florida rivers cut across the main flow of population. Most new immigrants traveled east or west, but the St. Johns, Suwannee, Chattahoochee, and Apalachicola rivers all flowed north or south.

Floridians, as a result, by the 1840s had developed widely varying political interests, especially over the issue of statehood. Many Floridians could appreciate the advantages of statehood—more effective representation in Washington and local stability that would attract more settlers. An explosive legacy from the Adams-Onis Treaty that ceded Florida to the United States, however, helped formulate the first Florida political parties. Should Florida be admitted into the Union singly *or* carved into two separate states?

East Florida tended to favor two-state admission; Middle Florida preferred single state status; West Florida was split between those favoring single statehood and those who wanted annexation to Alabama. Different frontier experiences in each section produced these differing opinions, and

Self-reliance and independence were characteristic of the lives and politics of the frontier. An early Florida photographer captures the pioneer spirit in a north Florida setting.

the political parties that were formed to express them. West Florida had always felt closer to Alabama than to Middle or East Florida, geographically, economically, and politically. Annexation was defeated at the time of Florida entry into the Union, but the idea continued to attract West Floridians through the Civil War and Reconstruction. Even today many West Floridians can find little common political ground to share with their fellow Floridians to the south. East Florida defined its future in terms of two states because of its Atlantic border and because of the unique conflicts in the Seminole Wars. Only Middle Florida, bound by the Suwannee and Apalachicola rivers, saw the clear advantages of immediate, single state admission, perhaps because it was by 1845 the wealthiest and most populous section of the state.

Generally Whigs in Florida supported statehood, and Democrats stood for continued territorial status until two Floridas could enter the Union. These differences were important. Not only did they indicate how the frontier could be perceived differently by Floridians living apart from each other, these differences to some extent cleave Floridians politically today. Whigs were often considered "respectable" gentry. In Florida most were to be found in the cotton plantation belt of Middle Florida. Florida Whigs tended to be men who envisioned future state growth commercially, and viewed immediate statehood as the best way to achieve it. According to the Whigs, statehood would attract new immigrants and new business. Less than 60,000 people lived in Florida in 1845, and immigration was vital for further development. Many Whigs also pointed out that as a territory Florida lacked political strength and influence in national government. Permanent representation by congressmen and senators could resolve that weakness.

Democrats tended to view the politics of statehood from another perspective. The balance of free versus slave states arising from the 1820 Missouri Compromise was in jeopardy. The Democrats argued that two Floridas could swing the balance to the South as sectional feelings heightened, and they seemed willing to postpone statehood indefinitely to achieve it. Perhaps the most critical issue that divided Whigs and Democrats politically in 1845 was more a question of economics, one still smoldering from the panic and depression of 1837. Nationally, the banking policies of Jacksonian Democrats had brought about a continued inflationary spiral. In Florida it also produced a class struggle related to the issues of statehood and the 1838 constitutional convention at St. Joseph. A line had been drawn between Florida Whigs representing larger plantation owners and friendly bankers who shared the planters' interests, and Democrats who were mostly small farmers and businessmen and afraid of bank power.

If the issues of banks and statehood divided Floridians politically, there were others that united them with equal strength. Florida Whigs and Democrats did not disagree fundamentally over slavery or the need to preserve their "peculiar institution." Nor did Floridians disagree over their need to increase the population, develop natural resources, and generally

Richard Keith Call, twice Territorial Governor of Florida, issued a pamphlet condemning Florida legislators for their secession vote on December 1, 1861.

Cartoons are used, then and now, as a graphic expression of political opinions. This one, subtitled "The One Qualification for a Whig President," shows opposition to the war Democrats felt could not be stopped if a Whig were elected president.

AN AVAILABLE CANDIDATE.
THE ONE QUALIFICATION FOR A WHIG PRESIDENT.

John Milton, a Georgian, fought as a volunteer in the Seminole War and then moved to Florida in 1846. As fifth Governor and an ardent States-Righter, he guided Florida during secession and the War Between the States and committed suicide as the Confederacy collapsed about him in 1865.

Winfield Scott in this cartoon is shown in his role as a general in the Union Army. He is slaying the serpent of the Confederacy which has many heads, all recognizable as Confederate heroes. Hercules in classical mythology is a god possessing exceptional strength.

THE HERCULES OF THE UNION,
SLAYING THE GREAT DRAGON OF SECESSION.

strive *to improve the quality of life on the frontier*. While there was much disagreement over statehood, the original Florida state constitution, written at St. Joseph in 1838, was more a product of political agreement than of bitter rivalry.

Politics changed, however, for Floridians who lived through the Civil War and the Reconstruction. Florida seceded from the Union and then joined her sister southern states in the new Confederacy in 1861. Little political division was seen on the surface, but former United States senator David L. Yulee's comment that Floridians were "no more Whigs and Democrats, but Confederates all" belied a deeper truth. Slavery and secession did manage to bridge the political chasm that had separated Whigs and Democrats; but the misfortunes and hardships of war, especially a losing war, gradually brought to life new political differences among Confederate Floridians. Disagreement with Governor John Milton's administration and conduct of the war often ran deep. Numerous Floridians opposed the state draft for militia troops, provisioning foodstuffs below market value for the Confederate armies, and even the overall relations of Florida with the Confederate government of President Jefferson Davis at Richmond. Not all Floridians suffered bitterness in defeat in 1865; some in fact were relieved and willing to help the Republican Party accomplish its Reconstruction task of returning Florida to the Union.

The story of Florida Reconstruction is the story of much besides politics. Emancipation and dislocations of war were felt socially and economically as well as politically. Indeed, politically considered, the Florida Reconstruction era under the Republican Party was relatively free from disruption. Although most Florida Whigs remained "Conservatives" and aligned with Democrats after the Civil War, other moderate whites were inclined to join with and lead the Florida Republican Party. Their moderating influence on the radicals was most effective: a moderate, not radical, state constitution was written in 1867; there was no period in which Blacks "ruled" Florida state government, no widespread disfranchising of ex-Confederate leaders. Republicans were unable to prevent steady Democratic electoral gains from 1870 onward, and Black Floridians were unsuccessful in developing and preserving their own political potential that a radical commitment to racial equality and progress could have produced.

Despite these facts, the Florida political legacy from Reconstruction resembled that of sister states of the ex-Confederacy—avowedly anti-Black, anti-Republican, and pro-Democratic. Yet even before, Democrats stripped any possible Republican (Black) resurgence to power in the 1885 state constitutional convention by incorporating white primaries, poll taxes, reductions in spending for Black education and for government services generally. The Florida Republican Party already had been reduced to an impotent organization by internal factional disputes among Blacks, white native-born Floridians, and Republican carpetbaggers from the North. Bourbon Democrats led by William D. Bloxham captured political control. Thereafter, Republicans became more interested in political patronage than in state politics. National nominating conventions and federal appointments took precedence as chief Republican concerns. Nearly one hundred years would go by before another Republican would replace Reconstruction Governor Marcellus Stearns who left office in

Print showing a scene of the assassination of President Lincoln was issued by the lithography firm of Currier and Ives, first established in 1835 and specializing in prints of American history, life, and manners.

1876, and Claude Kirk's election seemingly was more an anti- Robert King High (liberal Democrat from Dade County) campaign than it was pro-Republican.

Internal party harmony at this time was not much better for the Democrats than for their Republican predecessors. Much of this new Democratic splintering, however, was a carryover from old political disputes between Whigs and Democrats. There were also new conditions, created not only by the continuing factor of the Florida frontier, but also by the rapid growth the state experienced as it marched into the twentieth century.

Marcellus Stearns, acting governor 1874–1876, came to Florida from Maine via the Union Army. After losing an arm at the battle of Winchester, he was transferred to the Freedman's Bureau and then to Quincy, Florida. Active in organizing newly freed Blacks he also served in the Constitutional Convention and the Legislature.

Beginning in the 1870s and 1880s and running through the remainder of the century, Florida was swept by waves of farmer protest. The Democratic Party found it difficult to absorb, much less resolve, this steady torrent of agricultural discontent. The depression of 1873 affected farmers in the South and West longer and more harshly than others. Prices for foodstuffs and other farm products recovered less rapidly than did non-agricultural businesses. First it was the Grange and the Farmers' Alliance, and then it was the Independent Party and the Populists who tried to strengthen agricultural interests in Florida politics. Working against them, however, were the commercial forces that would eventually create modern-day Florida—businessmen, railroaders, and the captains

Despotic Governments must be sustained as they have ever been, by force; but the force of reason and science and virtue can only —

Likenesses of presidents Herbert Hoover and Franklin Roosevelt are familiar to many Floridians. Political issues surrounding their elections and policies from their terms in office still affect the life and times of people in the Sunshine State.

of the fledgling industries of lumber and mining. Although many of these political conflicts occurred within the framework of the state Democratic Party, in the cases of the 1884 Independents and the 1890s Populists, new political organizations appeared. They proved not to be lasting nor overly successful.

If old issues divided Florida farmers from Florida businessmen and others, new issues created new political arrangements as the state moved into the new century. A whole new frontier was encountered during the first few years. Rapid population buildup and an economic boom marked most of Florida in the early 1920s, but nowhere as significantly as in South Florida. With the opening of the southern peninsula to transportation, tourism, and settlement, Florida governmental services under the Democrats had to be expanded. Huge increases in railway mileage, a network of new public roads, and new cities and counties came about almost overnight. Here schools were needed, regulation of land sales and development, fencing for livestock, and countless other new problems. As urbanization, modernization, and industrialism developed in modern Florida, politics inside the Democratic Party attempted to keep pace. During the 1924 campaign public roads became the key issue for the five Democrats running for governor. John Martin won out, in part because he had called for expanded road building. Governor Martin's election, however, also marked the peak of the Florida boom of the 1920s and the inflationary spending by Florida governors to nurture it along. Martin himself increased school appropriations, provided free school texts for all elementary students, established a wildlife conservation program, and urged that convicts in the state prison be better utilized to provide non-competitive service for all Floridians.

By 1925, however, the boom in Florida was over, harbingering the national crash that would come four years later. The state election in 1928 revolved on how Florida should deal with the depression and economic collapse. This was a new issue, but it rested upon a traditional break among Floridians. When Al Smith of New York won the Democratic nomination for the Presidency, old-line Floridians were faced with voting against everything they stood for or voting for a Republican, Herbert Hoover. Smith's Roman Catholicism, anti-prohibition, and big-city nature alienated many rural Floridians. Prejudice won out against political affiliation, and Hoover carried Florida by a sizable margin. Democrats won state offices handily, however, by more than a two-to-one margin. This particular election demonstrated clearly the growing political estrange-

Cool, deliberation, and forbearance in debate, with union in promoting the great interests of our infant Country, will be the surest means of obtaining the objects desired, and meeting the Approbation of our fellow Citizens

Your fellow citizen

Wm P DuVal

ment of South Florida. In that section, people were far more concerned about hurricane damage from the two severe storms of 1926 and 1928. Recovery from the damages and from the general economic decline were of far greater importance politically than either Smith's religion or his preference for liquor.

Following the depression, there was considerable political controversy in Florida over President Roosevelt's New Deal programs. Governor David Scholtz' New Deal administration came under attack from many Democrats across Florida. When the Supreme Court ruled in *Brown v. Board of Education of Topeka* in 1954 that schools were to be desegregated, race was renewed in Florida politics to a degree unparalleled since Reconstruction. Fortunately, the next four governors of Florida, all of whom had to cope with the civil rights revolution, were more racially moderate than their counterparts elsewhere in the South. Violence did break out, most notably in Tampa and St. Augustine, but it was less by comparison with other states.

Throughout all the turmoil, Florida grew and has continued to grow faster than any other state in the Union. By 1966 it had become apparent that the 1885 constitution no longer could serve adequately the needs of a vastly more modern Florida. A new constitutional convention was called and the state government was reformed and modernized. Governors could run for reelection; lieutenant-governors were reestablished; state funding for capital projects was improved; and provision was made for periodic constitutional revision and updating. Other reforms equalized property rights for married men and women, placed budget responsibility in the governor's office, and smoothed legislative functions. Non-partisan support for the new document assured its acceptance by Floridians of all political persuasion. At a time when other states declined to modernize their state government, the new constitution and legislative reapportionment proved that Florida political parties could adjust to the changing needs of the state.

Considering Florida political parties from 1845 to the eve of the Bicentennial, Frederick W. Maitland's musings about the possible misuse of historical perspective comes to mind: "Too often we allow ourselves to suppose that, could we but get back to the beginning, we should find that all was intelligible and should then be able to watch the process whereby simple ideas were smothered under subtleties and technicalities."

—PETER KLINGMAN

Presidential Parade

Probably no state in the Union in the past century has hosted more presidents of the United States than Florida. Most came for relaxation, among them Theodore Roosevelt, Grover Cleveland and Herbert Hoover. Franklin D. Roosevelt had his favorite Floridian fishing guides, including an old timer named "Cap'n Sam" from a pioneer Miami family.

Harry Truman established his winter White House in Key West; John F. Kennedy spent time throughout his life at the family home in Palm Beach; and Richard Nixon operated from the winter White House on Key Biscayne.

A number of presidential candidates have also been seen walking the beaches, including Alf Landon, Adlai Stevenson and previously William Jennings Bryan who also orated on the golden assets of southern Florida during the boom days of the 1920s.

THE TRAUMA OF RECONSTRUCTION

Illustration for newspaper story covering the Civil War in Florida shows Fernandina Island, with terminal of Fernandina-Cedar Keys Railroad in the background and ships of occupying Union troops in the harbor.

Floridians who had worked tirelessly for admission to the Union in 1845 were just as anxious to secede from it in 1861. Much had happened to bring about this change of attitude. Florida was acquired by the new American nation from Spain just as cotton was becoming king in southern agriculture. The settlers who rushed into the new land found it ideally suited to cotton production on large plantations using slave labor. By 1845 the Florida plantation economy identified the new state with the agricultural South in a growing dispute with the rest of the United States over the morality of racial slavery, foreign trade policy, and Congressional administration of federal territories.

During the next few years a southern nationalism emerged; Floridians and other Southerners came to regard themselves as culturally different from people outside the South. Not only was racial slavery important to their economy, but it was considered necessary for their way of life, making possible the peaceful coexistence of Blacks and whites. With this view of slavery widespread in the South and increased pressure from abolitionists, events of the 1850s—Harriet Beecher Stowe's *Uncle Tom's Cabin*, the struggle over Kansas, the rise of the Republican party, the *Dred Scott* decision by the Supreme Court, and above all, John Brown's raid on Harper's Ferry and his subsequent martyrdom—widened a gap between the various sections of the United States. By the late 1850s, Southerners felt that their way of life was in danger if someone opposed to slavery—for example, a Republican—should win the presidency.

When Abraham Lincoln was elected President, most Floridians willingly followed their secessionist governor, Madison S. Perry, out of the Union and into the Confederacy. As a geographic appendage to the Confederate States of America, Florida was far from most of the Civil War battlefields, but most Floridians pledged themselves and their resources to the cause. From the Atlantic to the Mississippi River and from Shiloh to Appomattox Courthouse, Florida troops fought and died in every major battle of the war.

While most of the men were in the army, women managed plantations, made clothing for the army units, nursed the wounded, anxiously watched the growing casualty lists, and managed to maintain morale on the home front as hope of a Confederate victory gradually dwindled. With few exceptions, the slaves remained at home, identified with the cause of

Governor Madison S. Perry, a planter from Alachua County, warned the legislature that the election of Lincoln would lead to secession.

"Cotton is King" as Florida and the South thrive on a slavery-based plantation economy, producing and processing the plant fibre that has clothed people around the world for thousands of years. A staple for clothing in China, India, and Egypt, it was spun, woven, and dyed in the Americas long before the arrival of the white man.

their owners, and tilled the soil as they had in better times. From its broad fields and open ranges, Florida sent great quantities of beef, pork, staple foods, and fodder to the army in Virginia. Hundreds of Florida salt works supplied most of that scarce commodity used in the Confederacy.

The war that pitted brothers and fellow citizens against each other took a heavy toll, not alone in the death of one of every eight white male Floridians. Bitterness increased between those who held differing ideas about secession and the war. While most of the Unionists of 1861 had supported the Confederacy out of loyalty to the state, some had refused to do so. Others lost their enthusiasm for the Confederate cause as hope of victory diminished. Still others expressed Unionist sentiments when it was to their advantage to do so.

The Union invasions and occupations of Fernandina, Jacksonville, St. Augustine, Key West, Apalachicola, and Pensacola, provided bases for Floridians who opposed the Confederacy. As the Union blockade of the 1200 miles of Florida coastline increased, Unionists and others who opposed state policy began cooperating with the United States Navy, providing important information and raiding inland plantations for supplies.

Two regiments of Union cavalry were raised along the Gulf Coast from Florida Unionists and Confederate deserters. These troops fought numerous skirmishes with Confederate units, like Captain J.J. Dickison's independent cavalry. As hope for the Confederacy waned, deserters be-

Commerce Triumphs Over the Mason-Dixon Line

Although a Yankee citizen, Henry Plant, who had an efficient express business in the South, was given a special dispensation by Confederate President Jefferson Davis to continue his service during the Civil War. Plant's company not only was operated efficiently for the Confederate Army; after the war Plant was still the owner. He quickly amassed a fortune, and began buying railroads in the Southeast. During the 1880s, he put together a railroad system in Florida that is today part of the Seaboard Coast line.

He planned to develop a major port at Cedar Key, but when he discovered that he had been rooked—that his contract to buy a railroad did not include the terminal—he kissed Cedar Key off and went to Tampa. There he built a port, established a steamship line, and built the Tampa Bay Hotel, of Moorish-Arabic design. One of the most unusual buildings in the nation—bizarre is a better description—the hotel is today part of the University of Tampa. Still going strong at 78, Plant in 1897 opened the Belleview Hotel at Belleaire. He died in 1899, leaving an estate of $10 million.   —N.S.

Confederate cannon battery.

Italians

Gangs of Italian workingmen carried out much of the hard physical labor that was performed in Florida after the Civil War. Though often unnoticed, the Italians worked on railroad construction, in the turpentine camps, on plantations and naval stores farms, wherever large laboring crews were needed. The St. Cloud Sugar Plantation of Hamilton Disston, for example, employed several hundred Italian workers. The Florida East Coast Railway had regular contracts with Italian labor agents in New York City to supply the line with a continuing stream of recently arrived immigrants. During the height of the phosphate boom in Florida, when wild-cat mines sprang up like spring weeds and labor was at a premium, mine owners imported Sicilian peasants directly from the island. These hands commonly worked as "pickers" on the conveyor belt for forty-five cents a day wages. **G.E.P.**

Francis P. Fleming, on leave from his military unit in Virginia, defended home soil at the Battle of Natural Bridge. Later elected Governor of Florida, he held office from 1889–1893.

came an ever greater problem for civil and military leaders. When Governor Milton tried to control the deserter bands by burning their houses and arresting their families, he was discouraged to find that he had also destroyed the property and arrested the dependents of Confederate soldiers who were fighting in Virginia. This policy produced more desertions and further weakened the morale of Floridians. While most white inhabitants never wavered from the Confederate cause, those who did helped create an intense bitterness among neighbors, a bitterness which was difficult to resolve once peace was restored.

May 1865: some six long weeks after Lee's surrender, General Edward McCook accepted the surrender of 8000 Confederate soldiers in Florida. A few weeks earlier, anticipating the end, Governor Milton committed suicide. Many others talked of leaving the country, but only a few left, and some of those returned after a brief time. Most Floridians set out to pick up the pieces of their shattered lives. With some crops already in the ground, anxiety about the effect of emancipation was relieved when General John Newton ordered Florida planters to make contracts with the freedmen, and called on the former slaves to stay on the plantations and work for wages. The United States army repaired railroads before returning them to their private owners and even loaned army wagons to the planters so they could obtain supplies and market their crops.

Despite serious doubts that Blacks would adapt to a free labor system, the 1865 crop was planted and harvested, and the high prices it brought raised hopes for the future. Unfortunately this happy situation was only temporary and, in a few years, both freedmen and many of their former owners were gripped by perpetual debt in a failing cotton economy.

White Floridians were encouraged by President Andrew Johnson's reconstruction plans. Asking them only to renounce secession, slavery, and debts incurred in support of the Confederacy, Johnson pardoned all former Confederates willing to take an oath of loyalty to the United States and guaranteed that they could keep all of their property except slaves. Quickly complying with his mild requirements, Floridians approved a new constitution, elected officers, and prepared to resume normal relations with the United States. Believing that Blacks were incapable of full citizenship, most Floridians were relieved that Johnson had asked so little of them with regard to the rights of their former slaves.

Johnson and ex-Confederate Floridians, however, reckoned without the Radical Republicans who thought the war had been fought for human equality, and moderates who desired some guarantee of civil rights

Members of the Florida Legislature gather on steps of the capitol for a group portrait, as civil government is re-established following the Civil War.

"Stars and Bars," emblem and rallying point for the Confederacy, continues into the present as a symbol of sympathy for "the lost cause."

or Blacks before restoring the former Confederate states to their former sovereignty in these matters. When President Johnson resolutely refused to compromise with Congress, overwhelming majorities in both the House and the Senate overturned his reconstruction program and replaced it with a more stringent one of their own. Military rule was restored to the South under a Congressional plan requiring enfranchisement of adult male Blacks and ratification of the Fourteenth Amendment before Florida could be restored to the Union.

Freedmen's Bureau agents and other United States officials, a handful of ministers, and some promoters interested in developing the sparsely populated state—immediately dubbed "carpetbaggers"—joined a small number of natives—known derisively as "scalawags" by their incensed Florida neighbors—as leaders of the emerging Republican party of Florida. Shouting "the bottom rail is on top," freedmen rallied to the party of Lincoln in a campaign for delegates to yet another constitutional convention.

Angered that Johnson's mild program had been overturned and new requirements imposed on them nearly two years after the end of the war, white Floridians were uncertain how they should react to the Radical Republican legislation. Unwilling to accept Black suffrage and fearing that they were themselves disfranchised under the new laws, many of them boycotted the election. The result was an overwhelming majority of Black and white Republicans in the 1868 constitutional convention.

The convention was a disorderly brawl resulting in a constitution guaranteeing Black suffrage but providing a legislative apportionment favorable to the native whites. In an allegedly corrupt election, the con-

65

The KKK, still active in Florida and throughout the South, no longer has wide popular support as in the days of Reconstruction.

"All of the actions of an individual bear the stamp of his community as assuredly as does the language he speaks."
—JOHN DEWEY

Guard against the postures
of pretended patriotism.
—GEORGE WASHINGTON, 1796

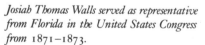

Josiah Thomas Walls served as representative from Florida in the United States Congress from 1871–1873.

stitution was ratified and a Republican slate of officials elected. The military commander of Florida turned over control of the state to Republican Governor Harrison Reed on July 4, 1868, and reconstruction was ostensibly accomplished.

Native Floridians had no intention of accepting this situation. Vowing not to recognize the Republican party or the Black suffrage on which it was based, they resisted the new government with every means they could muster: by dilatory tactics in the legislature; by disparaging editorials in the press; and especially by organizing night-riding regulator bands similar to the Ku Klux Klan. Blacks and white Republicans were threatened, intimidated, beaten, and finally murdered. Elections were disrupted to prevent Blacks from voting, and Republican officials countered by fraudulently counting the votes. Law and order and democratic processes suffered tremendously. The most serious violence subsided in the early 1870s, but cheating and fraud in the electoral process continued.

Calling themselves Conservative-Democrats, Florida natives gradually gained strength against the Republicans who spent much of their time and energy in wasteful bickering. By 1876 the Conservative-Democrats had gained a bare majority of the legislature, elected one United States senator, and were in control of many of the county governments; but Marcellus L. Stearns, a staunch Republican from Maine, still sat in the governor's office. The Conservatives were determined to change that in 1876.

National policy toward reconstruction of the South had changed. Many Radicals had faded from prominence; others were no longer as adamant about the elevation of Blacks to full citizenship. The nation turned to other matters including a disastrous economic depression. Many Congressmen and the people who had elected them were anxious to settle the "Southern question."

The presidential election of 1876, between Republican Rutherford B. Hayes and Democrat Samuel J. Tilden, was challenged. The national crisis of no clear election to the presidency was caused by disputed electoral returns from South Carolina, Louisiana, and Florida, the only three southern states where Republicans still controlled the governorships. The Florida canvassing board, with a majority of Republicans, counted the votes in favor of Republicans at both state and national levels, but they acted so unfairly that the state supreme court ordered a recount. The recount resulted in a victory for Republican Hayes as President and George F. Drew, the Conservative-Democrat, as governor. In a lengthy Congressional struggle, Hayes was finally seated over Tilden, but not before Southerners exacted from him a promise that he would remove all United States soldiers from the South and, thus, end the "Southern question." This compromise was hailed as the "end of Reconstruction" and the "restoration of home rule" in Florida.

Left to their own devices white Floridians soon disfranchised the Blacks and eliminated the Republican party as a force in the state. Blacks continued to farm the land, tied to it now by tenancy and crop liens and mounting debts instead of bonded servitude. The people who had led the state before the war resumed their leadership. But things were not quite the same. Cotton declined as a money crop and the old planter families turned to railroad promotion and land development, inviting Northern investors to the state and trying to attract more permanent settlers. Impressive commercial growth in Central Florida during the 1870s often has been obscured by historical emphasis on reconstruction of the older, cotton-producing part of the state.

If the Civil War and Reconstruction era was the end of the plantation-slavery economy it was also the beginning of modern Florida with its advertising for Northern tourists and potential settlers. Railroads were beginning to inch southward, hotels were built on the St. Johns, orange groves were planted, and winter vegetables became a new money crop. In some ways there were two Floridas: the old rural northern area which was similar to the rest of the South; and peninsular Florida with its new settlers and new types of activity. Yet both sections were much alike. Many members of older plantation families moved south and mingled with the new settlers. Regardless of background most adopted Southern attitudes about the traumatic Civil War, the abortive efforts of Congress to change Florida society afterward, and the growing myth of the "Lost Cause." All—at least all of the whites, and no one asked the Blacks—were satisfied with the settlement worked out during the 1876 election dispute. The completion of the Radical Republican program of the 1860s regarding Black rights was left for later generations.   JERRELL H. SHOFNER

The Civil War, together with bond issues floated by state administrations immediately after the war, plunged the state of Florida into debt. By the 1880s it faced bankruptcy. A Philadelphia tool-maker, Hamilton Disston, came to the rescue with a million dollars and saved Florida honor. For his million, Disston received four million acres of "swamp and overflow land," including the entire Kissimmee Valley as well as most of the Caloosahatchee Valley and all the land on the west bank of Lake Okeechobee.

With Kissimmee as headquarters, he proceeded to drain his land and develop it, as required under the sales contract. He improved the flow of the Kissimmee and Caloosahatchee rivers and made boat travel possible all the way from Fort Myers to the town of Kissimmee. He planted 20,000 acres of sugarcane on the rich, shallow lake bottom land from which the water was drained in the upper Kissimmee Valley, and he tackled the drainage of the rich muck lands about the south shore of Lake Okeechobee.

Just as it appeared that he was succeeding, just as settlers were pouring into Kissimmee to farm on the ten-acre plots they had bought from Disston's land agents in the North, a major depression swept the nation in 1893. Disston went broke. He shot himself to death in 1896.   —N.S.

_____

Flags of the United States and the State of Florida flap in the breeze and the top of a sabal palm, the Florida state tree, rises above the wall of old Fort Clinch. Partially completed by the time of the Civil War, Fort Clinch was occupied by both Union and Confederate troops.

Paintings of the Seminole War reveal pastoral beatuy of the Florida lands for which whites and Indians fought.

FLORIDIANS GO TO WAR

Major Francis L. Dade, marching his men through hostile Indian country during second Seminole War, is surrounded by Seminoles and all but one are killed in Indian ambush on Christmas Day, 1835. Battle took place near Bushnell but Dade's name lives on far to the south in Dade County on the tip of the peninsula.

Chekika

Dade County was four years old, and the county seat was at Indian Key, an 11-acre island retreat for wreck salvagers in the Florida Keys. Captain Jacob Housman, leader of the wreckers, kept a store there. Although the Seminoles and the U.S. Army waged war on the mainland, it must have seemed remote.

But at dawn on August 7, 1840, seventy residents on the key were aroused by the whoops and yells of a band of Indians. When the Indians departed in their thirty canoes, loaded with loot, they left behind thirteen dead whites and island dwellings in ashes. Among the dead was Dr. Henry Perrine, the first U.S. plant explorer, who had received a federal grant of land to establish a tropical agricultural center in southern Florida.

The leader of this Indian band was no Seminole; he was Chekika, a Calusa, who, like his forebears, was of almost giant proportions. According to Army sources, the Calusa, remnants of a once powerful tribe, took advantage of the Seminole War to pillage and murder.

The year before, Chekika and Sam Jones' lieutenant, Billie Bowlegs II, attacked a party of thirty-two troops under Colonel William S. Harney, sent to guard a store set up on the Caloosahatchee River to trade

with "peaceful Indians." The Indians, suspicious of Army intentions, set upon Harney and his men in a dawn attack, slaying eighteen. Harney escaped in his underwear, swearing vengeance as he swam the Caloosahatchee to save his life.

Harney's chance to even the score came after the Indian Key massacre. With a former slave as guide, he left Fort Dallas (now Miami) with a troop of ninety men, dressed and painted like Indians, to hunt down the Calusa leader. Thirty miles west of the Miami River, Harney surprised Chekika and his followers. Chekika was shot dead on the spot, but his body was hanged along with captured warriors, while his mother, wife and children watched. With the death of Chekika, the Calusas disappeared into history.   —NIXON SMILEY

The Perrine massacre at Indian Key in 1841 not only kept the Seminole war going, it aroused the imagination of the best known American writer James Fennimore Cooper. His *Jack Tier, or the Florida Reef* was first published as a magazine serial under the title "The Islets of the Reef or Rose Budd." Whether he had actually seen the country or not was unimportant—it was a "pot-boiler."
    —M.S.D.

Billy Bowlegs II bears a name famous throughout Seminole Indian history.

*Seminoles, reading signs on the land, used
tactics of guerrilla warfare.*

Engravings in illustrated newspapers brought Civil War close to readers before photographs became common.

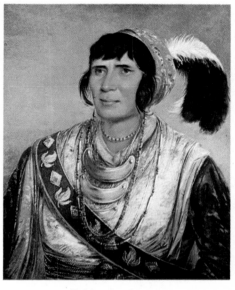

Defying the white man, Seminole chief, Osceola, pinned treaty to conference table with his dagger.

Cape Florida Lighthouse, scene of Indian attack in 1836, still stands at the tip of Key Biscayne.

Salt works at St. Joseph, here attacked by Union troops, supplied the Confederacy.

Fernandina, target of Union troops, was a major supply terminal for Confederacy.

PHALANX RIVER PICKETS DEFENDING THEMSELVES.
Federal picket boat near Fernandina, Fla., attacked by Confederate sharpshooters stationed in the trees on the banks.

A grimly factual study of the real causes of the Seminole war was written by a visiting Congressman, Joshua T. Giddings. *The Exiles of Florida* was too real to be popular in a country of slave-owners although it is the stuff of history that broke over the South in the thunder of the Civil War.

—M.S.D.

Builder's half model of C.S.S. Florida.

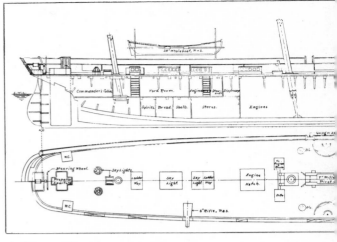

*Architectural line drawings
of C.S.S.* Florida *show hull shape
and interior design.*

Confederate blockade runner Florida
chasing Union ship Star of Peace.

C.S.S. FLORIDA

"Having few vessels in their own ports suitable for commerce-destroyers, the leaders of the Confederacy purchased, through their agents and middlemen, vessels in England, which, sailing without guns, ammunition or crews, were met, sometimes at sea and other times in out-of-the-way places, by another vessel laden with armament and stores, and thus became Confederate cruisers. . . . The conditions under which these vessels were secured, equipped and commissioned were sufficiently like those obtained by Benjamin Franklin in France during the Revolution to warrant the designation 'cruisers.'

"The first of this class of Confederate cruisers was the *Florida*, built at Liverpool, 1861 – 62, exactly on the lines of the British gunboat of that day, under the name of *Oreto*, ostensibly for the Italian Government. Although our minister to England, Charles Francis Adams, laid conclusive evidence before the British Government that the *Oreto* was in reality a Confederate cruiser, and in spite of the fact that the Italian consul disclaimed all knowledge of the vessel, she was allowed to clear from Liverpool, March 22, 1862, consigned to Adderly & Co., of Nassau. . . . On April 28th the *Oreto* arrived at Nassau, where she was joined by the English steamer *Bahama* from Hartlepool, England, laden with guns, ammunition and a complete outfit for a cruiser. In order to keep up a

semblence of complying with the laws of neutrals, the *Oreto*, when she began taking aboard her armament, was libeled, but was quickly released by the sympathetic jury, and on August 7th, under Commander John Newland Maffitt, sailed for an uninhabited island in the Bahamas, where her two rifled 7-inch guns and six 6-inch guns, together with the ammunition, were taken aboard, and she began her career as the Confederate cruiser *Florida*. At this time the vessel had only twenty-two men for a crew, and this number was reduced by yellow fever to only three or four efficient men.

"Touching at Cardenas, Cuba, where he got a re-enforcement of twelve men, Maffitt stood over to Mobile, sighting that port September 4th. The blockading squadron, under the command of Commander George Henry Preble, at that time consisted of the *Oneida* and the *Winona*. As the *Florida* was constructed on the lines of the English cruisers that were constantly inspecting the blockade about that time, Maffitt hoisted English colors, and in broad daylight stood for the Union vessels. Deceived by this, Preble went to quarters and approached the *Florida*, believing her to be an English man-of-war. When near enough he hailed the stranger, but no attention was paid to it. The *Oneida* then fired three shots in succession across the *Florida's* bow without getting an

answer, upon which Preble fired his broadside, but the *Florida* still continued on her swift course. The *Oneida*, the *Winona*, and the schooner *Rachel Seaman* (the last having just arrived off the port) fired as rapidly as possible, but the *Florida* was speeding away at fourteen knots an hour to the seven of the Union vessels, and although somewhat damaged she gained the port.

"Speaking of the injuries the *Florida* received from this fire, one of her midshipmen, G. Terry Sinclair, records: "We received one 11-inch shell opposite our port gangway, near the water line. It passed through our coal bunker, painfully wounding one man and beheading another, thence to the berth deck, where our men had previously been ordered as a place of safety. Fortunately this shell did not explode, the fuse having been knocked out, probably by contact with the ship's side. Another shell entered the cabin and, passing through the pantry, raised havoc with the crockery. The ship to the day of her destruction bore the marks of upward of fourteen hundred shrapnel balls. Our additional casualties were two men slightly wounded."

"Having shipped a crew, Maffitt, at two o'clock in the morning of January 16, 1863, boldly steamed through the Union blockading squadron and escaped, in spite of the additional vessels that had been detailed

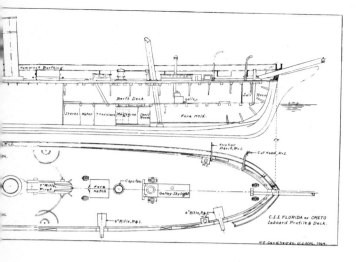

*Commander John Newland Maffitt,
first captain of the* C.S.S. Florida.

especially with a view of capturing him. Taking three prizes, the *Florida* was chased for thirty-four hours by the *Sonoma*, Commander Thomas Holdup Stevens, but escaped by the superior speed. Running into Nassau, she was received with every demonstration of joy by the British inhabitants, and was permitted to remain in port thirty-six hours, or twelve more than allowed by Government instructions. She also took aboard coal for three months, although the authorities had forbidden a larger supply than would suffice to carry her to the nearest Confederate port.

"Cruising between Bahia and New York, Maffitt in five months took fourteen prizes. . . .

"The *Florida* had sailed from Brest, where she remained six months, and being completely overhauled was placed under command of Captain Charles Maniguelt Morris. She then crossed the Atlantic, and, after being allowed by the British authorities to coal at Bermuda, continued her depredations on American commerce in the Atlantic Ocean. The peculiar nature of this service is interestingly revealed by Midshipman G.T. Sinclair when he says: 'Another of our captures, a vessel from the East Indies, contained a rare character in an old lady, who we were told, was a missionary on her return home for a vacation. As usual, Captain Mor-

ris gave this lady one of the staterooms in his cabin; but it was not long before she had the entire cabin, and, I think, had she stayed much longer, would have been captain. She was intensely Union, and had little use for 'rebels,' nor did she hesitate to tell us so. We got in the habit of watching for her head as it came up out of the cabin hatch, when there would be a general scamper; but the poor officer of the deck was compelled to stand and take her tongue lashing. The old lady usually promenaded the deck with a green cotton umbrella raised, and on one occasion one of the retreating ones returned and found that Lieutenant Stone, who was in charge of the deck, had gone into the rigging, where he remained, looking very much like a cat up a tree with a dog watching him.'

"After touching at Teneriffe, Morris, on October 5, 1864, anchored at Bahia (intending to take in supplies and then pass around Cape Horn to make a raid on American whalers in the Pacific), where he found the United States sloop of war *Wachusett*, Commander Napoleon Collins, of Wilkes' flying squadron. Fearing that a battle might be precipitated in the harbor, a Brazilian corvette anchored between the two vessels. A little before daybreak, October 7, 1864, Collins crossed the bow of the corvette, intending to ram and sink the *Florida* at her anchorage. Captain Morris and many of his officers

and men were ashore. Failing to strike square on, the *Wachusett* carried away the *Florida's* mizzenmast, main yard, and some of the bulwarks. After an exchange of a few shots, Lieutenant Thomas K. Porter, the senior officer in the *Florida*, surrendered with sixty-nine officers and men. Collins, who had only three men injured in the affair, took the cruiser in tow and carried her out of the harbor, in spite of the remonstrances of the Brazilian authorities. . . .

"The act of Commander Collins was a flagrant violation of the rights of a neutral port but in view of the fact that England, France, Spain, and many of the South American states had repeatedly, outrageously, and to a far more serious extent violated their neutrality toward the United States, his course does not seem so unjustifiable. . . .

"The *Florida* was taken to the United States and was accidentally sunk in port. While under Captain Maffitt's command the *Florida* and her tenders captured fifty-five vessels, and under Morris some twenty were added to the list."

—EDGAR S. MACLAY
A History of the United States Navy

Battle of Olustee, largest, bloodiest Civil War battle fought on Florida soil, ended with Confederate victory.

Forts and lighthouses, war-important, dot the long Florida coastline. Oyster shells at tabby-constructed Ft. Clinch at Fernandina shine in the sunlight. View from inside fort could be "light at the end of the tunnel," but is light at the end of the stairwell.

America fought three major wars during Thomas Edison's lifetime, yet he made virtually no direct impact on military technology. This is not surprising. A man who placed bird houses on posts offshore in the river to effect a truce between birds and cats is not likely to devote his energies to weapons of destruction. "Making things which kill men is against my fiber," Edison once said. "I would rather make people laugh."

—G.L.

Man-O-War Bird.

Time passed slowly for soldiers at Tampa during the Spanish-American War. Awaiting ships that would carry them to Cuba, some of their famous companions were Theodore Roosevelt and his Rough Riders and Major William Jennings Bryan.

75

MAN AND NATURE

Florida is a land filled with sunlight. Some say it had a cataclysmic beginning in volcanic eruptions that phased into tranquility. And out of cataclysm came an earthly Eden, and tales of gopherwood and arks. The unique climate and geology of Florida, in fact, did attract a marvelously varied assortment of living things: plants and animals that grew in the sunlight and rains, inland, along the coast and within fresh and salt waters. Some flourished, as native things will if conditions are right; others were hunted, harvested, or mined. Useful animals were fed and bred; agricultural and ornamental plants were given nutrients, irrigation, and encouragement. Their number and kind was increased by bold plant and animal explorers who traveled the world to bring new breeds and seeds and cuttings to Florida.

The changes would have surprised the Spaniard Fontaneda who recorded his impressions of Florida in 1575 after roaming the peninsula with the Indians for more than a quarter of a century. His words are filled with wonder as he describes the grand wilderness of land, lakes, and offshore islands drenched in sun. He could have no premonition that today land and coastal management would become a reality as Florida acknowledges the inland and on and off shore need to protect its economic and natural resources.

Like the fragile border that separates land and sea, man and nature have always been interdependent. In Florida, man discovered ways to take abundant harvests from the earth and sea. Only in the recent years did he realize they were not infinite sources, and paradise was only in the imagination. Man discovered that Eden was filled with a host of serpents. Some greeted the discoverers, the frontiersman, and the permanent settlers: poisonous plants and animals in the water or land or air; sudden storms, some tropical hurricanes; floods, lingering droughts, unexpected freezes. Then man recently discovered other serpents: he could over-harvest, over-build, over-cut, over-mine, and over-expend energy. He could muddy his own waters and lay barren his own lands. As man and nature enter a new period in history with an increasing awareness of obligatory relationships, the use and misuse of Florida resources is being reviewed five hundred years after its first reporter described the richness of this natural heritage.

— J.E.G. — B.R.R.

Migrant farmworker picks beans near Homestead.

He Lived and Wrote the First Book

No one will ever know how many Spanish people from the provinces of the New World died in Florida, burned alive in the festivals of the Glades Indians who had captured them from wrecks along the east coast. Only a few escaped. One was a boy, thirteen years old and from Cartagena, merry and quick-witted, who pleased his Indian captors when he guessed rightly that their chief had ordered him to dance. Escalante de Fontaneda, with his little brother, was on his way back to Spain carrying gold enough for their education, when he was shipwrecked. Only he, of that fleet, was saved.

Brought up as an Indian boy, Fontaneda learned all the skills of hunting and fishing in the lower Florida wilds, passing with his companions the tests of his manhood. Learning several Indian dialects, he moved about watching and listening and remembering everything he could about the Indians and Indian life in the rare region at the end of Florida. *Circa* 1575 Fontaneda wrote about Florida. This book is the sole documentary source for present knowledge of the civilization of those Indian people who had lived for centuries about the coasts and the sawgrass river of southern Florida.

Fontaneda's small book is startlingly vivid, rich with his reactions to the land and lives and ways of his Indian captors and the stories of the shipwrecked Spaniards.

—M.S.D.

View from on high of St. Petersburg peninsula, Clearwater Beach, and Tampa Bay with the city of Tampa in the distance.

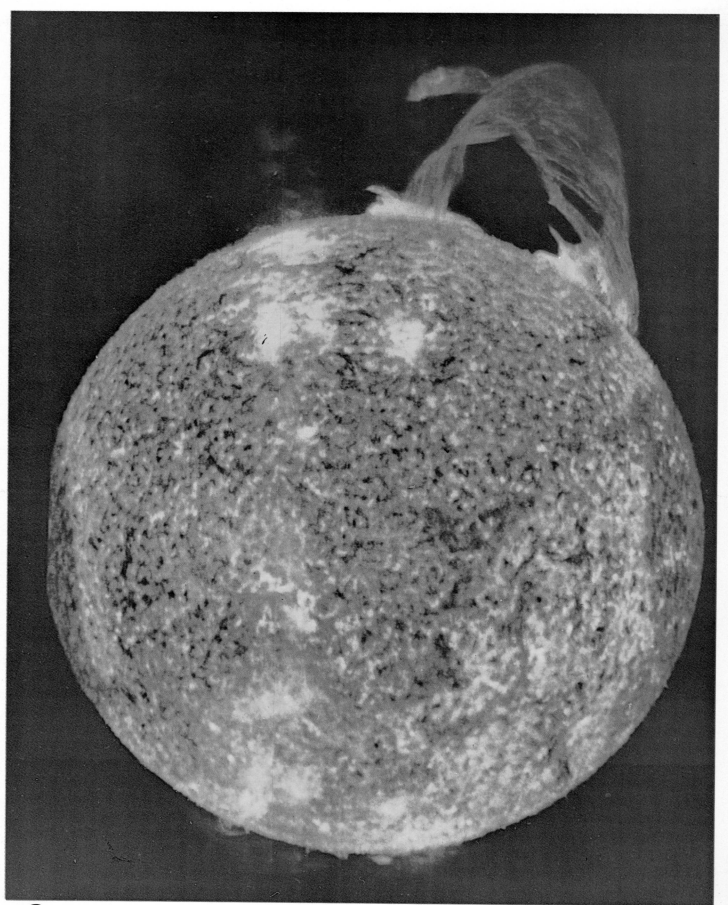

78

FIRE, WATER, AND AIR

In the beginning, the beginning of the earth, the land now known as Florida did not exist. But, when was "the beginning," the time of origin of the Earth and other members of the Solar System? Probably about 4.6 to 5 billion years ago, possibly from a cataclysmic cosmic event.

As the materials of the Earth cooled and a crust formed, a record was left of the changes that occurred. This record was preserved in the rocks.

The world of air and water peculiar to the planet Earth evolved through time, largely as internal changes occurred and unstable materials were released by volcanoes. The original atmosphere of the Earth probably was primarily ammonia, methane, hydrogen sulfide, and other foul gases. The evolution of life and then photosynthesis changed the atmosphere to one rich in nitrogen and oxygen.

The Earth originally was largely covered by oceanic crust. The record of the history of the earth preserved in the rocks formed at different times in its evolution proves no continents existed in the beginning. The continents have grown. The light weight earth materials, like granite, gneisses, and sedimentary rocks, composing the crust of the continents have changed through time and the action of the geological processes. This process of change into continents and ocean basins has been occurring for three and a half billion years or more. The oldest rocks, originally volcanics and impure sands and muds similar to those now forming in the Aleutians and other volcanic island archipelagoes, have been altered to schists, gneisses, and greenstone by the action of heat and pressure in our dynamic earth.

Rocks from deep oil test wells in peninsular Florida are not unlike the oldest rocks known from the "basement" of other areas of the North American continent; however, they are younger. There may be some rocks under Florida one billion years old; most are believed to be less than one-half billion years old. The volcanics forming the basement in south Florida may be younger. Continental type rocks, granites, gneisses, and sedimentary rocks, that form the "basement" of north Florida changed in the way a volcanic island archipelago along the southeastern portion of the North American continent would have, in the same way that Cuba, Hispaniola, and Puerto Rico have arisen. The Yucatan peninsula of Central America is the same geologic age and may be related. This common

Rocks from the "basement" of Florida are similar to this volcanic lava located in Hawaii, suggesting to some cataclysmic beginnings.

79

About five million years ago vast reserves of phosphate-bearing sediments accumulated in a chain of river mouths and embayments along the Florida west coast. The largest is called Bone Valley. Fossil bones and teeth in these phosphate deposits reveal Florida history at that time. Extensive phosphate mining activities turn up diverse kinds of sharks teeth, including *Carcharodon megalodon*, the largest shark that ever lived, sea-going relatives of the manatees belonging to the family Dugongidae, extinct horses, two kinds of rhinoceroses, three kinds of mastodons, and four kinds of camels. Several bizarre cloven-hoofed animals have recently been discovered in Bone Valley, including *Synthetoceras tricornatus* a slingshot horned species distantly related to the camel family; *Hexameryx simpsoni*, a six-horned antilocaprid; and *Subantilocapra garciae*, a near ancestor of the American Pronghorn Antelope.

—S. DAVID WEBB

origin is an unproven hypothesis. Other geologic clues suggest the volcanic chain extended to the southeast and formed the platforms upon which the Bahama limestone banks and islands were deposited. There are those who believe the Americas were once adjacent to Europe and Africa and have subsequently drifted apart. If so, Florida was once part of Africa.

The three areas, Florida, Yucatan and the Bahamas, do have a similar later history and all have been sites of extensive accumulation of limestone during the last 160 million years. Great thicknesses of shells, coral, and other sediment composed of calcium carbonate have accumulated in the warm tropical seas that covered these submerged platforms. As these platforms settled, limey deposits built upward and outward. They are in excess of 18,000 feet thick in south Florida.

Terrestrial Florida consists of two major parts, the panhandle and peninsular Florida. The climate and geology of these two parts merges between the Apalachicola and Suwannee Rivers.

Underlying the Florida panhandle is a thick sequence of detrital sediment, largely quartz and clay. Just as rivers are now carrying eroded materials from the soils of watersheds, so have bygone rivers carried materials into the northern margin of the Gulf of Mexico during the past 180 million years. The Gulf Coastal Plain and the adjoining continental shelf have been built from these sands and mud deposits.

The Gulf of Mexico has surely existed as a nearly enclosed oceanic basin since Jurassic time, 190 million years ago. This period, most commonly known as the time of the dinosaurs, was also the time of the origin of

MAJOR EVENTS ON EARTH AS RELATED TO FLORIDA

EVENT	MILLIONS OF YEARS BEFORE PRESENT
Oldest Moon rocks.	4600.0
Oldest Earth rocks.	3500.0
First organisms.	3000.0
Plants with chlorophyll and evolution of free oxygen.	2000.0
Evolution of skeletons.	600.0
Oldest rocks known from the Florida basement, appearance of fish.	500.0
First amphibians.	375.0
Time of vast coal swamps and the first reptiles.	345.0
Last major mountain building episode in Appalachians and possibly in Florida.	250.0
First dinosaurs.	225.0
Beginning of limestone deposits on Florida platform. Cuba, Hispanola and Puerto Rico come into existence. Gulf of Mexico contains a supersaturated salt brine.	180.0
Uplift of Rocky Mountains.	80.0
Dinosaur extinction.	65.0
Beginning of elevation of continents with influx of sand and clay over Florida peninsula.	25.0
World cooling and glaciation in Antarctica.	15.0
First man.	2.0
Continental glaciation began in temperate regions.	.5
Man in Florida, extinction of mammoths.	.01

GEOLOGIC TIME SCALE FROM RECORD IN ROCKS

ERA	PERIOD	EPOCH	MILLIONS OF YEARS BEFORE PRESENT
Precambrian	The Beginning		4600.0?
Paleozoic	Cambrian		570.0
	Ordovician		500.0
	Silurian		430.0
	Devonian		395.0
	Carboniferous		345.0
	Permian		280.0
Mesozoic	Triassic		225.0
	Jurassic		190.0
	Cretaceous		135.0
Cenozoic	Tertiary	Paleocene	
		Eocene	
		Oligocene	
		Miocene	
		Pliocene	
			65.0
	Quarternary	Pleistocene	2.0
		Recent	.01

Cuba, Hispaniola, and Puerto Rico as a youthful volcanic island chain. Warm tropical seas began to invade the southern-most portion of the platform that now forms the basement of peninsular Florida and the now submerged West Florida Shelf. Great salt deposits were precipitated from sea water throughout the Gulf. These deposits are known to underlie portions of the Gulf Coast from Panama City, Florida, westward, the continental shelves, and even the depths of the Gulf of Mexico. This vast deposit of salt could form only if the Straits of Yucatan and the Florida Straits were greatly restricted. The Florida Straits between Florida and Cuba may not have existed and certainly did not exist between Florida and the Bahamas. Then, even as now, the Gulf was characterized by lack of rainfall; the salt was deposited from supersaturated brines in the restricted Jurassic basin.

It is the plastic, light weight rock salt evaporite deposits that have floated upward into the overlying heavier sand and clay deposits to form the salt domes and plugs so characteristic of the margins of the Gulf of Mexico. Even the oil trap in the Jay Oil Field of northwestern Florida is associated with this type of salt-related structure.

Peninsular Florida, the West Florida Shelf, the Bahama bank and Yucatan have been covered by shallow tropical seas during most of subsequent time. The Cretaceous and Early Tertiary limestones underlying Florida all bear evidence of having been deposited in shallow water in spite of being over 3000 feet thick in the vicinity of Gainesville in northern peninsular Florida and much thicker eastward, westward and especially

Florida emerged from the sea about 30 million years ago. And almost from the beginning, rich accumulations of fossils have recorded the history of the land animals that lived here. The oldest terrestrial fossils were discovered in Gainesville in 1965 by a student, Mervin Kontrovitz. An even richer locality, known as Thomas Farm produces one of the most concentrated samples of land vertebrates in the world. An ancient sinkhole, the site gradually filled with sediments bearing bones of most kinds of animals living in that area, everything from bats and lizards up to rhinoceroses, three-toed horses, and huge bear-dogs.

—S. DAVID WEBB

Map of ocean floor showing the relationship of Florida to the North American Continent, Central America, Cuba and the Bahamas.

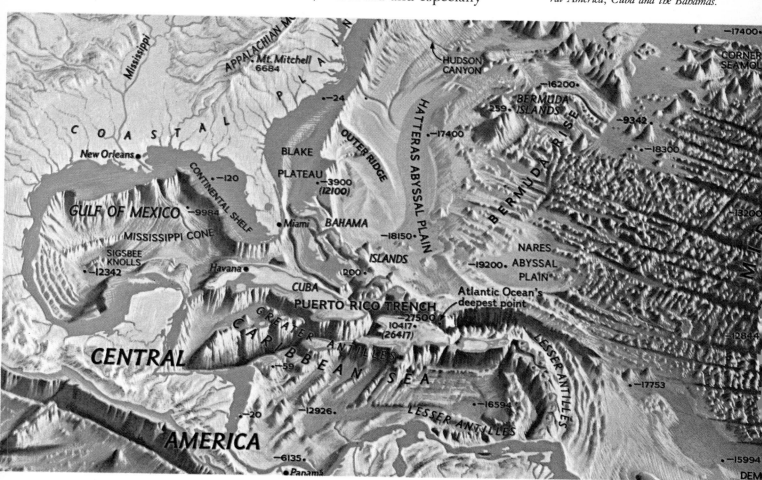

*Divers recovering mammoth bones from
Warm Mineral Springs.*

southward. The Felda and Sunniland Oil Fields in south Florida are producing from a Cretaceous limestone reservoir at a depth of about 12,500 feet.

Conditions that favor the formation of reef rock and other types of limestone have occurred over an ever smaller area during the last 25 million years. Florida, however, still has a coral reef extending from Miami, south and westward to the Dry Tortugas. In the shallow areas back of these reefs, extensive deposits of carbonate skeletal material of both plants and animals are accumulating. Geologists from all over the world come to south Florida to study limestone in the making.

Warm tropical seas covered part or all of peninsular Florida for the last time about 30 million years ago. Even at this time, some changes were occurring. A few sinkhole deposits have been found in Alachua County containing the bones of Oligocene land vertebrates. Some land must have existed. During the Oligocene and the two longer previous epochs of the Tertiary, the Eocene and Paleocene, thick deposits of limestone were deposited that now form the Floridian aquifer. This is the principle source of fresh water in most of Florida. Solution of this rock by the circulating water frequently causes the ground above to collapse forming a "sinkhole."

The Early Tertiary limestones are the most ancient rocks to outcrop naturally in Florida. Because of structural warping and uplift in northwestern peninsular Florida and near Marianna, the lithology and fossils of these formations can be collected and studied from natural outcrops and man-made exposures in road cuts and quarries. The most ancient fossils ever collected from these exposures anywhere in Florida are the marine sea shell and plant remains in the Paleocene limestone in Citrus and Levy Counties. The exception is the coral rock dredged from the steep escarpment along the West Florida Shelf; these fossils were Cretaceous in age, but they were from an outcrop under 8000 feet of Gulf water.

Sedimentary deposits that have accumulated in Florida during the last 25 million years attest to dramatic changes in sediment types, fossils, and climate. The Great Ice Age, the Pleistocene, often is thought of as the

Artist's version of early hunters attacking a mammoth.

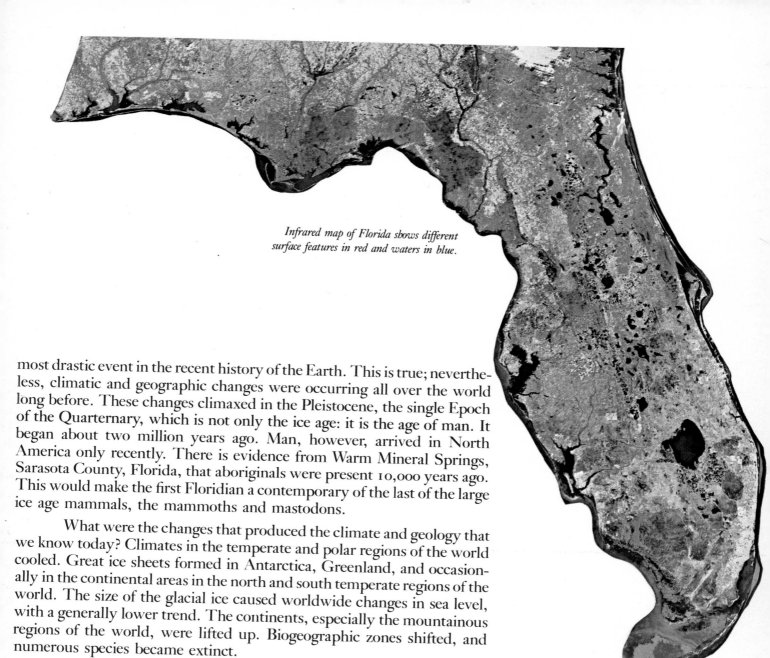

Infrared map of Florida shows different surface features in red and waters in blue.

most drastic event in the recent history of the Earth. This is true; nevertheless, climatic and geographic changes were occurring all over the world long before. These changes climaxed in the Pleistocene, the single Epoch of the Quarternary, which is not only the ice age: it is the age of man. It began about two million years ago. Man, however, arrived in North America only recently. There is evidence from Warm Mineral Springs, Sarasota County, Florida, that aboriginals were present 10,000 years ago. This would make the first Floridian a contemporary of the last of the large ice age mammals, the mammoths and mastodons.

What were the changes that produced the climate and geology that we know today? Climates in the temperate and polar regions of the world cooled. Great ice sheets formed in Antarctica, Greenland, and occasionally in the continental areas in the north and south temperate regions of the world. The size of the glacial ice caused worldwide changes in sea level, with a generally lower trend. The continents, especially the mountainous regions of the world, were lifted up. Biogeographic zones shifted, and numerous species became extinct.

Large volumes of sand and clay were transported into Florida from the land areas to the north during the Miocene. These covered the earlier limestones with an overburden from 100 to more than 600 feet thick. The highest areas in Florida, the plain north of Paxton at an elevation of about 345 feet, and the sand hills forming the central axis of peninsular Florida with a maximum elevation nearly 300 feet, are relic from Late Miocene time. The surface sands of west Florida are largely deposited by moving water, whereas in peninsular Florida these sands are similar to a gigantic marine sandbar. The outline of this sandbar, the Lake Wales Ridge, can easily be seen on the images of the earth taken by NASA satellites. When these sands were accumulated, sea level was probably about 200 to 240 feet higher than it is now. It just so happens this is approximately the amount of water that would cover Florida if all the glacial ice in the world were to melt and return to the oceans.

The land of Florida emerged from beneath the sea slowly and intermittently. Local uplifts, the Ocala Arch in northwestern peninsular Florida and the Marianna Arch west of Tallahassee, occurred, and erosion

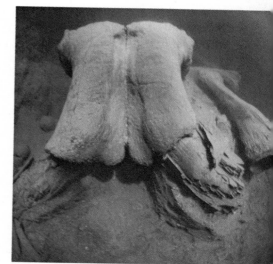

Geologic map of Florida.

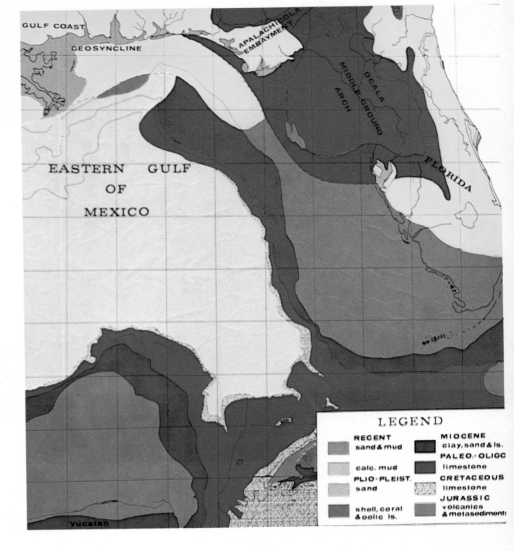

GULF COAST
GEOSYNCLINE

APALACHICOLA
EMBAYMENT

MIDDLE GROUND

OCALA ARCH

FLORIDA

EASTERN GULF
OF
MEXICO

Yucatan

LEGEND

RECENT sand & mud	MIOCENE clay, sand & ls.
calc. mud	PALEO.-OLIGO. limestone
PLIO.-PLEIST. sand	CRETACEOUS limestone
shell, coral & eolic ls.	JURASSIC volcanics & metasediments

Sinkholes and caves contribute to preservation of fossils. They act as natural "traps" into which many animals fall and die, and in turn attract carnivores and scavengers which themselves become trapped and preserved. The skeletons of these animals remain in virtually the same area where they died or were killed, and are not transported, fragmented, and dispersed as they are in streams.
Lime-saturated ground water passing through these sinkholes and caves acts relatively quickly to preserve the skeletal parts, and the deposits are generally not as subject to erosion.
— S. DAVID WEBB

A mammoth skull with its tusks slightly dislocated is being jacketed with plaster-soaked burlap. It was discovered on the bank of the Peace River by a group of Boy Scouts from Wauchula.

revealed the early Tertiary limestone. Most of Florida emerged from the sea as the glaciers reduced the volume of water in the oceans. Florida land features at elevations below 100 feet are beach, dune, lagoon, marsh——clues that it was recently under water. "Recently" in this case, means the last two million years. Coastal ridges are evident on the satellite image south and eastward of Orlando.

Miami is built upon a ridge composed of small spherules of calcium carbonate, called "oolite," precipitated when all of Florida south of Pompano Beach was submerged. The islands of the Florida Keys are reef and associated limestone materials formed at the same time when sea level was 18 or so feet above its present stand. The famous linear belt of coquina rock that occurs along the east coast of Florida is an old beach deposit composed of shell and sand representing the same interglacial event. We know this last major higher stand of sea level occurred 120 thousand years or so ago and preceded the last spread of glacial ice over the northeastern portions of our continent. The last glacial ice sheet melted in the northern United States about 10,000 years ago; it persisted in northeastern Canada as recently as 4500 years ago. Sea level is still adjusting and we are suffering the consequences in the form of beach erosion.

The most important relics of a higher stand of sea level still existing in Florida are the deposits of pebble phosphate. These deposits were formed by rivers which eroded and reconcentrated these materials from off the Ocala Arch, an uplift which occurred during the Pliocene. The redeposit of concentrated pebble phosphate at the mouth of rivers when the sea level was 120 to 140 feet higher than it is now created the great economic wealth of phosphate in Polk, Hamilton, Union, Alachua, and other counties along the edge of the Ocala Uplift. A wealth of remains of bones and teeth of exotic animals, the shovel-tusked mastodon, river rhinoceros, primitive grazing horse, river porpoise and dugong (relative of the modern manatee), also are found in the phosphate deposits, along with an abundance of teeth of marine and estuarine sharks.

During the multiple glacial stages, sea level was repeatedly 350 feet, or more, lower than present. It was during these times that Tampa Bay, the St. Johns River estuary, Choctawatchee Bay, and other areas, were eroded by the action of streams. Now that sea level is up in post glacial times, portions of these river valleys are flooded.

Present sea level and climate conditions have existed for a very short period of time. Truthfully, both are still changing, even within the past few years. The panhandle of Florida now has a temperate, humid climate with an excess of rainfall of about one and one-half feet per unit area. In peninsular Florida, the climate generally becomes less subject to frost, but is drier southward. Although the Kissimmee-Okeechobee-Everglades area is one of the most vast wetlands in the world, it is subject to droughts.

Most of central and southern Florida is in a precarious position relative to rainfall. It is a narrow peninsula, without significant changes in elevation. Situated between 25° to 31° North and bordered by the Atlantic Ocean and the Gulf of Mexico, its climate is highly dependent upon sea water surface temperature. For example, it has been determined a sea surface temperature of 2°C warmer could increase hurricanes fourfold, whereas cooling by 2°C may eliminate them altogether. Hurricanes are an important source of water; they can, however, be disastrous to those who are ignorant of or unprepared for their forces and coastal flooding from tidal surges. Summer thunderstorms generated by heating of the land are the main source of rain in Florida. Hurricanes provide the supplement in the southern portion of the state; winter frontal systems generate large amounts of rain in the northern portion. There is an interplay of temperate and tropical influences. The Florida climate from year to year is capricious to the point that it is neither completely tropical nor temperate, neither wet nor dry.

The aboriginals arriving in Florida about 10,000 years ago had problems finding water. The lakes, swamps and even the Everglades were dry. Lakes and wetlands have existed for less than 6000 years. Florida was in the past, and may be in the future, a land with little water. Some solace for Floridians can be found in the fact that even when glacial ice covered Ohio, no significant temperature changes took place—nor have they occurred in about half a million years.

—H. K. BROOKS

Restored skeleton of Synthetoceras tricornatus, *found in phosphate deposit called Bone Valley, is from an exotic and extinct animal that once roamed Florida.*

Many-horned pronghorn from Bone Valley.

Satellite shot shows thunderstorms over Florida.

85

Devils Eye Spring.

A Florida spring is a magical place.

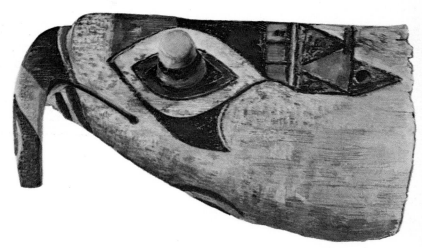

Marine and fresh water turtles have always been important to Floridians. This old turtle-head effigy was carved of soft wood, and excavated at Key Marco. It is said to show a pre-Colombian character and is credited to the early Key dwellers who showed craftsmanship and creativity in their animal carvings.

EDEN CHANGES

The history of man and nature in Florida has not been a wholly happy one. Very recently it has become possible to balance some of the violence we have done to the natural world with a few signs of good-will; but the change has been slow in coming and the delay has cost us heavily.

The irony of this is that, more than almost anywhere else in America, it was nature that drew people to Florida to start with. Partly the early violations were a sign of the times. To our forebears, cleared land was better than forests, and killing non-human creatures was only natural. Besides that there was from the beginning an obsession with the goodness of population growth. From the outset, the natives saw profit in visitors who could be overcharged for a side of bacon or a mule, or guided to good shooting in a heron rookery. This helped generate the heady magic of growth and made the word synonymous with progress.

When a naturalist whose delight is wild creatures and unworn country sets out to write about Florida, it is hard to refrain from bemoaning lost wilderness, as John Small did in *From Desert to Sahara*, or Thomas Barbour in *That Vanishing Eden*. Garment-rending seems out of place in a Bicentennial year; and actually, if you look around for them, there are pleasant things to be told.

It is no good trying to hide the fact that the history of Florida has been a desperate sort of striving for growth and development. The result of this has been the most protracted crowding in of outsiders that any state has had. Inevitably, this has dimmed or destroyed much of the natural charm that originally drew people here. There is no way that the favors of wild nature can be infinitely shared about, like loaves and fishes. The climate has not so far been materially hurt, but all other ecologic assets have to some extent been changed, and some have been forever lost.

Florida panther is a rare creature.

87

Currier and Ives drawing of Adam naming the creatures.

Otters, once hunted to near extinction like the plume birds, are again multiplying and playing their age-old sliding and swimming games in Florida streams and marshes.

Recently the statistic appeared somewhere that Florida and Bangladesh have almost precisely the same area. There are seven million people in Florida; Bangladesh has 70 million. To judge from the way the exploiters oppose curbs to their schemes, Bangladesh is the model they strive toward. But it is no longer a walkaway for the fast-money chaps, and though they still have a lot to learn, they seem to be learning it.

Meanwhile, there are things to be thankful for. The return of the manatees to the limestone springs, for instance. Thirty years ago it was next to impossible to see a manatee in the primordial winter-time habitat of the species—the big springs of the central peninsula. Manatees are good to eat, and they were hunted out of the springs long ago. Those not killed for meat were idly shot by duck hunters or by kids with 22s. Today the poachers and irresponsible gun-toters are fewer, and manatees, though still an endangered species, are back, in some of the springs, at least. And that is a blessing because manatees are neat, very neat.

It is somewhat the same with alligators. When Bartram was here, there were alligators galore. By the late 1800s, however, hide hunting and recreational slaughter were going on everywhere, and alligators had disappeared from much of their natural range. Even in Florida populations declined drastically, and tourists could count on seeing alligators only in the alligator farms. A few years ago the alligator was declared an endangered species. Under protection it has proved surprisingly resilient. In a few parts of its original range the species is obviously no longer endangered. A visitor who looks around can now usually see wild alligators in natural habitat; and in some suburban bodies of water they have even become a nuisance. The existence of these localized sites of abundant, brash alligators, has generated an incredibly hairbrained and retrogressive scheme to reopen a hunting season. The potential for harm in this proposal

Native Americans in Florida
carved crocodile heads for tools.
This one was excavated in Key Marco.

No state in the union has been more haunted by myths than Florida. Widely believed, the stories have endured. Christopher Columbus found islands but never heard of the land beyond. Spaniards quickly peopled the islands and built stone cities. River gold mines and plantations were worked by the peaceful and enslaved Taino Indians captured in the Bahamas.

In those years a story blew about the Spanish islands, whispered by Indians dying of hard work and homesickness, that on an island called "Bemimy" or "Bimini" there was a fine spring of water in which old men bathed to become young again. It was called, "The Fountain of Youth."

A hard-working provincial governor of Spanish Hispaniola, by the name of Ponce de León, was in his active fifties, had two daughters he could marry off if he had rich dowries for them, and no fortune at all. After coming to the islands with Columbus on his second voyage as an impoverished son of a great Spanish house, he had been content, as probably his wife bitterly reminded him, with his ill-paid official position while men more adventurous than he held better jobs on richer islands to the west. But on that legendary shape to the north, island or continent no one knew, there must be gold and certainly Indians for slaves of an equal value.

Ponce de León persuaded the Spanish King to give him the right to conquer, rule, and exploit the legendary land at his own expense, as Adelantado. With two ships, he sailed north, tacking and beating among the known Bahamas, almost stripped of people by the slavers. There is neither hint nor proof, that Ponce de León had ever heard of the legendary fountain or of Bimini. If he had heard he paid no attention. He sent only the smaller ship to Bimini to bring back a man who could pilot them across the Gulf Stream to the coast beyond.

Ponce de León's ships were anchored off the sands below St. Augustine Harbor for several days, but there is no proof that he made any explorations. It was not long, however, before the great myth was born that he was looking for the Fountain of Youth. Ponce de León later was wounded unto death on the lower west coast of Florida, perhaps Fort Myers Beach. So Florida brought him no good—only a leading role in the oldest and most enduring, most universally believed myth the new country would ever know. —M.S.D.

is complex and one can only hope that nothing comes of it. Meantime, having visible wild alligators in the landscape is a thing to be thankful for in a Bicentennial year.

Besides that, there are otters. During the first half of this century otters were heavily trapped and shot, and seeing one became a rare occurrence. Today hunting pressure has relaxed, and the main enemy of otters is the highway. Otters are very bright, but for some reason their brain copes poorly with automobiles; they are often found dead on any stretch of paved highway through marsh country. Away from the fast cars, though, they are much more numerous now than they were thirty years ago, and their return is cause for celebration.

So is the return of the beavers. Beavers probably never entirely disappeared from the panhandle of Florida but, as far as most Floridians could tell, they might as well have been completely gone. Now they are increasing their range and abundance in the state. A few singleminded entrepreneurs have even begun to cry out for beaver control, on the grounds that timber land is being flooded by their work. But most people probably would figure beavers in Florida are worth a few drowned planted pines.

Another pleasant change, more conspicuous to the casual visitor than the return of sea cows, alligators, otters and beavers, is the spread of long-legged wading birds. A part of the new look that these produce is contributed by the cattle egret, an Old World species that, for some wholly unknown reason, began crossing the ocean three decades ago and is now a common sight standing with cows in pasture lands. But these new immigrant white egrets being here should not obscure the important fact that other water birds too have returned as a regular feature of the landscape, in the roadside ditches and out on the wet prairies. It took many years for

The Florida Myth-Taken Identity

Florida, a myth-haunted land, is still spawning myths. There is the myth that the garden of Eden was located on the Apalachicola River. There is the myth that the mysterious Everglades, drained, could become "the Empire of the Sun" and that everybody buying land there, sight unseen, could be rich forever. The great myth still exists that Florida is the golden land, rich in every possible resource, where everyone will live happily ever after.

Florida is only a flat low land between the sea and the gulf. It reaches from the tropics to the south temperate zone, with a fragile interior environment of strange and curious and undramatic beauty, and a shifting and variable coast forever at the mercy of the great salt tides. The true Florida has been used and broken down, drained and trampled by hordes of people who know little of the land and want only myths, not reality. They have not seen what Florida is and *might be* because of its strange, four-century old, myth-taken identity. —M.S.D.

Wild hogs roam the Florida wilds. Fierce in appearance, they are the descendants of domestic pigs that escaped from early Florida frontier settlers and are hunted for food and sport. Their capture often occasions a barbeque over an open fire.

Black bears, perhaps best known for their antics in Yellowstone and Smokie Mountain National Parks, also roam Florida woodlands.

them to recover from the plume hunting massacres, finally stopped by the Audubon Society wardens in the early 1900s. Now, again, however, the herons decorate the wet places. Even roseate spoonbills can be seen with little searching, and this was undreamed-of only a while ago.

There has been another pleasing change in the look of much of the landscape of interior Florida. Wherever there is open country free of people and agriculture this is more lush and comforting to the eye than it used to be. This change has come about because of the decline of the cracker habit of letting wildfire loose in any patch of woods any time it would burn. Planned, monitored burning of pinelands is a useful tool for keeping out hardwood seedlings that would turn pine woods into hammock. In fact, it is altogether essential to the maintenance of pine flatwoods, and other pineland as well. But unless the burning is done with skill it makes a shocking mess of the land. The old Floridians burned heedlessly, only aiming to be rid of debris from timbering or to stimulate the growth of new grass that would rescue their cattle from a winter diet of palmetto fans. Or if they had no cows, they burned to kill ticks and rattlesnakes or to flush out game.

Some people just don't like the look of flatwoods anyway. Dr. Motte, an army surgeon of Charleston, South Carolina, who arrived in Florida during the Second Seminole War, was appalled by the appearance of the pinelands around the Georgia-Florida line. They seemed to him "a dull, insipid pine barren, where the listlessness of blank vacuity hung upon the flagging spirits." Dr. Motte was probably just prejudiced. Most naturalists would give a lot for a chance to see what those pinelands looked like before they were cut down. But later on the flatwoods were cut over, most of them more than once, and the crackers burned them into blackened bare-floored semidesert, devoid of animal life except for razorback hogs that ploughed up the bayheads and thin sooty cattle that stood around in the road or wandered through the unfenced country foraging morosely for scattered sprigs of wire grass.

Now the ritual burning has stopped. In some cases the protection is overdone, but a new and pleasantly lush look has come over the land. It is not a wholly natural look. Even before the crackers and Seminoles came to

Florida the woods used to burn over, in natural fires, and the present fire-free regimen will make hardwood hammock of much of what once was pineland. Meantime, however, what you see from a traveling car is far greener and more opulent country than what they used to see from the Model T Fords.

So there are bright spots in our relationship with natural Florida. When you think of the abuse much of our heritage has suffered, however, it is not easy to stay cheerful. Take the decline of the big springs, for instance, the biological communities in the limestone springs of the state. The ecological degradation of these incomparable springs is one of the major losses the state has suffered and one that clearly illustrates the problem of saving the diverse values of natural landscapes.

Florida is underlain by soluble limestone. Where this lies near the surface, solution has formed caves, chimneys and sink-holes, and much of the drainage of the region goes into subterranean streams rather than running over the surface to the sea. Rivers disappear into the ground and emerge a mile or more away; lakes gurgle out overnight through newly opened holes in their bottoms. Such terrain is known as Karst topography, after a region in Hungary. There are numerous Karst regions in the world, but nowhere are big river-making springs as abundant as they are in Florida.

And nowhere in the Florida landscape is natural beauty distilled to its essence as it is in the big springs—wherever their natural biologic organization has been spared. There is a dreamlike quality to the appeal of these places. It is a stirring thing to come upon one of them unexpectedly, whether you walk in overland and find it suddenly glowing in shadows of liveoaks and magnolias, or you paddle up a cypress-bordered run, wondering where the run comes from, and then all at once see the trees open in a circle and live water surging up like liquid blue crystal. When William Bartram wrote of his journeys through the limestone country in the late 1700s the springs evoked some of his most rhapsodic prose. Three hundred years before that, it was surely rumors of the supernatural beauty of the springs that generated tales of the Fountain of Youth.

Each spring is different from all the others; but in the intensity of

Of Cormorants and Bears

An old nonsense verse celebrates two forms of Florida wildlife, the double-crested cormorant and the black bear. The cormorant's nickname, "shag," comes from the crest upon its head.

The common cormorant or shag
Lays eggs inside a paper bag.
The reason you will see no doubt
It is to keep the lightning out.
But what these unobservant birds
Have never noticed is that herds
Of wandering bears may come with buns
And steal the bags to hold the crumbs.

Double-crested cormorant.

The World Grows Round My Door

"The tall royal palms. . .stood for many years and were part of the picture our friends saw as they walked through the archway into the house. But with the constant lowering of the fresh water table beneath us and the gradual seeping in of more and more salt water, the beautiful palms died off one by one leaving only two for the hurricane of 1945 to decapitate.

The spring by the side of the path has, alas, become salty and it is hard to realize, as I look down into the hole, that it once played an important role on this coast, furnishing drinking water to small sailing ships that passed."

—DAVID FAIRCHILD

Fins and fresh spring waters are fine go-togethers.

Sand sparkles through the waters of a Florida spring as tiny plants struggle to take root in the rushing stream.

its grace and color each is a little ecologic jewel in which geology and biology have created a masterwork of natural art. In all of them the water wells up in shades of blue and silver that vary with depth and the slant of your view. In the unviolated basins there are submarine beds of water plants of half a dozen kinds, each a different shade of red-brown and green, waving slowly in the current, or spreading over quiet bottom like patchwork quilts of velvet. Where the flow is too fast for plants to hold, the bare sand of the bottom shows white, and in some of the springs white chips of fossil shell or flakes of marl swirl up like snow with the roiling newborn water.

It would be hard to find a better example than these springs to show the kinds of troubles that hinder the preservation of biological landscape. The springs are still there, most of them. Fountains still surge up out of rock caverns and make sudden streams that give a strange look to the contour map. But all of them are distressingly fragile treasures that have without exception suffered damage, in some cases irretrievably.

At Jody's Spring, near Silver Glen in the Ocala National Forest, there is a charming bit of the world, described by Marjorie Kinnan Rawlings in the opening chapter of her book, *The Yearling*. It is a place where you can sit for a while in the dim cool of a scrap of hammock surrounded by sand-pine scrub, and marvel over a superb small gem of the natural landscape.

Jody's Spring is unique. There is no one big, river-making out-pouring but instead, a scattering of gentle little geysers of crystal water and snowy sand bubbling in the bottom of a shallow pool surrounded by evergreen hammock. Each sand-boil makes a lively snow-white pit in the leaf-strewn bottom. Some of the boils are no bigger than your fist, some are the size of a washtub. Killifishes cruise about among them and wherever one is big enough to hold him, a young bass or a half-grown red-breast bream is usually ensconced, working his gill-flats and eyeing any visitor through the air clear water. Thin, conical snails creep across the brown

leaves on the bottom of the pool; and dragonflies course above it or bask on twig-tips in splashes of sunlight. Where the outlet leaves, there are patches of cress and lizards tail, and neverwets spread velvet leaves about the banks, their flowers glowing gold in the gloom. The pool feeds a stream that wanders away through the woods to join Silver Glen Run a short way off. In any setting Jody's Spring would be an enchanted place. Set out there in the heart of the vast hot scrub, with the little bubbling boils gleaming white and silver in their quiet patch of deep, cool shade, a marvelously unreal aura is generated.

There are ecologic lessons to be learned at Jody's Spring. The hammock is a striking variant of the scrub community where, because of the presence of the springs, the sand pine forest gives way to a moist woods of broadleafed trees. There is an abrupt transition, a narrow ecozone, where tall cabbage palms can be seen standing almost side by side with the closely related dwarf-sabals that grow only in scrub. And yet if you go there and sit in the cool quiet for a while, the important thing you will see is a work of natural art.

As you sit there admiring it, however, as likely as not a car will come tearing up and stop out on the road. Doors will slam and people will charge down through the hammock, thrash out into the pool, and enter into a raucous competition to see who can sink down deepest into the heaving sand of the little springs. To a quiet watcher on the bank the invasion seems a stupidly violent assault. The worst of it is, to the people engaged in the assault it is harmless horseplay and a lot of fun, an offbeat and stimulating thing to do. So the predicament of Jody's Spring clearly exemplifies the intractability of wilderness preservation when both aesthetic values and opportunities for physical recreation are involved—which they almost always are.

This dilemma hinders most efforts to save wild places to which the public is admitted. In the case of the springs, their unique value is a fragile loveliness that depends on their integrity as biologic landscape. They are

A Legendary Land is Named

Ponce de León, a provincial governor of Hispaniola, was commissioned by the King of Spain to explore and exploit a legendary land to the north. Using his own funds he set out in two ships and sailed through the Bahamas. At Bimini he sent the smaller ship ashore to find a man who could pilot them safely across the north-surging current to the coast beyond.

They celebrated Easter Sunday, when the ship returned, with bells ringing and as much ceremony as they could with no priest on board. Then they crossed the current and went north along its western edge, looking for a harbor, peering beyond the line of white surf flashing always on their left hand. The low line of sand slipped behind them for several days, until they came to sand dunes yellow in the blazing light and a break that revealed a watery passage within.

They went ashore in their small boats just south of what we know as St. Augustine harbor, jumping with their heavy boots into wave edges and struggling up through the hot sand to the dunes, among sea-oats and sandspurs. It was still the month of May, the season of "Pascua Florida" or "Flowery Easter." The great red and gold banner of Spain flapped out over their heads as Ponce de León, his bright sword flashing, took possession of all and much, much more than he could see, for Spain and himself as Adelantado. Since he had no priest there was no formal ceremony or mass.

He had no idea yet what the land was but he named it "Florida" not because he saw flowers on that everlasting beach, but because of Easter. All he could see to the west, over inland water, was what his chronicler Herrera called "many and cool woodlands."
—M.S.D.

The American Flamigo, painted by John James Audubon when he visited Key West a century and more ago, is now extinct. His cousins, imported from Africa, are here in carefully tended captive flocks. Coots and gallinules are still common, but their beautious relative, the Purple Gallinule, is now on the protected list.

all attractive for other reasons too; and many of the people drawn by these other qualities often miss the real point completely.

Long before Florida settled up so badly, the springs had begun to suffer. Those located in farmland were used for irrigation. The moonshiners liked the water for their stills. Springs near towns made superb swimming holes, and some of them became popular spas, to which people from other parts of the South came every summer to take the waters. So the wear and tear began long ago, but more recently it became much worse. Madmen in outboard powered boats have raced round and round in the boils, making deserts of the basins. And into the deepest and most enchanted the scuba divers have gone. They come from everywhere, by the hundreds, to test their skills in enchanted caves and fountains, and by the mere passing of their countless bodies and the bubbling of their regulators scour and scare to lifelessness some of the best of the spring communities.

With most of the Florida rheocrene springs already damaged and some utterly wrecked, any that remain in anything like natural ecological diversity and organization ought to be made inviolate sanctuaries, kept perpetually free of contact with either boats or human bodies. That is tough, because a part of the artistic appreciation of springs is getting into them, putting on a face mask and going down and looking through airlike water at nuances of light, life and color never thought of back on the bank. One human quietly flippering about in a spring or spring run does no harm to speak of. But as viewers multiply, even reverent ones, the place begins to wear. So there is really a cruel dilemma to be faced, if even the handful of unspoiled springs is to be saved. And while the trouble reaches a peak in the special case of the springs, it is much the same wherever the complex organized interplay of animals, plants, and their living space, is the treasure to be preserved.

In listing some reasons for optimism over the state of nature and man in Florida one favorable development outweighs all the rest. It is not another species on the mend, or a new park or preserve or sanctuary established. It is rather a change in the heart of the people. Although original Florida is still undergoing degradation, an assessment of the trends would show the rate of loss being overtaken by the growth of a system of ecologic ethics, by a new public consciousness and conscience. There was a time when "preservationism" was a dirty word, a name for visionary folk whose aim was to keep the world the way the Indians had it. But now the farsighted kinds of people who saved the white birds in 1913, and three decades later generated the Everglades National Park, have multiplied and are influencing the whole political climate for conservation and preservation. By a 65 percent majority, Floridians recently voted to tax themselves for a 200 million dollar Endangered Lands Program, set up to purchase outright wild land threatened by development. These changes in the public mood are reflected in government policies as well.

The rise of this new stewardship gives heart to opponents of ecologic ruin everywhere, and brings promise of better times for man and nature in Florida in our next two hundred years.

—ARCHIE CARR

Thomas Moran painting is of the coast of Florida along Ft. George Island in 1878.

PENSACOLA

It is said that Pensacola was named for the long haired or "panshi," people or "okla," living in the area when the Spanish arrived.

Flags of many nations have been raised in triumph over the old city of Pensacola.

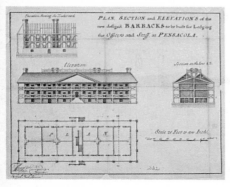

Plan for new British barracks at Pensacola, prepared as Britons take over rule of Florida from Spanish.

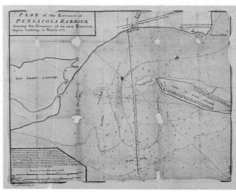

Early map of Pensacola Bay is from Public Record Office, London.

Lavalle House

Red cliffs of Pensacola.

Pensacola harbor attracted the first Spanish explorers in 1540 when the de Soto expedition arrived in Florida. Nineteen years later, the temporary settlement established here by the Spanish gave Pensacola its claim to being the first settlement in the United States. Throughout its early history, the Pensacola area was marked by rivalries and claims by international powers including Spain, France and England. Discoveries, pirates, traders and naval fleets have frequented the bustling port town.

Engraving of Pensacola city and harbor midway in nineteenth century.

Union Navy defends Ft. Pickens from Confederate attack at Pensacola.

Port of Pensacola

COMMERCE AND TRADE

Commerce and trade was the motivation which first enticed Christopher Columbus in a westerly direction across the waters which terrified many of his fellow seamen who feared they would fall off the edge of a flat world. Columbus was searching for a new easier route to the Indies, from whence came the spices which made tasty the often ill-cooked and ill-preserved foods eaten by most Europeans. Only a tortuous desert and mountainous land route then existed over which these highly prized commodities of trade could be brought from the East Indies to the European merchants and markets. By sea the ships and sailors must sail far south around the tip of Africa and travel many seas and oceans, the Pacific, the Indian, and the Atlantic. How easy it would be to ship the spices directly across the waters from west to east!

Columbus and those who followed were disappointed that the islands he found were not the Indies for which he was searching and the Atlantic was not a new trade route to the Orient. On the new islands and in the continents beyond they found, not the spices for which they were hoping, but numerous other things, new and old, which sparked a lively commercial trade that has never since ceased to flow back and forth across the Atlantic and beyond.

Ponce de León, seeking a fortune in gold or silver or slaves under a grant from the Spanish king, discovered Florida in 1513. Disappointed that the long peninsula, Florida, did not yield the mineral treasures of Mexico and Peru, the gold and the silver so avidly sought by all the *conquistadors*, the Spaniards only half-heartedly attempted settlement here. They did use Florida timber and rosin and tar and turpentine to build and maintain the plate ship fleets that carried New World treasure to the Old. The ships rode the Gulf Stream current past treacherous Florida shores to shorten their voyages by many days.

Ultimately, after the shiny minerals had been stripped from the New World and moved into the mainstream of the known world of commerce and trade, it was the small things the Europeans found that were more important than the gold and the silver. New plants and foods and wondrous inventions they found here—corn, potatoes, squash, tobacco and tobacco pipes, swinging hammocks, and hollow rubber balls.

Here in the commerce and trade of feeding and housing and entertaining the peoples of the world lay the commercial destiny of the "land of flowers." The land and the climate and the minerals for fertilizing the plants that produce food exist in abundance in Florida. From the long pier peninsula, products and people now radiate back and forth to all points of the globe over the land and the sea and through the air. Florida has become a trade link to the world.

— J.E.G. — B.R.R.

CHRISTOPHER COLUMBUS.

CHARTING NEW LANDS AND WATERS

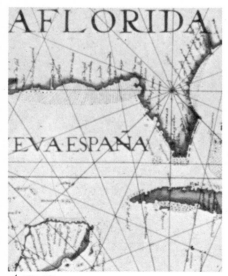

A mountain chain down the peninsula is shown on some of the earliest charts of Florida. The cartographers, no doubt, assumed that Florida was similar to Cuba and other islands in the Caribbean. Some charts show it as a large island or group of smaller ones. These early charts show that little was known of Florida; but even the earliest maps indicate that sailors knew of the Florida Current and Gulf Stream. Together these currents form one great ocean current, and sailors soon learned the advantages of that route for the homeward passage to Europe.

Ponce de León had discovered it in 1513, crossing the Stream near Cape Canaveral while on a voyage from Puerto Rico. For centuries the treasure fleets from South America and Mexico would assemble at Havana prior to following the Stream home to Spain. During the century prior to

the American Revolution, that body of water between Florida, Cuba, and
the Bahama Islands was commonly known as the Gulf of Florida or the
Florida Gulf and Stream (to northward). It is from that body of water that
the Gulf Stream appears to have come by its modern name.

By the time of the Revolution this stream had been crossed and
followed countless times, and various charts had been drawn of its course
and to explain its cause, with varying degrees of correctness. The sharp
temperature contrast of its western boundary had become well known,
but poorly understood. This was the age of imagination for scientists.

Some authorities define the Gulf Stream as only that part of the
great current that flows eastward from about Cape Hatteras, but names
are established by common usage. It would be difficult to convince most
Floridians that the Gulf Stream does not pass off the southeast Florida
coast and, indeed, there is some historical basis for this common usage.

—DONALD C. GABY

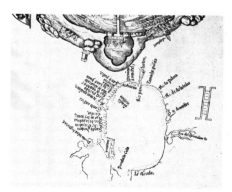

101

R E M A R K S

Upon the Navigation from

NEWFOUNDLAND TO NEW-YORK,

In order to avoid the

GULPH STREAM

*On one hand, and on the other the SHOALS that lie to the Southward of
Nantucket and of St. George's Banks.*

AFTER you have paſſed the Banks of Newfoundland in about
the 44th degree of latitude, you will meet with nothing, till
you draw near the Iſle of Sables, which we commonly paſs in latitude 43. Southward of this iſle, the current is found to extend
itſelf as far North as 41° 20′ or 30′, then it turns towards the E.
S. E. or S. E. ¼ E.

Having paſſed the Iſle of Sables, ſhape your courſe for the St.
George's Banks, ſo as to paſs them in about latitude 40°, becauſe
the current ſouthward of thoſe banks reaches as far North as 39°
The ſhoals of thoſe banks lie in 41° 35′.

After having paſſed St. George's Banks, you muſt, to clear Nantucket, form your courſe ſo as to paſs between the latitudes 38° 30′
and 40° 45′.

The moſt ſouthern part of the ſhoals of Nantucket lie in about
40° 45′. The northern part of the current directly to the ſouth of
Nantucket is felt in about latitude 38° 30′.

By obſerving theſe directions and keeping between the ſtream
and the ſhoals, the paſſage from the Banks of Newfoundland to
New-York, Delaware, or Virginia, may be conſiderably ſhorten-
ed; for ſo you will have the advantage of the eddy current, which
moves contrary to the Gulph Stream. Whereas if to avoid the
ſhoals you keep too far to the ſouthward, and get into that ſtream,
you will be retarded by it at the rate of 60 or 70 miles a day.

The Nantucket whale-men being extremely well acquainted with
the Gulph Stream, its courſe, ſtrength and extent, by their con-
ſtant practice of whaling on the edges of it, from their iſland quite
down to the Bahamas, this draft of that ſtream was obtained from
one of them, Capt. Folger, and cauſed to be engraved on the old
chart in London, for the benefit of navigators, by

B. FRANKLIN.

Note, The Nantucket captains who are acquainted with this
ſtream, make their voyages from England to Boſton in as
ſhort a time generally as others take in going from Boſton
to England, viz. from 20 to 30 days.

A ſtranger may know when he is in the Gulph Stream, by
the warmth of the water, which is much greater than that
of the water on each ſide of it. If then he is bound to the
weſtward, he ſhould croſs the ſtream to get out of it as ſoon
as poſſible.

B. F.

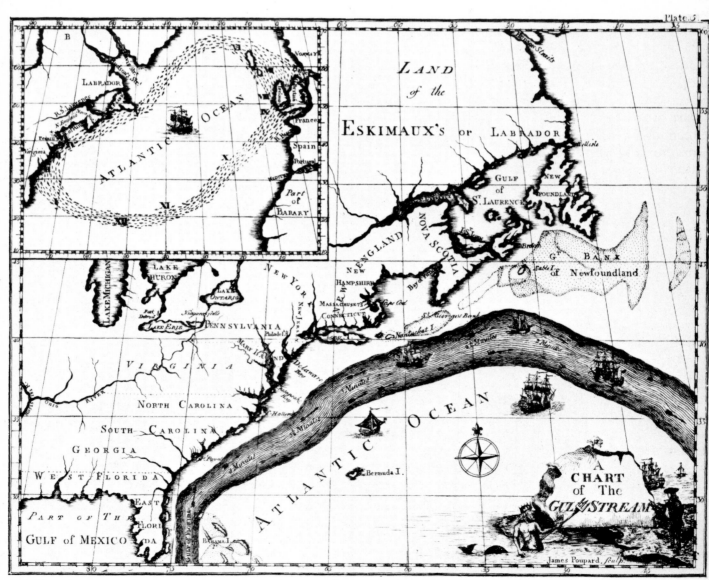

SATELLITES DISCOVER SEA SECRETS

The Harangus Volans, or Flying Fish.

American fishermen, principally whalers from New England, had a large store of marine knowledge that was passed down by word of mouth. They would find their whales to either side of the Gulf Stream, but never within its warmer waters. Often they would see the mail packets stemming the current unawares. It was from one of these whalers, Captain Folger of Nantucket, that Benjamin Franklin, then Deputy Postmaster General for the North British Colonies in America, learned the course of the Gulf Stream, and had it engraved on an old chart in London. Franklin's famous Chart of the Gulf Stream was first published in 1769, with Franklin's directions for navigation. Unfortunately, his location of the narrow current returning westward across the ocean appears to have come from some earlier navigator's foggy notions.

Franklin's estimates of the velocities of the Gulf Stream turned out to be remarkably good. He suggested the use of a thermometer to locate the Gulf Stream by temperature. This technique might save sixty to seventy miles per day in crossing the North Atlantic. On his last three voyages—aboard the Pennsylvania packet, Capt. Osborne, in April and May 1775; on the *Reprisal*, Capt. Wycks, in October and November 1776; and on the London packet, Capt. Truston, in August and September 1785—Franklin made the first scientific observations of sea temperature, using a thermometer in a sample of sea water collected by bucket over the side of the ship. Together with other scientists he made many similar observations to improve navigation. Besides the sea temperatures, Franklin also noted the presence of "Gulphweed" in the Stream, the color of the water, and that it sparkled at night.

On his last voyage home in 1785, at 79 years of age and with a large stone in his bladder, he even attempted to measure subsurface temperature down to about 100 feet using a cask fitted with a valve at each end. A fellow passenger, Mr. F. Williams, kept his journal and made all the experiments "with great exactness." One result of Benjamin Franklin's early measurements was the discovery of pockets of cold water, large eddies that are now known to retain their identities and to drift for long periods of time.

Even with modern methods and a great many ships, not until the arrival of the space age were oceanographers able to view the Gulf Stream in its entirety, at once and with all its great complexity. The first American

Benjamin Franklin crossed the Atlantic often as a diplomat for the new American nation. His inventive mind used this opportunity to explore the mysteries of the Gulf Stream and to produce the Franklin Chart of the Gulf Stream.

BENJAMIN FRANKLIN

I join with you most cordially in rejoicing at the return of peace. I hope it will be lasting, and that mankind will at length, as they call themselves reasonable creatures, have reason to settle their differences without cutting throats; for, in my opinion, there never was a good war, or a bad peace.

—BEN FRANKLIN, 1783

Cape Hatteras ———————
St. Johns River ———————
Lake Okeechobee ———————

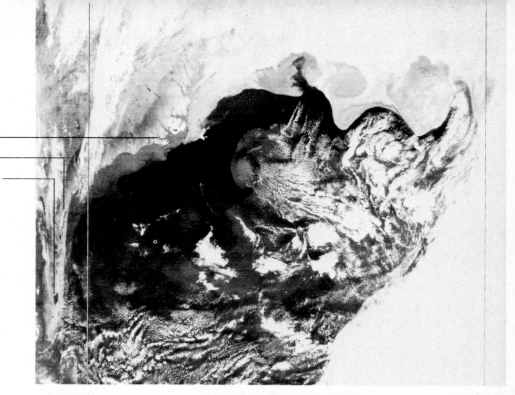

Satellite temperature picture by infrared sensor "camera." Warm water of Gulf Stream is almost black in striking contrast to cooler coastal waters off the Carolinas which appear gray and cooler waters of the Atlantic Ocean north of the Stream which are quite white. In this picture Florida appears somewhat foreshortened in the lower left margin with Lake Okeechobee, the St. Johns River and Cape Hatteras clearly visible. Large mass of white in lower right corner is cold cloudiness of a weather front.

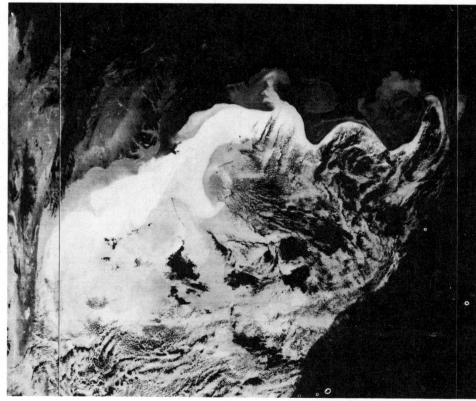

Reversal of colors shows Gulf Stream, Lake Okeechobee, and St. Johns River as white.

Analysis of temperature pictures notes warm eddy, marked "W.E.," cool eddy to the south-west of it, and the meandering of the Gulf Stream.

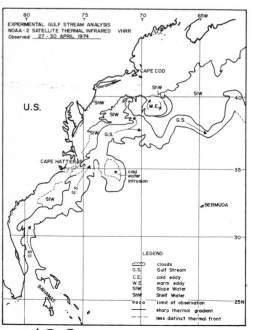

"weather" satellite was launched in April 1960. Improvements quickly followed. Within a few years the satellites were observing ocean surface temperatures with infrared imagery. These early "temperature" pictures clearly defined the Gulf Stream and showed for the first time the tremendous amount of fine detail and structure that lies within the broad current.

The polar-orbiting NOAA satellites now routinely observe the oceans of the entire world. Daily depictions of temperatures and pictures of the temperature fields are produced by the National Environmental Satellite Service. The polar-orbiting satellite is only able to view the Earth

A very high resolution picture in the visible spectrum taken by SMS-1. "Visible" picture *shows the Earth by reflected sunlight, much as a man sees it looking down from a spacecraft.*

Infrared weather picture of the Earth with continents outlined.

at any particular location twice each day, with the unfortunate likelihood that the ocean will be covered with cloud just when it is time to see it.

In May 1974 the United States launched the first of a series of "geostationary" satellites with infrared observing capability, presently known as Synchronous Meteorological Satellites (SMS). Future satellites will be known as Geostationary Operational Environmental Satellites (GOES). These satellites are placed in orbit above the equator, going around the Earth from west to east once each day, so that they appear to stand still. From a vantage point 35,800 kilometers (22,300 miles) up, these SMS or GOES satellites take a picture of most of a hemisphere every 30 minutes, day and night. Although the spacial "resolution" of the infrared is not so good—one can not see fine detail so well—these satellites have the great advantage of viewing the entire Atlantic Ocean every 30 minutes and, thus, can "catch" the Gulf Stream whenever it is not covered by cloud. Future generations of geostationary satellites, expected near the end of the decade, will have the same high resolution as the present polar-orbiting satellites, while viewing an entire ocean every 30 minutes or so.

The National Aeronautics and Space Administration also by this time will have built and launched the first satellite designed especially for viewing the oceans. To be known as SEASAT, this satellite will carry a variety of sophisticated sensors, including a precision altimeter. SEASAT will be able to measure the height of the ocean surface with an accuracy of about 20 centimeters.

Now, contrary to popular belief, the Gulf Stream is not a current of warm water flowing through the ocean. It is a western boundary current in the ocean, where the Coriolis force, an effect of the rotation of the Earth, is balanced by the difference in density of the warmer waters of the Sargasso

Early satellite infrared high resolution picture of the Gulf Stream is from Nimbus II, launched from Kennedy Space Center at Cape Canaveral.

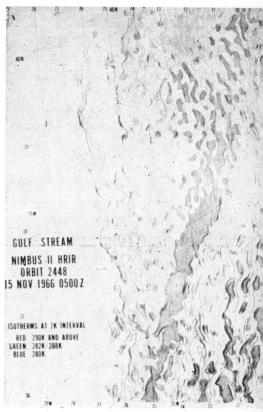

GULF STREAM

NIMBUS II HRIR
ORBIT 2448
15 NOV 1966 0500 Z

ISOTHERMS AT 2K INTERVAL
  RED 290K AND ABOVE
  GREEN 282K-288K
  BLUE 280K

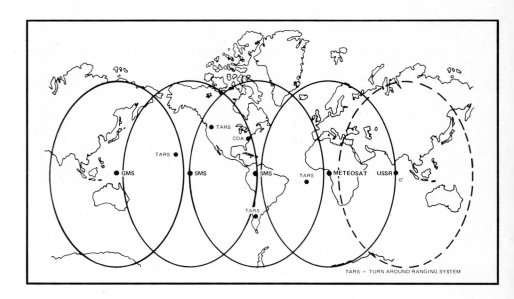

International cooperation by governments and scientists around the world will make possible worldwide coverage when all the planned weather satellites have been launched and are in orbit. These environmental satellites will help predict weather and add to scientific knowledge and understanding of the Earth.

TARS = TURN AROUND RANGING SYSTEM

Frequent satellite observations of both sea surface temperature fields and weather systems are used in up-to-the-minute operational support of ships at sea. Satellite meteorologists from a satellite field station in direct radio contact with ships can provide the very latest information to guide the ships on the safest and best course.

Seven satellites in this relationship to the Earth will be in orbit and sending back pictures of the entire globe in the near future.

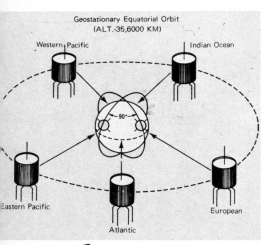

Geostationary Equatorial Orbit
(ALT.-35,6000 KM)

Western Pacific
Indian Ocean
90°
Eastern Pacific
Atlantic
European

Sea on the one hand and the colder waters of the inshore regions and northern ocean on the other. This difference in density causes a difference in height of the Gulf Stream from one side to the other. The difference is thought to be about one meter (39 inches). This difference in height across many miles of open sea may seem slight to the layman, but it is expected to be well within the accuracy of the measurements from this new satellite. A whole new range of knowledge will, thus, become available. With the ability to measure precisely the slope of the sea surface, it will be possible to calculate the speed of these ocean currents wherever they might be. Combined with the more accurate measurements of sea surface temperature also expected, man will indeed have taken another giant step forward in his viewing of the Gulf Stream.

Several nations of the world are joining with the United States to install a satellite system that will provide continuous infrared and visible pictures of the entire planet. This system will have five geostationary satellites spaced at intervals above the equator to observe continuously all but the polar regions. These satellites will be complemented by two polar-orbiting satellites that will observe the low latitudes four times a day and the polar regions about once per hour. The first two of these geostationary satellites have already been launched by the United States and are in place over South America, viewing all of the Atlantic Ocean, and over the eastern Pacific Ocean. Japan will soon place a similar satellite above the western Pacific Ocean. A Russian satellite will follow above the Indian Ocean and one above the Equator and the Greenwich meridian will be provided by the European Space Agency. The first of the polar-orbiting satellites has already been launched by the United States and is in daily operational use.

Who can imagine what the Third Century will bring? Doubtless our knowledge of the oceans will be vastly increased—perhaps just in time. Man needs additional resources to cope successfully with an ever increasing world population. Old Ben should be pleased to see that his successors have followed so well the fine example he set at the time of the birth of our nation.

—DONALD C. GABY

Of Myths and Names

Low-lying in sun-haze beyond a strong-running mysterious great river of sea-water, the land of Florida or what they could see of it, was a myth to the earliest white explorers, probably from the Portuguese Azores, who in their tiny ships, were poking about the warm seas. Rude maps, copied in Europe from some forgotten scrawled charts show island shapes, like Puerto Rico and Hispaniola and Cuba as we know them, long before they were ever named. On one map a shape to the north was drawn that can be nothing but the tip end of Florida.

Other ships came groping down from the north on the current within the great stream, like blind ships manned by blind men, trying to feel out a coast in unknown and dangerous waters. Some turned and gained the stream to flee homeward on it, not knowing what they had found but leaving marks and charts for other mapmakers.

—M.S.D.

Astrolabe, recently recovered from Spanish ship sunk off Florida Keys in seventeenth century, is old instrument used in navigation to measure altitude of sun and stars.

The fate of Ponce de León as a mythical character was recently reestablished. At the time of the assassination of President John F. Kennedy, the great Florida east coast cape, shown on even the earliest charts and now the site of a sprawling space center, was renamed Cape Kennedy in honor of the late President. The new myth grew up after the name change, when the State of Florida launched and won a struggle to have the cape restored to its original name, Cape Canaveral. It is now said that Ponce de León named the cape "Canaveral" on his first voyage. It is not true.

In 1513, on his way south, Ponce de León saw the great sandy cape which is a landmark on the Atlantic coast of Florida. Early historians say that Ponce de León named it "Corrientes" because of its turbulent currents. Later researchers say the maps that copy Ponce de León's last map indicate that he named it "Cabo de Arecifes." He put "corrientes" on a lower cape nearest of all to the Gulfstream; here the coast turns due south and he nearly lost a ship in the northgoing stream near the northern shore of Lake Worth inlet or Palm Beach.

Whatever the truth of "Corrientes," certainly Ponce de León did not name the greatest cape "Canaveral." The name "Canaveral," meaning "canebearer" for the great reeds then in the swamp at the southward bight of the cape, appeared on Florida maps after 1520. That was the year when a Spanish official from Hispaniola named Vasquez de Ayllón was sailing about the Bahamas exploring, with smaller ships beside his flagship, looking for more Indians to enslave. Ayllón was the man who presently was blown north by a hurricane and so discovered what the English later called the "Carolinas."

One of his slave-ship captains, Francisco Gordillo cruised over to the coast of Florida and probably fought a battle with the savage Indians near the great cape. Gordillo's men were killed or wounded by Indian arrows made from the canes or reeds of that swamp. The arrow tips, hardened over a fire, split on contact with chain mail and made grievous wounds with the keen splinters. It was Gordillo, therefore, it is thought, who named the cape, "Canaveral," the oldest continuous place name on the Atlantic coast of the North American continent. It is clear that Ponce de León had nothing to do with that name at all, but it is not his fault that the name has recently been ascribed to him. It is only the latest development in the Ponce de León myth.

—M.S.D.

Treasure map from archives in Seville, Spain. Letters show where seachers failed to find silver treasure from ship sunk in 1623.

Treasure map

Spanish inscription describes the Keys: sandy, come and go with the weather, inhabited by Indians, fishermen. In 1623 three galleons owned by Marques de Cadereita carrying silver and many souls were lost. Nicolas de Cardova was sent from Mexico to look for ships and silver and found two of the ships and some bullets but did not find the main treasure, more than a million, which was a shame because the ships were not really deep and their divers had reached them easily.

"There are yet other islands, nearer to the mainland, stretching between the west and east, called the Martires; for the reason that many men have suffered on them, and also because certain rocks rise there from beneath the sea, which, at a distance, look like men in distress. Indians are on these islands, who are of a large size: the women are well proportioned, and have good countenances. On these islands there are two Indian towns; in one of them the one town is called Guarugunbe, which in Spanish is *pueblo de Llanto*, the town of weeping; the name of the other little town, Cuchiyaga, means the place where there has been suffering."
—*Hernando D'Escalante Fontaneda, circa 1575*

COLONIAL ROADS AND TRAILS

An artist's vision of travel in colonial Florida. A Paradise of birds and plants is easy on the eyes but hard on the feet.

A few homesteads and struggling plantations were located along the St. Marys and the St. Johns rivers in the East when the United States acquired Florida from Spain in 1821. Even more isolated were the settlers on the upper reaches of the Escambia, the Yellow, and other rivers in western Florida. The only notable settlements were the Spanish administrative and military posts at St. Augustine and Pensacola. Travel and communication between the two regions was almost nonexistent. Indian trails in the northern part of the territory were little known and less used by white men. The larger peninsula area was still an unexplored wilderness. Three hundred years of colonial history had failed to bring settlement and development to Florida.

Accounts of the early explorers emphasize the extreme difficulties and hardships of travel through the Florida wilderness. Both Narváez and de Soto occasionally made use of Indian trails. With rare exceptions these trails were mere paths by which one or a few men could travel through the forests; they were totally inadequate for the passage of large bodies of men encumbered by armor and accompanied by cavalry horses and pack animals.

The 1693 journal of Torres y Ayala in West Florida vividly describes the difficulties of his march from St. Marks to the shores of Mobile Bay in search of a suitable site for a military outpost. Aside from the normal labors

of cutting through undergrowth and bridging streams, his party spent many days probing the swamps and hammocks in search of a practical route of travel. Even the Indians employed as guides sometimes seemed to be as much lost as were the Spaniards.

Spanish missions were established in 1608 in the Timucua area between the St. Johns and Suwannee rivers. In the 1630s this chain of missions extended into the Apalachee region between the Suwannee and Ochlockonee rivers. By 1675 the fortified mission town of San Luís, established some twenty years before near the present city of Tallahassee, had become the most important post in Apalachee. Its population numbered nearly fourteen hundred Indians, plus a considerable Spanish garrison assigned to man its fortifications. San Luís served as both the western anchor of the chain of missions stretching eastward to St. Augustine, and as a gateway to the otherwise isolated missions near the junction of the Chattahoochee and Flint rivers some forty miles to the northwest. Increasing travel and communication between the missions resulted in a well defined and improved trail that eventually connected St. Augustine with San Luís. Long after it had been abandoned and in many places obliterated, this trail came to be remembered as the Old Spanish Road.

Pensacola was not established until 1698, only six years before the destruction of the Spanish missions by Colonel James Moore of Carolina during Queen Anne's War. There were no Spanish settlements in the two hundred miles separating Pensacola from San Luís, and all communication between these two posts was carried on by sea by way of St. Marks, and was very much subject to the vagaries of the weather.

Diego de Florencia carried out a mission to Pensacola and Mobile in November and December 1702, seeking military relief for the besieged fortress at St. Augustine. He reported after his return to San Luís that "the winds were so contrary that the outward journey was extended to ten days and the return to fourteen."

Jacinto Roque Perez, reporting on a similar voyage in May 1703 stated: "The journey . . . is very slow, and urgency cannot be assured; the coast is very wild and a slight wind raises a heavy sea and it is necessary to shorten sail, as happened to me on the outward journey, and the seams

Pocahontas

One of the greatest myths of American history, still believed by almost everyone, originated in a true Florida story. It is the legend of Pocahontas and Captain John Smith.

A Spanish youth by the name of Juan Ortiz, going ashore on the lower west coast of Florida from an exploring vessel, was captured by Indians. Condemned by their chief to be burned to death, he was saved by the pleas of the chief's daughter. Ortiz lived for years as an Indian but was rescued by the expedition of Hernando de Soto. De Soto promptly put him to work as an interpreter. Before the expedition discovered the Mississippi, Juan Ortiz, on horseback and in armor, was drowned crossing a river. But the anonymous Portuguese "Gentleman of Elvas," who was writing an account of de Soto's great adventure, had already heard and recorded Ortiz' story.

A French translation was read by the famous English reporter, Richard Hakluyt, who was a friend of dashing Captain John Smith. In Hakluyt's book, *The Principal Navigations and Discoveries of the English Nation*, the story of Juan Ortiz is retold as having happened to Captain John Smith in Virginia. Yet John Smith was a guest of Powhatan, not a captive, and was courteously used by the Indian chief. Powhatan's daughter, Pocahontas, was then a little girl four years old.

John Smith did not repeat or endorse that colorful story for ten years, until *he* wrote a book about Virginia. He evidently saw Pocahontas after she had married John Rolfe and, in England, was a favorite of the Royal Court. Pocahontas never repeated any such story, and saw John Smith only once, in private. Nothing they said was recorded. So the Pocahontas legend is only another great myth that perhaps had its origins in Florida.   —M.S.D.

French engraving records storms
and shipwrecks that challenged travellers

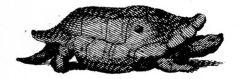

Some travellers complained
that travelling on colonial roads
was "as slow as a turtle."

In 1821 ships were still being made of wood,
and, except on rivers and canals, usually
were powered by sail. Live oak was a valuable shipbuilding timber because of its
strength and the curved limbs which were
sought for ribs. The United States
Government tried to reserve certain stands
of live oak for the navy, but it was cut from
the Florida woods almost without hin-
drance. It would have required an army of
enforcers to protect the oaks. Extensive
stands of the valuable wood grew in the
sandy soils of the peninsula. By the middle
of the eighteenth century and the period of
the United States Civil War, iron and steel
for shipbuilding and steam power were replacing wood and sail and the live oak lost its
importance in the timber industry.

– CHARLTON W. TEBEAU

opened so it did not appear the boat would survive. We fixed them the best
we could and arrived at Pensacola sixteen days after our departure from San
Marcos [de Apalachee], and from there to the French five, and five on the
return to Pensacola, and eight from Pensacola to San Marcos. I was only two
days in Mobile and four in Pensacola, with which all of the time of my delay
was on the sea."

A surplus of corn and other foodstuffs was produced in Apalachee.
Some of this was shipped by sea from St. Marks to supply the Spanish
settlement at St. Augustine, but trade between Apalachee and Havana and
Vera Cruz appears to have been of far greater importance.

The "Old Spanish Road" was a well maintained route for travel on
foot or horseback, as was amply demonstrated by events that occurred
during Queen Anne's War. Open hostilities in this conflict were initiated in
the Timucua district on May 20, 1702, when a party of Apalachicola
Indians under English influence, if not leadership, made a dawn attack on
the mission village of Sante Fe. After repulsing this attack in a three hour
battle, Juan Ruíz de Canicares led a small force in pursuit of the enemy. Ruiz
and his men covered a distance of some eighteen miles before overtaking the
Anglo-Indian force after dusk on the same day. Having thus demonstrated
their valor and stamina, Ruíz and most of his men were killed in the ensuing
fight. But their effort clearly indicates that an open and easily travelled route
existed through the Timucua region. Exhausted as they must have been
from the morning battle, they could hardly have covered so great a distance
over anything but a good road.

The initial onslaught against the mission towns in Apalachee, in
which several towns were destroyed, was carried out by Colonel Moore in
January 1704. This was followed six months later by a series of attacks on
the remaining missions. Destruction of the mission system in Apalachee
was virtually complete. The Indian population throughout the region was
either captured or driven out, and Fort San Luís, its undermanned garrison

having already been defeated once in the field, was threatened with imminent destruction. On July 8, Joseph del Pozo left San Luís with a letter reporting this situation, addressed to Governor Joseph de Zúñiga y Cerda at St. Augustine. He delivered the message at about six o'clock in the morning on July 12, having averaged over fifty miles a day in covering the distance of nearly two hundred miles. He must have had little if any opportunity to rest or obtain a fresh mount at one of the remaining missions along the way. This feat could only have been accomplished if the route were clear and in good condition for travel.

The destruction of the missions in Apalachee and Timucua put an end to effective Spanish occupation of interior Florida. Both Governor Zúñiga and his successor, Francisco de Córcoles, were well aware of the strategic necessity of settlement and defense of these regions. Even as he reported to Madrid the withdrawal from San Luís, Zúñiga suggested that Apalachee be resettled by bringing two hundred laboring families from the Canary Islands. Francisco de Córcoles later suggested Galicians from Spain instead of Canary Islanders for this purpose.

Although no such colonizing efforts were made, Diego Peña was sent in 1716 with a small band of Spaniards and Indians to reopen the road to Apalachee, and to reestablish relations with the Indians in the Apalachicola region. Peña's progress was slow and painful. He left St. Augustine on August 4, and, after ferrying his men and horses across the St. Johns by canoe, for lack of any better transport, he found little remaining of the road through Timucua. Nearing the natural bridge of the Sante Fé River, the party traveled for two days without a road, got lost, and went some seven or eight miles out of its way. The one hundred mile journey from the St. Johns River to the Suwannee River required nineteen days. Thirteen days were actually spent in traveling, at a rate of about seven miles per day, while six days were spent in camp, as the trip was extremely hard on both men and horses.

West of the Suwannee River conditions were just as bad, if not worse. Fallen trees obstructed and in some places obliterated the road. A hurricane swept the region, adding to the tangle. Peña reported that the party was often obliged to retrace its steps because of fallen timber. Rivers were swollen with rain, and in crossing the Aucilla, Peña lost his horse and narrowly escaped drowning when he was swept into the branches of a tree that had toppled into the stream. The Ocklochonee River was crossed in a boat made from green buffalo hides, and the Little River on a log raft.

The twenty years of British control of Florida following the treaty of 1763 saw little improvement in internal communication. British activity in East Florida was first aimed at consolidating military control over the area. The fortress at St. Augustine was augmented by the construction of an extensive barracks with materials brought in at great expense from New York. This extravagance prompted Bernard Romans to speculate in his contemporary *Natural History of Florida* that "the contrivers of all this having a sum of money to throw away, found a necessity to fill some parasite pockets." He went on to suggest that "the money spent on this useless parade would have been better laid out on roads and ferries."

In 1766 Governor James Grant raised a subscription of two hundred guineas, and began construction of the King's Road from St. Augustine to the St. Marys River. Only a few small plantations were scattered around St.

William Bartram during his Florida journey in the 1770s took care to detail his observations in pictures and words. Here is a drawing of the Great Golden Speckled Bream of the St. Johns River, signed by the artist in East Florida, 1774, during his travels.

The buffalo.

*Trails through Florida wilderness,
like those which served the Indians,
are quickly overgrown.*

The First Florida Developer

The first Florida developer was a Scotch physician, Dr. Andrew Turnbull, who recruited some 1200 Mediterraneans, mostly Minorcans, and in 1768 established a settlement at what is now New Smyrna Beach. The colony failed, but the survivors settled in St. Augustine to contribute many colorful pages in the history of Florida and of the United States during the next two centuries. Some customs and architectural styles are evident, and their pride in Minorcans includes celebrating descendant and author Stephen Vincent Benet who won the Pulitzer prize with his famous poem, *John Brown's Body* in 1929. Benet's brother, William, founded the *Saturday Review of Literature*. "Nor more motley group ever to set foot on America," according to Leonard Usina, a present-day Florida banker and another descendant of the early Florida Minorcans.

———

None of the Spanish owners of Florida could be called developers. Indians bent on defending their territory turned back the early Spanish colonists. But once the Spanish discovered that Florida had no precious metals and would produce neither grapes nor wheat, without which no Iberian could exist, the peninsula henceforth was to Spain no more than a hinterland, which the king held onto only as a military outpost to prevent inroads by the ambitious English and French.

—N. S.

Augustine and southward along the coast and the King's Road became an important link between these scattered plantations and the more mature colonies to the north.

A post road was opened in British West Florida between Pensacola and Mobile in 1770. Communication with the rest of the colony was maintained by way of the Gulf, lakes Maurepas and Pontchartrain, and the Iberville and Amity rivers. Travel in the interior from Mobile and Pensacola was confined to canoes on the various rivers of the region or by packhorse over woodland trails.

In 1773, the Colonial botanist William Bartram accompanied a trading expedition from the St. Johns River to the Indian towns along the Suwannee River. Well supplied with riding and pack horses, this party seems to have had little difficulty in following the general route of the old Spanish road through Timucua. The good condition of this and other trails in the region at that time, as Bartram describes them in his *Travels*, may be attributed to the fact that the Seminole Indians who then inhabited the region possessed good horses in large numbers, and travelled widely.

Barely able to populate her military and administrative posts at St. Augustine and Pensacola, Spain from 1783 to 1821 was no more capable of settling the interior regions than she had been before. So tenuous was her grip on the restored provinces that she attempted through liberal land and immigration policies to attract Americans to settle around St. Augustine and in West Florida, and licensed the Panton, Leslie Company, an English trading firm, to conduct trade with the Indians in the vast area in between. Both measures were partially successful. But both created more problems than they solved, stimulating, on the one hand, political intrigues and military incursions by the Americans, and contributing, on the other, to the virtual abandonment of mid-Florida to the refugee Indians and fugitive slaves who made up the Seminole population.

By 1821, travel routes in the interior of Florida had reverted to a changing network of Indian trails. Use of these trails by white men was limited essentially to that by traders, slave catchers, and assorted adventurers. The deterioration or disappearance of direct routes of communication and travel was summarized by John Lee Williams in his contemporary description of *The Territory of Florida*: "When Florida was ceded to the United States, there was but one road of any consequence in the Territory. That called the King's Road extended from St. Augustine to the River St. Marys. It had been well constructed by the English, and at first extended to New Smyrna, but the lower part was wholly grown up, and the balance much out of repair. Trails leading from Pensacola to Mobile, and up the Escambia, were scarcely passable for carts."

Throughout the period of Florida colonial history, and indeed for many years after, efficient and reliable travel and communication depended on the availability of convenient waterways. The only water route between St. Augustine on the Atlantic and St. Marks and Pensacola on the Gulf was around the peninsula. This route was not only long, it was also difficult and hazardous. The low lying coastline offered few landmarks to guide the mariner, inlets and bays were too far apart and often too shallow to afford shelter to vessels in distress, and the many sand bars, reefs, and keys took a heavy toll of shipping. Rivers, so useful in other regions, presented serious obstacles to inland transportation, because their north-south courses ran athwart the east-west travel routes required. Thus, Florida was denied efficient use of the primary mode of travel in colonial times.

Roads could be cut easily and maintained through the areas of relatively open and well drained pine barrens, but swamplands and tangled live oak hammocks posed serious problems requiring causeways and a continual battle with encroaching undergrowth. In Apalachee rainy weather turned the rich clay soils into quagmires in which horses sank to their bellies and wagon wheels to their axles. The sand hills east of the St. Johns river made a firm roadbed all but impossible. It is not surprising that wheeled vehicles were conspicuous by their absence in colonial Florida.

Roads could be maintained only where frequent travel kept them open and where a prosperous or ambitious population could afford the labor and expense. These conditions occurred in the Spanish mission period, when the concentration of Indian population channelled travel and communication along the old Spanish road. With the destruction of the missions and dispersal of the Indians, the road quickly deteriorated. In the years that followed, neither Spain nor England was able to establish a colonial population in Florida; Spain because she lacked the expansive energy, and England because she lacked time to consolidate her position in the new province. As the Indians filtered back into Florida in the late eighteenth century, they made use of woodland trails for hunting and trade, but these were of little value to later inhabitants. Permanent Florida roads did not appear until the American acquisition opened Florida to permanent settlement by a dynamic population.

—WILLIAM N. THURSTON

Andrew Turnbull is a controversial person in Florida history. When he brought over ships filled with workers from the Mediterranean area to labor on his planned plantations, he was soon under criticism: in 1775, Romans wrote: "About 1500 people, men, women and children were deluded away from their native country, where they lived at home in the plentiful cornfields and vineyards of Greece and Italy, to this place, where instead of plenty they found want in its last degree, instead of promised fields, a dreary wilderness; instead of a grateful fertile soil, a barren arid land; and in addition to their misery, were obliged to indent themselves, their wives, and children for many years. . .The better to effect his purpose, he granted them a pitiful portion of land for ten years, upon the plan of the feudal system: this being improved and just rendered fit for cultivation, at the end of that term it again reverts to the original grantor, and the grantee, may, if he chooses, begin a new state of vassalage for ten years more."

West Indians

Large numbers of non-American blacks, mostly French and British citizens from the West Indies and other locations, have settled and worked in Florida. Jamaicans have served as migrant laborers during the harvest seasons, most often in the cane fields of the glades area. Bahamians have done likewise; they have also worked as domestics who stay for a short period of time and return to the home island. So great has been the mobility of these laborers that many have described them as "commuters."

G.E.P.

Contemporary scene along King's Road.

Multiple modes of transportation on land and sea were used by people of the southernmost city in the United States, Key West.

Dredging Santa Fe Lake.

Roadbuilding by chain gang, 1925.

Corry Field at Pensacola reminds present day naval airmen that Lt. Com. W.M. Corry, Jr. was the first Floridian commissioned at Pensacola Naval Air Station, when the hazards of flying, if not worse, were certainly closer.

John Glenn, a pleased pioneer in space flight from Kennedy Space Center on Cape Canaveral.

Bridges or no, early Floridians usually were able to go from bank to bank across shallow Florida rivers. Most Florida rivers were flowing in the wrong direction for early Florida travellers, so they were forced to cross a river rather than use it as a waterway. Cows in Trenchard engraving ford Indian River in 1788.

OPENING THE FRONTIER

Resourceful skipper pilots steamboat along unmarked Florida waterway.

A vast wilderness wretchedly served by a few Indian trails and old colonial roads, this was Florida when it was acquired by the United States in 1821. One of the immediate concerns of the Congress was to improve the transportation system of the new territory. A St. Augustine to Pensacola road was authorized in 1824. The eastern part closely followed the old Spanish road, crossing the St. Johns River at Picolata. Built under contract by John Bellamy, using slave labor, the road bore his name. The portion from Pensacola to the Apalachicola River was built by the Army and became known as the Military Road. A Tampa Bay to Jacksonville road was completed but authorized roads to Cape Sable and to Cape Florida were never constructed.

The canal craze caught on in Florida but proposed projects far exceeded functioning canals. Limited federal appropriations improved the principal rivers, including the Apalachicola, the St. Marks and the St. Johns. The territory chartered scores of ferry boat corporations to bridge these streams for the new roads. As early as 1822 Secretary of War John C. Calhoun ordered Army engineers to explore the possibility of a cross-Florida canal and in 1826 Congress appropriated twenty thousand dollars to survey a canal route. The early surveys, however, reported that a canal was not practicable.

The first steamboat service on Florida waters was on the Apalachicola River in 1827. Steamboats soon appeared on most inland waterways, usually woodburning side- or stern-wheelers. These efficient colorful little boats quickly replaced sailing vessels for carrying both passengers and goods, although the sailing ship held its own on the high seas

Floridians through the years have found different ways to bridge the watery wilds for purposeful and social activities, close by or distant.

for another seventy years. Within ten years thirty steamers were operating on the Apalachicola alone, serving Florida, Georgia, and Alabama, and soon regular service was in operation on the Suwannee River.

The Charleston-built *George Washington* arrived in Jacksonville in May, 1831, initiating east coast steam transportation. Regular packet service was established on the St. Johns in 1834 between Savannah and Picolata, with stops at Darien, St. Marys, Jacksonville, and Mandarin, but the ancient city of St. Augustine usually was reached by stage overland from Picolata. In 1852 direct service from Charleston reached far up the St. Johns River valley to Enterprise.

The second Seminole War (1835–1842), although in most aspects tragic, boosted transportation facilities in Florida. The Army relied on steamboats operating in the St. Johns and its tributaries to supply and transport the troops. Naval vessels also frequented these waters. More than forty steamboats were chartered by the Army, five were purchased, and Army needs sometimes disrupted normal civilian traffic. The Army also built a network of roads connecting its forts and supply depots. The further south the Indians were driven, the further south the roads penetrated. Marked by temporary bridges or causeways, never paved and rarely graded, these roads were little more than cleared openings through the forest.

The little river steamers penetrated all the streams and coastal waterways of the state after the Civil War, running through the Indian River, the Kissimmee, the Caloosahatchee, the Withlacoochee, the exten-

Engineering and determination created a "railroad that goes to sea" for Henry Flagler.

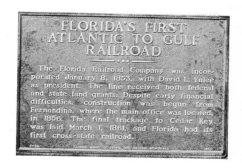

FLORIDA'S FIRST
ATLANTIC TO GULF
RAILROAD

The Florida Railroad Company was incorporated January 8, 1853, with David L. Yulee as president. The line received both federal and state land grants. Despite early financial difficulties, construction was begun from Fernandina, where the main office was located, in 1856. The final trackage to Cedar Key was laid March 1, 1861, and Florida had its first cross-state railroad.

*Local dignitaries greet the
Orange Blossom Special.*

sive bays and rivers of the "pan-handle" Gulf coast area, and the scores of Florida lakes connected by rivers and canals. In the last ten years of the nineteenth century even the ocean sailing vessels began to give way to steam powered ocean liners with New York to Florida passenger and freight service.

The earliest railroad lines date from the mid-1830s. The St. Joseph to Lake Wimico road, operational in 1835, was the first, followed by the Tallahassee to St. Marks line, opened in 1836. The Tallahassee Railroad, operated until 1855 with horse powered cars, survived and is still in use today as part of the Seaboard Coast Line system. In the next seventy years one hundred and seventy-four railroad companies (of four hundred and twenty-nine actually incorporated) built railways in Florida. The most important was the Florida Railroad, from Fernandina to Cedar Key. The moving force behind the line was U.S. Senator David L. Yulee, its president. Receiving aid from both state and federal governments, it was begun from Fernandina in 1856 and was completed to the Gulf at Cedar Key in 1861.

Deterioration and military destruction of the Florida railroads resulted from the Civil War; further physical deterioration, bankruptcy, financial manipulation and consolidation marked the post-war period. The state government regained some solvency by 1880 and renewed its efforts to promote railroads. Railroads were now the most promising means of opening Florida resources to settlers, developers, and tourists. With government aid the building of new railroads mushroomed all over the state.

Most Florida roads were either of three-foot or five-foot gauge rather than the "standard" 4'8 1/2" gauge common to Northern railroads. In a massive effort in 1886 almost all Southern railroads were changed to standard gauge; for the first time through service from the North to Florida was possible.

Three men emerged as state railroad giants: W.D. Chipley, with an empire based upon new construction and the old Florida and Alabama Railroad; Henry B. Plant, whose Savannah, Florida and Western pushed down the west coast of Florida; and Henry M. Flagler, who developed the east coast. The old Yulee road and the lines from Jacksonville to the Apalachicola were put together, with other short lines, as the Florida Central and Peninsular Railway, boasting 630 miles of track in Florida and service from Yulee to Savannah. Pride of this line in the 1890s was the "Flying Cracker," an express passenger train which ran, double-headed, from Jacksonville to Tampa in seven and one-half hours—plus a fifty minute stop at Silver Springs!

First interested in hotels, Henry M. Flagler became involved with railroads to transport building materials to his pleasure palaces. The rails could bring tourists as well as supplies, and Flagler soon put three short lines together in a road to Daytona. By 1896 he had pushed it down to the hamlet of Miami. His last monumental effort was the twenty-eight million dollar Overseas Railway from Miami to Key West completed in 1912. Sometimes called the "Eighth Wonder of the World," the Overseas Railway was severely damaged by a hurricane on Labor Day, 1935 and never rebuilt. Later sold to the state, its right of way and bridges form the southernmost extension of U.S. Highway 1.

The really revolutionary transportation development in the 1920s was the state system of public roads. By 1930, private automobiles and motor buses rolling over 3,254 miles of state highway were challenging the rail passenger business. Gradually rail passenger service declined and many short runs resorted to single coach gasoline powered rail cars as the only passenger service. A vast increase in both freight and passenger rail traffic occurred during World War II but by the late 1950s traffic declined again. The automobiles, trucks, and buses were joined by airline service to virtually every city in Florida.

One hundred and fifty-two passenger trains passed through Jacksonville in one day in 1913. By 1971 a quasi-governmental corporation, Amtrak, had taken over all passenger trains in the state and less than a dozen trains a day were scheduled through the new passenger terminal in the gateway city, a terminal considerably smaller than that provided for bus or air travellers.

The massive interstate highway system and huge jet aircraft of the 1970s seem to spell the end of the railroad role as a carrier of freight and passengers. Yet, as the twenty-first century approaches and the United States enters its third century as a nation, a world-wide energy crisis looms. The sources and uses of energy have put transportation problems in a new focus. Rail transportation now holds the promise of more efficient use of energy than the newer more popular ways of moving people and things.

—HERBERT J. DOHERTY, JR.

The Last Steamboat Skipper

Mark Twain immortalized the Mississippi steamboat captains, but Florida had its colorful steamboat skippers, too—on the St. Johns, the Oklawaha, the Suwannee, the Apalachicola, and on the Kissimmee, the Caloosahatchee, the Indian River, and Lake Okeechobee. Glimpses of early steamboating in north Florida have survived in the writings of Harriet Beecher Stowe, Sidney Lanier, and other travelers with a penchant for recording their experiences. The most vivid account of steamboat captains, right down to the last one, is told by Lawrence E. Will of Belle Glade, who in his later years discovered he had a talent for writing.

Will in 1964 immortalized himself in *Cracker History of Okeechobee*, then in 1965 immortalized Okeechobee steamboats and their skippers in a little book of that name. "They were a tough and hardy breed, for sure," he wrote of the steamboat captains, "and, brother, they knew all the tricks of shallow water navigation."

They "had to know" shallow water navigation because of the crooked rivers, dangerous snags, changing channels with every freshet, and, of course, changing sandbars. The Kissimmee River not only was "crookeder" than any snake can twist itself, but the main channel wound and twisted its way through a maze of false rivers that wound and twisted themselves in a flat basin a mile wide. When high water covered the valley, a captain had only his instinct to navigate by. Such a man was Captain Clay Johnson, who, according to Will, was "the last steamboat skipper."

"Now, if you're of a mind to picture the captain of one of them old smoke boats," wrote Will in Crackerese, "you'd most likely imagine him standing by his steering wheel, spare and straight, with a big white mustache acrost his lean, tanned face, with keen blue eyes, and a shock of snowy hair crowned by a battered boatman's cap. And so, I reckin you'd have a pretty accurate portrait of old Cap'n Clay Johnson, the last of Fluriday's steamboat skippers. And if'n you'd have told him he was the dead spit of old Mark Twain, he'd a-been your friend for life."

The steamboat Hiawatha *carried passengers and freight up the Oklawaha River to Silver Springs.*

Will, who worked on steamboats for a time after his arrival in the Lake Okeechobee area in 1913, remembered Captain Johnson steamboated where there were neither buoys nor beacons nor dredged channels; and he had no searchlight to pick up his marks at night, "nor ship-to-shore telephone to let his missus know he'd be an hour late in gettin' home." But Johnson could read the "face of the water like a parson readin' scripture. He'd never mistake a wind ripple for a sandbar, and he knowed the silver streaks that marks a hidden snag, and the lines and curves above a shoal." He knew the river changes in fog and rain and in pitch darkness.

The Kissimmee was opened to steamboats in the 1880s, after Hamilton Disston's crews removed the snags and connected the Caloosahatchee with Lake Okeechobee. A skipper could take his steamboat all the way from Fort Myers to Kissimmee, stopping along the way to freshen his fuel supply of fat pine cord wood. Captain Johnson's first smoke boat was the *Mamie Lowne*, a 35-foot sidewheeler. Then he bought the *Cincinnati*,

a 57-foot Mississippi paddlewheeler, and renamed her *Roseada*, after his daughters, Rose and Ada. Johnson then built his favorite, a paddlewheeler he named *Lillie* after his wife, and fixed her up with fancy cabins to make her the queen of the Kissimmee passenger boats.

Captain Johnson's largest steamboat was the *Osceola*, 74.6 feet long, which he built in 1910. It could carry 1,000 boxes of oranges, and, according to tradition, make 12 miles an hour upstream. The *Osceola* was another "wet tail boat," as the paddlewheelers were called.

Railroads put the steamboats out of business, first in north Florida, then in south Florida. Captain Johnson, Will writes, was the last, and when his *Osceola* hit a stump in the Palm Beach Canal at Loxahatchee in the 1920s and sank, that was the end of steamboating. "In October, 1931," writes Will, Captain Johnson "quietly slipped his moorings for his farewell journey on the River of No Return."

—NIXON SMILEY

Old Folk Song from Polk County.

Got on de train
didn't have no fare
But I rode some.
Yes I rode some.
Got on de train
didn't have no fare
Conductor ast me
what I'm doing there
But I rode some.
Yes I rode some.

Well, he grabbed me
by de collar and
he led me to de door
But I rode some
Yes I rode some.
Well, he grabbed me
by de collar and
he led me to de door
He rapped me over de head
with a forty-four
But I rode some.
Yes I rode some.

Early locomotive on the Jacksonville, St. Augustine, Halifax Railroad retired to power work train on the overseas railroad.

A railroad spans the sea as wooden frame for Long Key Viaduct rises above clear coastal waters of the Florida Keys.

Henry Flagler is surrounded by Admiral Young and other well wishers as he steps from the first train to Key West, on January 22, 1912.

He Used Railroads To Fill His Hotels

Henry Flagler, caught the Florida development fever in 1885 when he decided to build the Ponce de Leon Hotel at St. Augustine. He soon bought a short-line railroad to bring his guests from Jacksonville, and this put him in the railroad business. By 1890, Flagler's railroad extended to Daytona, and he had purchased the Ormond Hotel. In the early 1890s he extended his railroad southward to the Indian River section, but upon reaching the Indian River, he was ready to go even farther south.

Flager was 63 in 1893 when he started laying rails to Palm Beach, where the construction of his Royal Poinciana Hotel, the "world's largest hotel," was in progress. He was to continue with his developments for the next nineteen years, ending in 1912 with the opening of the overseas railroad to Key West. He rested the remaining year of his life, dying in his Palm Beach mansion in 1913. To Flagler's credit is the creation of Miami and the Palm Beaches. Although Flagler had dissipated millions in railroad and hotel building, he was still wealthy at the time of death. —N.S.

121

A TIMBER TALE

Cypress Logging

The series of etchings depicts a cypress logging operation at a log pond in Volusia County. Skidder logging was used whenever possible, but sometimes it was easier to take the mill to the logs: "pull boat" logging was used as a kind of floating sawmill in the deep swamplands of northern Florida. Operating in part water, part muck, and part land covered with thick underbrush, the logging crew could not see the pull boat engineers, so shrill steam whistles were used as signals. Over the noise of this operation, the incessant blasts spoke a simple and clear language to workers waistdeep in the muck.

In the 1750s royal timbers were cut in the colony for masts and spars with the enthusiastic encouragement of Ferdinand VI.

Two masts of yellow pine, each eighty-four feet long, were shipped from Pensacola to Havana in 1743—the first recorded export of Florida timber. The timber industry was off to a slow start, however, because the Spanish kings failed to recognize the importance of Florida forest products during most of the first occupation.

Logs and timbers were produced as needed for homes, fortifications, and plank roads. The Spanish also found that the forests yielded excellent timber for shipbuilding. Some Spanish officials recognized the potential for the production of naval stores, rosin, tar, pitch and turpentine, but little was done.

When the British came in 1763, they began to tap the products of this virgin forest. Pensacola, with its magnificent harbor, was surrounded by an estimated eighteen billion feet of yellow pine. At least one sawmill was soon established and Pensacola began exporting pine and cedar lumber, shingles, staves, and pitch in addition to cattle, salt, myrtle wax, and fish. The British also began producing naval stores in East Florida. By 1782 fifty thousand barrels of tar, rosin, pitch and turpentine were extracted every year from the areas surrounding the St. Johns and St. Marys rivers. A vast trading empire extended as far north as the Tennessee River and encompassing many tribes within the Creek Nation. Established during the last few years of the British period it continued to flourish for a time after the Spanish regained Florida in 1783.

When Florida became an American territory in 1821 exploitation of the forests resumed. As early as 1835, four million feet of lumber was shipped from Pensacola, and the first steam sawmill was built near the

"The years clawed at the house ineffectively, for it
had sturdy rafters and thick walls and its cypress
had served a long apprenticeship standing in
swamps, and cypress knows how to ignore time,
better than most things."

– JOHN KEASLER
Surrounded on Three Sides

In 1835 the Governor of East Florida is said
to have established a lumber and naval stores
industry producing pitch, tar, spars and
masts for Cuban shipbuilders.

town in 1841. Lumbering spread to Jacksonville. In 1853 there were
fourteen sawmills near that city and by 1860 the annual export of lumber
was valued at two million dollars.

Pensacola remained the lumber center of Florida prior to the Civil
War. The Florida lumbering industry, however, was largely backed by
Northern capital. During the War, most of the equipment was destroyed
or allowed to deteriorate. When peace returned, the manufacture of forest
products was one of the first industries to be re-established. Lumber was
sold locally to the railroads and for construction, but most of it was
exported.

The coming of the railroads changed the lumber industry. Sawmills now could be located away from the water and in stands of timber
that before had been unreachable. A resident of Micanopy, Alachua
County, wrote a letter in 1877 to Northern lumbermen describing the
unique opportunities available in Florida. "Mills can be located anywhere
and find ready sale for all the lumber that can be made. This is one of the
finest countries for that branch of business in the world. It can be carried
on throughout the entire season, and at less expense than at the North,
where the logs have to be cut in the winter, hauled to some stream and
floated down in the spring."

Northern capitalists and native Floridians heeded this message.
Most of the Florida virgin timber was cut in the next sixty years. Commercial exploitation, not conservation, was the keynote of the day. When Red
Cedar "of the very best kind" was harvested from the Cedar Keys and the
nearby mainland to make pencils, the population of this small group of

"These poets of the swinging blade! The
brief, but infinitely graceful, dance of body
and axe-head as it lifts over the head in a
fluid arc, dances in air and rushes down to
bite into the tree, all in beauty. Where the
logs march into the mill with its smokestacks
disputing with the elements, its boiler room
reddening the sky, and its great circular saw
screaming arrogantly as it attacks the tree
like a lion making its kill. The log on the
carriage coming to the saw. A growling
grumble. Then contact! Yeelld-u-uow! And
a board is laid shining and new on a pile. All
day, all night. Rumble, thunder and grumble. Yee-ee-ow! Sweating black bodies,
muscled like gods, working to feed the
hunger of the great tooth. Polk County!"

–ZORA NEALE HURSTON
Dust Tracks on a Road

Hardwood timber on the Florida Keys very early attracted the attention of people who also fished, caught turtles, and engaged in wrecking, or marine salvage, along the Florida Reef. Bernard Romans in his book refers to the "People from Providence [New Providence Island in the Bahamas] who came here for turtles or wood. . . . Having mentioned the cutting of the mahogany it may be proper to observe that little or none now remains here."

Andrew Ellicott who surveyed the boundary between the United States and Spain in the late nineties of the eighteenth century has left an interesting description of the Florida Keys made from his observations as he sailed around the lower peninsula when the Floridas were still Spanish territory. In 1799, he observed: "Some of the Keys or Islands were formerly well timbered, but the most valuable kinds, such as lignum vitae, fustick and iron wood, have generally been cut off by the inhabitants of the Bahama Islands."

When Florida became a part of the United States in 1821 Florida residents complained repeatedly that people from the Bahamas used the Florida Keys as a base for fishing, turtling, wrecking and timber cutting. Floridians were demanding that these activities be reserved for citizens of the United States.

In an article, "Florida's Clipper Ship," Edward A. Mueller notes that while most clipper ships were built in the Northeast, at least one was built in Florida. And the hull was made of mahogany. He suggests quite rightly that both the mahogany and the oak may have come from Florida forests. Christened the *Stephen R. Mallory*, the clipper ship was built in Key West in 1856.

–CHARLTON W. TEBEAU

A Self-destructing Industry

In several instances in Florida history, timbering has been carried to an extreme. The early Spaniards are said to have stripped the Florida Keys of hardwood including varieties of mahogany and lignum vitae used for shipbuilding. Latter-day Floridians in the west coast town of Cedar Key, once a strategic port and depot, began a lumbering operation related to the production of cedar pencils. The industry flourished, supplying the United States demand until the moment that all the trees were felled. Wooden houses with gingerbread carvings attest to its historical past.

islands off the Gulf coast reached five thousand in 1884. Fifteen years later all the cedar trees had been cut and the population dropped to twelve hundred people. Jacksonville, by 1890, was competing with Savannah, Georgia, as the leading world market in naval stores. Ten years later the value of the Florida naval stores industry approached a yearly value of eight million dollars.

Nearly all of the good timberland had been destroyed by 1930. Florida was left with millions of acres of idle, cut-over, burned-out forest lands. Thousands of people were without work as the mills closed or moved to new locations. New stands of "second growth" timber fortunately began to appear, and, very importantly, a new wood-using industry was developed. The pulp and paper industry thrives on what was once considered waste forest products. A pulp mill was built at Panama City in 1930 and three other mills were in operation by 1938: two at Fernandina, and one at Port St. Joe. Today, Florida is the third largest producer of pulpwood in the United States.

The Florida timber supply again dwindled in the 1940s. Improved management of timberland became imperative, including genetic improvement of forest trees, increased application of fertilizers, better land preparation, and better fire controls. Since 1930 almost two billion seedlings have been planted and about three million acres have been reforested. As more people come to Florida, other land uses compete with forests. In the press for urban development, citrus groves, crop land, and pasture land, better conservation practices will be needed in the future. Florida forests can become more productive and can provide more attractive areas for recreation. Sound forestry programs are needed and a more efficient use of state timberland. Florida forests, the second largest industry in the state, should last for many more years and continue to provide for the economic and esthetic needs of man.

–FRED BLAKEY

Cups, Gutters and Shouts in the Woods; Gum Turpentine and the Woods Worker

Turpentine, pitch, tar, and rosin were the products of one of the first colonial American industries. In time, the industry concentrated in the pineries of South Georgia and North Florida. By this time, production of naval stores, as the products were called, was basically in the hands of the turpentine Black. This was not an ordinary man but one set apart as "different." He was one who may have had both an aptitude for and a willingness to accept the life of the turpentine worker in the piney woods where near debt-peonage is said to have prevailed.

What kind of a man was content, or willing, to work ten or twelve hours a day under primitive circumstances? Mostly alone, but checked by the woods rider on his horse, he spent about two-thirds of his time just walking. He led a simple uncomplicated life, some have said happy in his ignorance, secure in the knowledge that the commissary in camp provided credit, that the "boss man" understood him and that the only law he need observe was that in the camp. He was far from the sheriff and from jail. For shelter, a miserable cabin with clapboard shutters over glassless windows to shut out the weather was provided for him, his woman, and a brood of children, but he did have safety in a kind of paternalistic system.

The woods are silent now but once they rang with the melodious half shout, half cry of the lonely worker. Some remember it as a Tarzan shout given in exuberance or to communicate. The woods workers also sang, but mostly it was their cries which distinguished them.

Out in the pines, the turpentine hand was expected to rake away the old needles and trash from the base of suitable trees. This was to protect the resinous faces from the frequent fires of that period. He selected large trees in the virgin forest but anything over nine inches in diameter in second growth. At a level close to the ground, two intersecting slashes were cut in an upside down chevron pattern. This was a face. The wounds or streaks, as they were termed, led to a resin or "gum" collector. In the days of large virgin pines, boxes were chopped into the bole of the tree for gum. Later, a round bottomed clay pot or "cup" was substituted. Later still, metal containers were often used to replace the heavier pot. Metal gutters were nailed below the face to direct the flow into the cups.

On the average around twenty suitable trees grew per acre, more in stands of smaller trees. Generally, one face per tree was prepared but larger ones may have had two or rarely three. Each face was visited and another half-inch wide streak cut every week. A maximum of about 3000 faces could be handled in a week. About every three weeks the cups were emptied. During the season, March through October, a tree might give up eight or nine quarts of gum. In three years, the faces could be expected to extend eight feet up and the tree was worked out unless it was large enough for another face.

The turpentine Blacks were considered to have been the most poorly paid workers of their period. They were concentrated in camps of maybe 160 individuals. Self-contained, isolated, often ten or twenty miles from a decent road, this camp afforded few amenities. With substitutes for and other ways of getting turpentine, prices fell, labor costs could not be lowered as they were already at rock bottom, and it became uneconomic to work the pines for gum. A picturesque period in Florida had closed.

Few trees are bled today. The cries or shouts of turpentine Blacks are no more. As one once said, "You are born into turpentine; you don't go into it; it's something you get out of." And they have. A scattering of those old clay pots and overgrown faces remind one of their time.
                                                    —CLARK I. CROSS

Signposts to Old Florida

Clues, even to the distant past, often remain in the landscape. People as they pursue their daily lives frequently erase the bolder patterns and features to leave the subtle—in the form of house types, fences, building materials, land use patterns and scars, and ways of doing things.

Florida is a pioneer land in spite of the St. Augustine claim as the oldest European settlement in the United States. For this reason the cultural inheritance contains little that is really old. Most of what can be observed of the past represents a rough, even crude, frontier.

The pioneer farmers relied upon the forests and prairies for economic support —employment in the woods, or a near subsistence form of agriculture in which a poor breed of scrub cow played an important part. The open woodlands offered an abundance of wildlife matched only by that found in the swamps, marshes, and prairies. Later cotton and corn became important and, in the north, tobacco. Pigs were introduced early. Soon escapees roamed the woods as half wild animals where they contributed to sport and food and were a part of the atmosphere of Cracker Florida into the 1960s.

Within a brief period of time, Central Florida passed through several stages: the Great Freeze of 1894–95 virtually wiped out northern citrus; virgin forests were cut over and the lumber industry vanished or changed; cotton production disappeared. As economics changed, some clues to the past remained in bold form, as the old hard rock phosphate pits attest to mining of sixty or more years ago. Evidence of other periods and of other activities may be found in simple items like an iron kettle. If shaped like the 1917 U.S. doughboy's helmet, it was used for making cane syrup. Although syrup making virtually disappeared in Central Florida in the late 1950s and early 1960s, the kettles and a few cane crushers remain to tell of the part cane once played in the local economy.

The cut-over stump lands have been reclaimed by natural forest or replaced by the regimental ranks of planted pine. Sawlogs have been replaced by pulpwood as the major item of lumbering interest. The echoing whistle of the logging locomotive or steam skidder disappeared a generation or longer ago but are suggested still by traces of railroad bed or scars in the vegetation.

The piney woods no longer know the songs of the turpentine worker. Where he once went his solitary way, cutting new faces, setting gutters and pots, gathering the gum and transporting filled wooden barrels to collecting station or still, there still may be forest. Now, however, the days of gum tur-pentine are almost over. Ceramic solid-bottom pots, galvanized gutter strips, faced trees with scars nearly over-grown, sometimes a stump which reveals a chopped box predating the manufactured gum collector, all tell a story of past turpentining—evidences of the past among those of the present.

In Cracker Florida the past is young and the pioneering spirit seems strong. Its people, shaped by their near self-sufficiency, are distinctive and characteristic of the land and the life which set them apart.

—CLARK I. CROSS

MINING WHITE GOLD

Newspapers all over the state headlined the find when Albertus Vogt discovered hard rock phosphate in Marion County, Florida on May 1, 1889. Phosphorus has no natural or synthetic substitute, yet is necessary for all forms of life and hard rock phosphate is the primary source of phosphorus. Thousands of would-be prospectors surged into Florida, and the Florida phosphate rush of 1889 repeated in miniature the California gold rush of 1849.

Middle Florida was swarming with phosphate adventurers. Trains were filled with prospecting parties armed with spades, chemicals, and camping apparatus. Thousands came by horseback, by wagon, and on foot. A few were experienced miners from the phosphate fields of other states and countries, but the majority were men who did not even know what the mineral looked like. But they were searching it. To their minds, ". . . anything more cohesive than sand and more resistant than putty was phosphate. It was true petrified bone when it was hard, and very valuable. When exceedingly soft it was decomposed bone and therefore more valuable. If unusually light-colored, it was amazingly rich, though if uncommonly dark-colored, it was richer."

Strange theories soon cropped up. Some prospectors said that the height or shape of a pine tree was a clue. There was also a "phosphate grass" which supposedly grew only over rich deposits of phosphate. Interesting explanations concerning the origin of the deposits were given. One ingenious prospector accounted "for the vast accumulation of animal remains by suggesting that that was the locality whence Noah's ark started on its voyage, and that the remains were of animals that failed to secure passage on her."

These wild exaggerations had largely disappeared by 1892, but the so-called "boom" cannot be said to have ended until 1896. The Panic of 1893 brought recession. The citrus industry was hard hit by a freeze

Like the 49ers in the Gold Rush heading West, phosphate prospectors swarmed down to the frontier towns of west Florida seeking the white powdered gold. Their tools were diverse; they had no idea what they sought; but the phosphate fever was strong in '89.

Millions of tons of concentrated phosphate rock are mined in Florida and return billions of dollars to the economy of the state. As world demand for food rises, and for phosphate fertilizers to increase crops, those millions and billions may become trillions.

Phosphate Pits
of Boom Time Days

The old style homes and aging store fronts of Newberry date back to the hard rock phosphate boom. Here some eighty years ago hard rock phosphate induced men to establish a town. And what a town it was! A town where ladies stayed off the streets at night and all day Saturday. Saturday when hard and hungry men, men hungry for diversion, whiskey and women, strode the streets, fought and sometimes died. Newberry, quiet and peaceful now, lived a productive life in which the wilderness was just a part. Nearly forgotten are Lexington, Wade, Clark, and other phosphate camps not far away. Of some there is little but a name on old maps to tell of their existence.

Out in the early phosphate mines, where the pits still recall the past, a past that still lives in the memory of a few, life was cheap and frequently brutally difficult. Steam shovels and dipper dredges were not designed for the deeper, steeper-sided pits. These are the monuments to the muscle of men, of the men with shovels and picks. Many were without any incentive other than to save life itself. These were convicts—chain gangs of black men—who sweated under the summer sun, intensified by the white glare of phosphate rock and limestone, unrelieved by the cooling breezes. It was better in the winter but the exhausting work was the same.

Gangs of black convicts were leased out by an economy-minded state to contractors to whom convicts were more chattel than human. Cheap labor to be poorly fed and housed, ruled by whipping bosses, these unfortunates dug many of the holes that are half masked by forest growth. But not all was unrelieved drudgery. View the pits too as peopled with men swinging and digging to a rhythm—songs and chants. A singing people may not be a happy people but in their songs hope was expressed as well as despair, and life was worth living—even in the phosphate pits—even as a convict. Conditions for free workers were frequently primitive and their toil too involved similar reliance on straining human muscles.

Time has softened the contours and vegetation has added interest and beauty to the excavations and piles of waste. The deeper pits are water filled, perhaps locally cherished fishing holes. Impressed deeply into the landscape are the signs of a productive, if frequently harsh, even brutal, interlude in Florida's history.

–CLARK I. CROSS

during the winter of 1894–1895; another severe freeze in 1896 ruined numerous crops. The new phosphate industry was crippled by the recession, increasing competition, and spiraling costs of operation. Many small companies consolidated into a few major ones. The number of mining companies dropped from over 400 in 1895 to fifty in 1900, and the great phosphate "boom" was over.

Years of experimentation followed, marked frequently by mismanagement and inefficiency as the infant industry struggled to achieve stability. By the end of World War I, Florida producers recognized the need for research and study to develop more efficient mining techniques and technological inventions.

Branching out, the Florida phosphate industry in the late 1940s began producing complete fertilizers and plant foods. Another "boom" flowered as world demand for phosphate products escalated. And almost

simultaneously there arose among Americans a concern for the conservation of natural resources, pollution, and the quality of the environment, its beauty and its recreational opportunities. The public demanded during the 1960s that the industry reclaim the mined-out phosphate lands, or "spoil banks" as they are commonly called. Today nearly seventy percent of the acreage mined is restored. Unsightly mining areas will still be visible for many years, however, because much of the mined-out area must be retained for waste disposal and water conservation.

The pollution of the air and water of central Florida was another problem facing the phosphate industry, a significant offender. Industrial and municipal wastes polluted Florida water resources in amounts equivalent to a population of over seventeen million people prior to 1969, and the air was polluted with an average of 870 tons of particulates every day by Florida industry. Two of the worst polluters were the phosphate industry and the pulp and paper producers. After spending over 165 million dollars for pollution control devices, the phosphate industry by 1973 had largely solved these problems.

Phosphate rock underlies almost all of Florida. It is found in marketable quantities only in Polk, Hillsborough, Hamilton, Citrus, Marion, Columbia, and Gilchrist counties. The heart of the three billion dollar industry is in Polk and Hillsborough.

Florida produces one-third of the world supply of phosphate rock. The future will confront Floridians with hard choices in the conservation and use of this vital mineral while preserving their environmental heritage. Enlightened use of the mineral phosphorus and all other natural resources is imperative as man makes increasing demands upon the land.

— FRED BLAKEY

"Polk County. Black men laughing and singing. They go down in the phosphate mines and bring up the wet dust of the bones of pre-historic monsters, to make rich land in far places, so that people can eat. But, all of it is not dust. Huge ribs, twenty feet from belly to backbone. Some old-time sea monster caught in the shallows in that morning when God said, 'Let's make some more dry land. Stay there, great Leviathan! Stay there as a memory and a monument to Time.' Shark-teeth as wide as the hand of a working man. Joints of backbone three feet high, bearing witness to the mighty monster of the deep when the Painted Land rose up and did her first dance with the morning sun. Gazing on these relics, forty thousand years old and more, one visualizes the great surrender to chance and change when these creatures were rocked to sleep and slumber by the birth of land."

— ZORA NEALE HURSTON
Dust Tracks on a Road

Ponce de León brought the first cows to Florida on his ship and the early Spanish imports became known as scrub cows. Four hundred years later the hardiness of the scrub cow was mixed with the virility of pure bred bulls from many parts of the world including Canada, France, and India. With plenty of blackstrap molasses, water, range land and a mild climate, the cattle industry has grown and Florida has become a large exporter of breeding stock .

HOME ON THE RANGE

The hunting-gathering way of life needs 20,000 acres to support a single person. By contrast the village style of living, with cultivated plants and domesticated animals, supports one person on 25 acres. Eight thousand years ago Near Eastern foods and planting methods appeared in south-eastern Europe and ended the hunting-gathering way of life there. Life, however, went on much as before, in the nameless place that was later called Florida, an ancient finger reaching from a warm sea to support the choking denseness of swamps, alligators, mosquitoes, sea oats, and peoples whose records are mostly lost. Here, somewhere, an anhinga stretched its wings to dry on a palmetto and an alligator at the edge of an unnamed stream snapped its teeth shut on a 'possum.

Cattle, originally hunted as game, were first domesticated in Europe and Asia. In the flourishing Mediterranean cultures and in Greek mythology, bulls played an important part. Julius Caesar, around 65 B.C., described B. *primigenius*, the ancestor of modern-day cattle breeds as ". . .approaching the elephant in size but presenting the figure of a bull. . . ."

The cow, this important friend of mankind, did not set foot on Western Hemisphere soil until 1493, some time during Columbus' second voyage. These animals, now a major source of food in Florida as in most of the western world, were brought as work oxen for colonists in the West Indies. Cortez, in 1519, took cattle from Spain to Mexico. Eighty-one years later, in 1600, more Spanish cattle were brought over as work animals and as dairy animals for the chain of Christian missions that extended from the east coast of Mexico, up the Rio Grande River and across the mountains to the Pacific Coast. Spanish mission priests by 1833 estimated their herds at 424,000 head.

How did cattle come to Florida? The important date for Florida cattlemen is 1521, the year that Juan Ponce de León sailed from Santo Domingo to Florida, arriving with six heifers and a bull. These Andalusian cattle are the ancestors of the Texas Longhorns, the Mexican fighting bulls, and most of the present-day Florida herds. The Plymouth Pilgrims had no livestock for three hungry years until 1624 when the Good Ship *Charity* landed a bull and three cows from Devonshire. Spanish tax returns from Florida, however, show that in the 1600s St. Augustine was supplied with beef from nearby ranches, unlike other early American colonies.

The seventeenth century was a time of expansion for the Florida cattle industry. With the eighteenth century came wars, raids, and the destruction of the Spanish missions and the agriculture that had grown up around them. St. Augustine again became dependent on imports for its survival. A group of Oconee Indians soon, around 1750, moved from Georgia and Alabama south to a place near Micanopy, Florida. They grew corn and had large herds of cattle which grazed the Alachua Prairie and Payne's Prairie.

After the Seven Years War, England became a supreme maritime power, and not only controlled the seas but also part of Spanish Florida. During this English period, 1763–1783, the population of Florida flourished and the herds of cattle expanded again. Though Floridians were dependent on England for manufactured goods, they did produce most of their food. The importance and abundance of cows can be detected in the name of a St. Johns River crossing which was called, simply and descriptively, "Cow Ford." The place has since grown and acquired a new name, Jacksonville. The September Treaty of Versailles in 1783 not only gave independence to the American colonies; on the same day Great Britain ceded Minorca and Florida to Spain. Hearing the news ten thousand British colonists left Florida with their cattle and all of their possessions they could carry.

The second period of Spanish rule over Florida was the time of the Spanish Land Grants. The grants ranged from a few thousand to more than a million acres, and were given to individuals and companies. Those

Cattle business was the big business on the West Coast. The Savannah News of Oct. 25, 1879 listed the following shipments of cattle to Cuba: "Ziba King, 6,000 head; Jake Summerlin, 7,000 head; Dr. Lykes, 10,000 head." This trade had a profound effect on the money in use in the area. Both Cubans and Floridians distrusted Spanish bank notes, and had little more respect for the American dollar. They dealt primarily in gold Spanish doubloons, worth $16.80 each. These bright, soft coins were always measured by weighing because they wore easily. McKay and Grismer, respected Tampa historians, each state that for about 20 years "gold Spanish doubloons became more common in Tampa and the cattle country than American dollars."

The stockmen, often termed "cattle kings," were the dominant figures of west Florida's most colorful era. The law of the open range prevailed from Palatka to Lake Okeechobee throughout the 19th Century. The Western Plains provided no more thrilling stories of cattle drives, open-range feuds and shoot-outs than did Florida. Newspapers carried "Cattle Warnings" displaying the owners' brands and ear croppings. These warnings usually could be enforced with labor and reasoning, but, when not, with revolvers.

The names of the famous cattlemen were equally picturesque—names like Ziba King of Fort Ogden, Captain John T. Lesley of Fort Brooke and Jake Summerlin, "King of the Crackers." Jake, among others, could handle an 18-foot bullwhip as well as any cowhand. The crack of this whip gave the "Florida Cracker" his nickname.

–J.M.I.

In recent times there has been a bull market for Florida cattlemen and cowboys on the range and in the rodeo.

who received the grants agreed to bring in settlers and clear a portion of the grant land. Spanish efforts to colonize Florida were never a success, yet part of the Spanish culture lives on in Florida in the giant citrus and flourishing livestock industries, as well as in the customs of her people.

At the outbreak of the Civil War Florida cattlemen were no match for those in Texas where there were ten cows for each Texan. When the Federal blockades became effective, however, Florida was tabbed to be the main supplier of beef for the Confederacy. Florida cattle provided not only army food rations, but also leather for equipment and tallow for candles. Cattle drives, lasting forty days or longer, were organized to herd cattle from the south Florida prairies to the one cross-state railroad running from Cedar Key to Jacksonville. Toward the end of the War the transportation system in the South was in chaos. Foodstuffs piled up in commissary warehouses while the Army of the Confederacy went without food and boots, and the civilian population was on the verge of starvation. The so-called "Confederate Tithe," a ten percent sales tax on beef did not help the fledgling Florida cattle industry. Neither did the Impressment Act of 1863 which authorized Confederate agents to seize food and other property useful to the Army at an arbitrarily low price. Some overzealous agents even took family milk cows and stripped Florida of food supplies and the means for agricultural production. Strangely, during Reconstruction thousands of cattle roamed Florida woodlands and grasslands in a semiwild state.

The Florida cattle industry in its present form began in the early 1920s. This was the beginning of the effort to control the cattle fever tick, a battle that did not end until 1950. Mineral deficiencies in Florida cattle were discovered and corrected as the cattle licked mineral blocks along with the traditional salt blocks. Pastures and management practices improved. Native or scrub cows, hardy animals which withstood the tough Florida range conditions, were "bred up" with purebred Brahman, British, and crossbred foundation bulls. Still, there was the screwworm, the two-winged fly that laid its eggs in the sores or wounds of animals, and even people. The larvae that hatched literally ate the living creature to death. Finally a new idea in pest control was tried in 1957—the sterile male technique. This technique wiped out the Florida screwworms in two years time. The campaign cost eleven million dollars but it stopped losses of twenty million dollars in years past and the horrible suffering produced by the screwworm in Florida.

Florida had less than ten purebred herds in 1929, but twenty years later there were nearly five hundred herds of Angus, Hereford, Brahman, Santa Gertrudis, Charolais, Shorthorn, and Brangus. Those herds have grown again and an enlarged breeding and crossbreeding program has introduced new exotic breeds like the Simmental, Limousin, Chianina, and the Maine-Anjou.

It staggers the mind: Juan Ponce de León sailed from Santo Domingo to St. Augustine in 1521 with six heifers and a bull, and from this small beginning has come a Florida cattle population that numbers over two million—a minor miracle never envisioned by the Spanish friars who tended the first Florida herds. —JANOS SHOEMYEN

132

Two Florida cowboys on tough little cowponies canter over grasslands near Lake Okeechobee in a Remington painting made near Arcadia in the 1890's.

Florida Cowboy

Bone Mizell

He was the cracker wag of the Florida cow country, kindling his pipe with dollar bills, branding cattle with his teeth and clowning his way to a permanent niche in Sunshine State folklore.

In short, Bone Mizell was just a typical cowboy—the way Paul Bunyan was a typical lumberjack.

Unlike the mythical Bunyan, though, ol' Bone actually did rustle cattle, guzzle booze and get himself immortalized in a Frederick Remington painting.

Bone had a Roman nose. He lisped and wheezed. Old-timers who knew him say everything he did was funny, and the stories told about him have been embellished since

Bone Mizell is believed to have been the model for the painting, "A Cracker Cowboy." Frederic Remington, famed artist and illustrator of frontier life, came to Arcadia in 1895 to paint and write about Florida cracker cowboys.

his death in 1921. He's a folk hero now, droller than life, and he's become an institution. The Peace River Valley Historical Society has erected a monument to Bone near the Pioneer Park Museum in Zolfo Springs.

Bone roamed the valley when it was one vast open range and Arcadia and Wauchula were boisterous little cow towns. He was head cowhand for Zibe King, a prominent rancher of the day, and though he couldn't read, write or do sums he carried King's accounts in his head while outriding every cowpoke on the range.

Gaunt, mean scrub cattle roamed freely across endless miles of swamp and palmetto flats, through swarms of mosquitos, searing sun and tropical torrents of rain. The rugged men who tended these herds worried little about stealing each other's cows unless they got caught at it. Bone's name appeared on the semi-annual docket of Arcadia's circuit court for many years, but he always managed to beat the rap—with one exception.

One day Bone was butchering a cow when its owner rode up. The man swore out a warrant, and Bone was in real trouble.

The judge asked him if he had anything to say.

"I shore do, yer honor," Bone declared. "I must of stole ten thousand cows for Mr. King and everybody laughs at that, but now I go and steal one leetle ol' speckled calf for myself and you want to send me to the pen."

The judge sentenced Bone to a year in Raiford. His friends arranged a pardon, but then discovered it could not be effective until Bone actually served time in the penitentiary.

He received a hero's sendoff as he boarded the train in Arcadia. At Raiford, prison officials gave him a tour and a banquet. He made a speech praising the management, received the pardon which was waiting for him, and—having "served his time"—boarded a train for home.

Then there's the time Bone arranged for one of his fellow crackers to serve as "guest of honor" at a Yankee funeral. An undertaker had hired Bone to dig up the remains of a young Vermont adventurer who died while camping in the Everglades during the dry season. The man's companions decided they couldn't haul the body out by flatboat across dry creek beds, so they buried it in a remote cemetery near Moore Haven.

The Vermonter's wealthy parents contracted with the undertaker to ship their son's remains home for proper interment in the family plot. When the rains came, the undertaker paid Bone to retrieve the body.

"Shucks, I got to thinking," Bone told his cowpoke friends years later. "Here was this Yankee who'd been all over the world and seen everything, and right next to him lay pore old Bill Redd who hadn't never traveled none and always wanted to take a train ride.

"I figgered it wouldn't make no difference to the rich boy nohow, so I said to myself: 'Bill, now's yore chance. I'm gonna give you that ride.'"

Bone died in the Atlantic Coast Line depot at Fort Ogden, south of Arcadia, on July 14, 1921. His death certificate states the cause as "Moonshine—went to sleep and did not wake up."

He was buried in Joshua Creek Cemetery, just east of Arcadia, in a grave which remained unmarked until the 1950s when some friends erected a small granite marker. It reads:

"Bone." N. Bonaparte Mizelle
1853–1921

The monument at Zolfo Springs commemorates the kooky cowboy's importance for Florida folklore, as a symbol of the Florida frontier period.

—GEORGE LEPOSKY

133

Kennst du das Land wo die Citronen blumen
In dunkel Laub die Gold-Orangen glühen.

Know the land where the citrus bloom
In dark foliage golden oranges glow.

—GOETHE

From the air citrus groves carpet the rolling
hills of central Florida.

GOLDEN GROVES

Sometime between 1513 and 1565 the official symbol of Florida arrived. It was round, green or orange in color, and came either with Ponce de León or someone else a bit later. On April 2, 1579 Pedro Menéndez, Marques of the Audencia (Court of Justice) of Santo Domingo, reported to the Audencia from St. Augustine: "There are beginning to be many of the fruits of Spain, such as figs, pomegranates, oranges, grapes in great quantity. . . ." Two hundred years later early settlers found wild citrus groves in many parts of the state, usually on hammock lands near lakes or rivers where Indians had established villages. Apparently the Spaniards had given some of their oranges to the Indians.

William Bartram, writing in 1791 about his travels in East and West Florida in 1774, said that when he was sailing down the St. Johns River alone in a small boat he looked for high land for his camp at night. At these camping places he always found wild orange trees in amongst the magnolia, oak, hickory, and bay trees. It was as if the Indians had deliberately scattered orange seeds around their villages so they would have their own orange groves. Bartram also mentions the town of New Smyrna established by a Mr. Turnbull on the Mosquito River near the coast. "I was there about ten years ago when the surveyor ran the lines or precincts of the colony, where there was neither habitation nor cleared field. It was then a famous orange grove, the upper or south promontory of a ridge, nearly half a mile wide, and stretching north about forty miles . . . ."J.S. Adams gives a physical description of these trees in his *Note on wild orange groves:* "The natural trees grow from 12 to 15 feet in height—not very large, interspersed with oak, hickory, bay et cetera." By 1791 William Bartram regretfully reported that most of the wild orange groves on the St. Johns River had been cleared to make way for indigo plantations.

In 1809 a Spanish nobleman, Don Phillippe, immigrated to Florida and settled in what is now Safety Harbor in Pinellas County. He brought grapefruit seeds and trees and set out a small grove. A.L. Duncan, a grower in the same county, wrote in 1892: "Phillippe fifty years ago planted seed which came from Cuba." Don Phillippe gave away a great number of seedlings as gifts to his neighbors and the Duncan grapefruit was a seedling from one of Don Phillippe's trees.

Florida became a part of the United States in 1821, and by 1835 a fledgling Florida citrus industry was going. D.J. Browne reports in 1857: "The number of trees owned by different individuals, prior to 1835 varied from ten to fifteen hundred. . . .There were many trees then to be found in St. Augustine which exceeded forty feet in height, with trunks from twenty to twenty-seven inches in diameter, and which probably were more than a century old." Suddenly the great freeze of 1835 halted the spread of citrus trees across the land of Florida. Colonel Dancy, a pioneer orange grower, reported: "Trees a hundred years old were killed to the ground. . . .In the spring, however, the trees grew up from the roots, and in two years bore fruit once more."

One of the first famous groves was on Fort George Island, where the grove spread over three or four acres. Planted in 1824 by Zephaniah Kingsley, sugar planter, slaver, author, and alleged pirate, the grove was based on sweet orange seedlings. The Dummitt grove on Merritt Island was established in 1830 and, as far as is known, was the first wild grove to be "top-worked." Top-working is a technique used to substitute a new variety on the root system of an older tree of the same type. The top-worked tree will produce more quickly than a newly planted tree because it has an already developed root system. Wild sour orange trees grew on the Dummitt plantation. The sweet orange to which Captain Dummitt's wild sour orange trees were budded came from a grove near New Smyrna. It is thought that this budding was the beginning of the succulent Indian River Orange that is shipped and relished around the world.

Marketing citrus out of the wilderness of Florida was a problem. Early groves were planted near or along rivers so that the oranges could be picked up by boat. The wharves were fragrant with the pungent odor of citrus as the barrels of fruit piled up waiting for the boats, but most of the Florida rivers were going in the wrong direction. When the railroads came along in the 1850s, the citrus industry expanded rapidly.

Growing grapefruit on a commercial scale began in Florida. The first shipments to Philadelphia were made between 1880 and 1885, and the going rate was five cents a barrel. Today the largest single agricultural crop in Florida is citrus. From this sun-filled land comes half of the grapefruit in

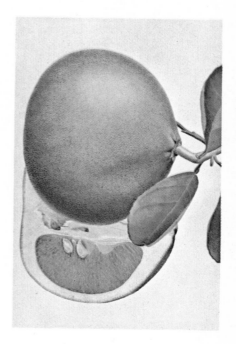

CITRUS MAXIMA
Fam. Rutaceae

Dutch:	Pompelmoes
French:	Pamplemousse
	Pomme d'Adam
German:	Adamsapfel
	Pampelmus
English:	Forbidden fruit
	Grapefruit
	Paradise-apple

According to a book on fruits of the Dutch East Indies written in the early 1930s by J.J. Ochse, the red grapefruit is the *citrus maxima* and those who like the legend that Florida was the Garden of Eden will be captivated by the suggestion that the grapefruit, after all, is the apple that tempted Adam and Eve.

The orange, the golden fruit of Florida by way of the Orient, has been called *citrus nobilis*, or noble fruit.

"Oranges, lemons, limes, and other fruits grow spontaneously over the country."
—The English Governor
St. Augustine
October 7, 1763

The Truth Tree of de Soto

The nation has the George Washington cherry tree story but Florida has the Hernando de Soto orange tree tale. It is said by some that the wild oranges in Florida took root from seeds unwittingly sown by de Soto and his shipmates. The legend credits them with spitting out seeds of Spanish oranges in central Florida soil from which scattered groves grew.

On December 25, 1717, the sloop *Swan and Eagle* arrived in Charleston carrying a cargo of oranges from St. Augustine.

Oranges were cultivated for commercial purposes during the British Period in Florida. Jesse Fish had a large plantation on Anastasia Island and grew dates, olives, and oranges. Oranges were also grown in other areas around St. Augustine. In 1764, 21 barrels of oranges were exported and 62 barrels and 3 casks in 1765; 21 barrels of squeezed juice, 49,000 oranges, plus 20 barrels, 30 casks and 6 barrels of juice in 1766. Shipments also included dried orange peel, lemons, and limes.

Chinese

During the turbulent years following the Civil War many Floridians urged that Chinese workmen be imported to alleviate a critical labor shortage. Newspapers and journals throughout the state praised their hard-working habits and frugality and many came to work in the state. The Paradise farm just outside of Gainesville, a large naval stores operation owned by Mr. C.W. Chase, counted several hundred Chinese among its work force. Florida's most famous Chinese immigrant, of course, was the noted horticulturist, Lou Gim Gong. A native born Chinese, Lou Gim Gong produced two of the best strains of citrus fruit grown in Florida (the Lou Gim Gong orange produced in 1888 and the Gim Gong grapefruit produced in 1892). He was awarded the Wilder medal by the United States Department of Agriculture in recognition of his discoveries.   G.E.P.

Lou Gim Gong.

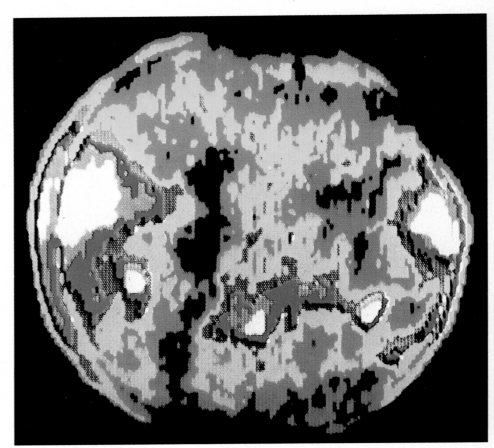

Florida oranges are a Florida gold first seeded by early Spaniards and still growing under a sun pictured in new ways by space age scientists from satellites and space ships launched on Florida shores. Color-coded image of sun recorded by Skylab, shows intensity of light from white down through yellow, red, blue.

the world, and nearly one fourth of the oranges. Here, nearly all of the frozen orange concentrate in the world is packed. These processing plants are recycling the waste products—peel, pulp, and seeds—into another product, cattle feed.

Where did the orange and grapefruit come from? Many probably are natives of Asia and the Malay Archipelago. The first news of citrus fruit in Europe comes from Theophrastus who lived from 372–287 B.C. About that time, a Chinese poet named Ch'u Yuan wrote in his verse called "Li Sao," Falling into Trouble, about many citrus trees and other trees and flowers. Years later, 1178 A.D., Han Yeh-chih, in "Chu lu," told all about the oranges of Wen-chu, Chekiang, and even describes varieties, grove management, diseases, and nursery methods.

In the Bicentennial year, 1976, millions of boxes of oranges and millions of boxes of grapefruit will be harvested in Florida. Because of a love for oranges and their faraway homeland by a handful of Spanish adventurers, again the northern pilgrims will pose in front of the green trees with their golden globes. Cameras will record again and again this historical moment in time, commemorating a marvel that has taken place on the Florida sand.

—JÁNOS SHOEMYEN

Colorful Cracker houses are disappearing as fast as the Florida wilds.

The Florida Cracker

From the north they came. Small farmers pushed out of Georgia, Alabama and the Carolinas by adversity or pulled to Florida by opportunity, they came with their livestock and their household and farming goods. They were mostly impoverished and poorly educated but they had courage, toughness, tenacity, and a strong moral code rooted in their Protestant backgrounds.

The Cracker, claimed by some people to be so-called because these were a whip cracking people, was a product of his environment. A hostile environment theirs proved to be. For all of its abundant game, its fish and timber resources, nature withheld, resisted, and attacked. The Cracker was molded in the struggle.

The abundance of wildlife included insect pests, the malaria-carrying mosquito among them. Dysentery, typhoid fever, yellow fever, hookworm to weaken, to sicken, and to kill were the early settlers common enemy. Soils were not so fertile as supposed, markets were distant and the roads were more correctly described as roughly cleared, barely passable wagon trails.

The Cracker was obligated to be self-sufficient and self-reliant, a close to nature farmer-woodsman. Isolation, however, drew the scattered Crackers together in a kind of mutual assistance neighborhood in which the needs of an emergency would be spontaneously met. The Cracker was a strongly independent, individualistic, yet generous frontier type, proud even in poverty.

There is no doubt that the stamp of environmental deprivation was carried by the Cracker. Barefoot children, as well as adults, and the frequent disposal of human wastes in the most convenient manner along roadsides, trails, and backyard fringes, combined to give Cracker Florida a high incidence of hookworm infestation. The pallid faces of its people may have also been a reflection of poor diet or malaria, but hookworm was a common cause. Soles of feet toughened to leather-like armor easily admitted the hookworm.

Screenless houses placed in a paradise for mosquitoes and yellowflies contributed to sleepless nights and daytime annoyance. A near-immunity to chiggers (or redbugs) may have come from longtime attack on human victims, but the scarred bare legs of the children gave evidence of past attacks of various insect pests.

Thin and toil worn, lean, lanky and tired, these terms, with no disrespect intended, could be applied to many of the backwoods inhabitants of the area. Teeth were lost early to give faces some of their pinched appearance, but even this implies environmental poverty. Life in Cracker Florida, and in other parts of Florida, too, may have provided enough to eat but it withheld from its people many of the amenities of life.

With greater opportunity in growing towns and cities the temptation to emigrate was strong. Some of the most energetic, enterprising, and footloose departed. They could not shuck the attitudes gathered in a lifetime and, in spirit, they remained Crackers still. Those who remained may have improved their lot as conditions changed and they too lost some of their most apparent physical marks.

There is an Old Florida, call it Cracker Florida if you will, where a distinctive way of life and attitudes persist, where houses and barns seem little changed but this Florida exists only in pockets and seems harder to find with every passing year.

—CLARK I. CROSS

"There is no easy definition for a Florida cracker. The literal-minded say he is simply a Florida-born native. This has nothing whatsoever to do with it. A man can be a Yankee and a Cracker in the same lifetime, although it is true only a limited number of men are equipped to do this. Most of these, however, end up as Crackers. The rest wonder all their lives what is wrong. . . . The term is not easy to define. You are or you aren't. A Cracker is inclined to gamble, and knows when it's going to rain."

—JOHN KEASLER
Surrounded on Three Sides

Back-packing her brood until they can fend for themselves, mother oppossum was always fair game.

Snowy egrets, painted by John James Audubon and nearly exterminated by "Plummers," are now protected by law.

Highly prized for their hides used for leather shoes, belts, and luggage, alligators were hunted and traded by the Seminoles.

Attracting fashion designers of the "Gay Nineties," the pink plumes from the roseate spoonbill brought top prices.

138

Plume, mounted and ready to be attached to my lady's hat.

PLUMES, PELTS, AND HIDES

In the "Gay Nineties," and even earlier, the fashion conscious ladies of New York, Paris, London, and other major cities wore feathered finery. The designers in this country and in Europe developed an ever-increasing demand for the silky plumage of the snowy egret and roseate spoonbill to decorate their gowns and fine hats. The soft fur of the fresh water otter was used in hats, coats, muffs. Not to be outdone, every well dressed gentleman sported alligator shoes, belts, and a set of matched grain luggage, with perhaps a fine otter collar for his Edwardian coat. Few of these *élégantes* knew where their adornment came from, or how it had been gathered and started on its way to the fashion centers. Actually, the bulk of the raw materials used for high style originated in the Everglades region at the tip of the Florida peninsula, and was brought to a handful of frontier trading posts by the Seminole Indians and a few white hunters. This traffic formed the basis for a unique partnership between the white traders and their Indian suppliers that lasted for over fifty years.

Until 1900 the state of Florida was hardly known to the rest of the nation, a land of exotic plants and animals and vast unexplored swamp lands, populated by a few settlers and Seminole Indians. By the 1870s tourists had begun to flock to north Florida, drawn by the warm climate and the possibility of relief from illnesses, as described by writers like

Fashionable furred and feathered lady of the "Gay Nineties" owes her adornment to Everglades wildlife and Seminole Indian trade in Florida.

Seminole woman in typical loose-fitting garb.

Seminole hunter scatters a flock of
wading birds as he poles his dugout canoe
through an Everglades cypress head
in search of pelts, plumes, and hides.

Harriet Beecher Stowe and Sidney Lanier. Ten years later vast areas of land north of Lake Okeechobee were opened for settlement through the drainage and development schemes of Hamilton Disston, and by the 1890s the railroads of Henry B. Plant and Henry M. Flagler were inching down opposite sides of the peninsula. Farms, groves, and cattle ranches followed, while small communities grew up along the railroad right of way and settlers took advantage of the cheap land offered by development companies.

Nevertheless there was almost no white population south of Lake Okeechobee except for small settlements at Miami on Biscayne Bay, at Fort Pierce on the Indian River, along Lake Worth, and at Fort Myers. These communities were built on the coastal ridges of Florida. In between lay a great shallow river flowing southward from Lake Okeechobee to the Ten Thousand Islands. The Indians called it "Pa-hay-o-kee," the "grassy water"—but the white man has always called it the Everglades. This broad, flat region of sawgrass, dotted by tree islands called hammocks, covered an area sixty miles at its widest, and almost 120 miles from Lake Okeechobee to lands-end in the mangroves of the Ten Thousand Islands. At the southwest corner of the Everglades region lay the Big Cypress Swamp, a tangle of cypress heads and hammocks, crossed at intervals by broad "strands" of navigable water. A watery wilderness, practically inaccessible to white men, this was the home of the last group of Seminole Indians to survive the Seminole Wars (1818-1858). By 1880 there were only 208 Seminoles left in Florida. The others had been sent west by the federal government to the Indian Territory in present day Oklahoma. Those who stayed evaded the military, retreating into the fastness of the Everglades, avoiding all contact with the outside world. When the Civil War began, this remnant group was soon forgotten by the government in Washington.

Left alone in the vast Everglades, the Seminoles made a swift and successful adaptation to a water environment. The elevated thatched-roof, open-sided "chickee" provided housing that was easily built from native materials. Long, shallow-draft canoes fashioned from hollowed-out cypress logs could be poled across the length and breadth of the Everglades; some were even fitted with sails and put out to sea or on Lake Okeechobee. This transportation enabled the Seminoles to hunt and trap over a broad area, and to trade at a variety of locations. Basically, though, the Indians were farmers long before the advent of heavy trading near the turn of the century. The garden plots at their hammock camps produced crops of beans, pumpkin, corn, and bananas. The Seminoles also had learned to harvest the wild Coontie (Zamia) root, which was used in making the thick gruel called Sofkee. These foods were supplemented with deer, bear, fish, and turtle, as well as a few hogs that were kept at most Indian camps. Indian clothing also was admirably suited to the environment and climatic conditions, with both men and women wearing light, loose-fitting costumes rather than traditional buckskins.

To provide a cash income the Seminoles hunted and trapped the abundant wildlife of the Everglades for pelts, plumes, and hides which they sold at trading posts. This trade became quite profitable in the 1890s as the demands of the fashion industry reached a peak. Otter pelts, which were brought in stretched on boards called "shingles," were the single most profitable item traded. A good otter pelt brought eight dollars on

"Left alone in the vast Everglades, the Seminoles made a swift and successful adaptation to a water environment."

Abstract Seminole doll (above), from the Southernmost state and dressed in distinctive patchwork dress and beads, contrasts vividly with heavily clothed Eskimo doll (below), from the Northernmost state.

the average, but occasionally a prime one could bring as much as twenty-five dollars to the trapper.

Alligator hides were measured out on long boards, and the Indians received ten cents a running foot on the average. Only the soft belly skin of the alligator was taken by the Seminoles, because the rest of the thick, horny hide was unsuitable for tanning. Generally they would "fire hunt" the 'gators at night, the light of their torches reflecting off the reptile eyes. The 'gators were dispatched by a rifle bullet between the glowing eyes, or by severing the spine with an axe. The Indians took a great many plume birds, like the snowy egret and roseate spoonbill, selling the feathers to traders for anywhere from fifty cents to five dollars each. In the early days the plumes were usually brought in by twos and threes, tied to crossed sticks. As the demand swelled and the price soared, however, hunters began bringing in great bundles every trip.

The Seminoles, even so, never were a major factor in the infamous plume trade, primarily because they were incapable of the wanton destruction of rookeries by organized gangs of "Plumers." These groups of white hunters, using 12 gauge shotguns, would invade the rookeries during the spring nesting period when the plumage was at its best, kill all nesting birds, and leave the ground littered with dying birds, hatchlings, and chicks. This barbarism was a violation of the Seminole's oneness with nature.

In addition to the products of hunting and trapping, the Indians also brought to the trading posts fresh venison, pumpkins, and bananas, Coontie starch (arrowroot), and even some livestock to sell to the storekeepers. What they did not dispose of at the trading posts was often sold door-to-door throughout the frontier settlements.

The way the Indian exchanged his goods for items at the stores was not actually a trade. One product was *not* directly bartered for another. The Seminoles received exact payment for their pelts and plumes, usually in gold or silver coins; they then selected the objects that they wanted from the store shelves and paid the merchant for each item. Some say that the Indians took their own good time in making selections, generally enjoying their infrequent visits to the white man's "emporium."

Store ledgers and the reminiscences of trading families reveal that the Seminoles bought a wide variety of goods. Food staples, coffee, sugar, grits, and canned goods were the big sellers. Rifles and ammunition, particularly Remington and Winchester 38 caliber repeaters, and 32 single shot rifles were popular. Hardware of all types for use in the camp sold briskly. So did kerosene used for mosquito repellant as well as for lanterns.

Women bought great quantities of cloth and ready-made appliques for their colorful clothes, along with hand-cranked sewing machines which could be used in the camps. White and Singer models cost about twenty-five dollars. The women were especially fond of great quantities of beads for necklaces. Men bought derby hats, watch chains with fobs, vests. They also bought train conductors' caps. Once in a while a Seminole would invest in ready-made trousers or shirts.

After the trading, the Indian families sometimes stayed near the stores for a few days. Often this was to give the men opportunity to buy liquor and indulge themselves for a time before returning to the wilds of the Everglades to resume hunting. If the Indians had camps nearby, they visited the trading posts on a more regular schedule and did not stay as

Beads, prized by Florida Indians from the days of the Spanish conquistadors, decorate this Seminole chieftain's belt.

An early air conditioner. Seminole fan made of wild turkey feathers.

Detail of typical patchwork and braid design on Seminole clothing.

long. Interestingly, many of the storekeepers were "teetotalers," and did not sell liquor, but some liquor dealers on the Florida frontier were ready and willing to part a Seminole from his funds. Some of the Indians even left their weapons and money with trading post operators before they began drinking.

The people who knew the Seminole best were the families which had permanent trading posts on the edge of their hunting grounds. It was to these stores that the Indians came, not only to sell their products and buy the white man's wares, but also to learn some of the storekeeper's skills. Many of the traders' wives taught Seminole men and women how to use the hand-cranked sewing machines that became so popular in developing the unique Indian pattern of dress. A few of the Indians also learned a bit of reading and writing in English, and enough of the spoken language to ease trading. Seminoles came to the trading posts when they needed medical help beyond that of their tribal medicine men. Epidemics of measles or influenza were particularly hard on the Indian population in Florida.

Over the years the Seminoles became an accepted part of the small communities which grew up near the trading posts, and generally going to local social gatherings, weddings, Sunday church services and Fourth of July celebrations! The Seminoles were particularly fond of church hymns, but few showed any interest in converting to Christianity until the present century.

Genuine friendships matured as the white families came to know and appreciate the Indian way of life, and learned how to survive in the Everglades. Many frontier homes were enriched by Indian herbal medicines, recipes for preparing manatee stew, turtle, and the heart of the cabbage palm, or knowledge of how to thatch a roof for shelter from the elements. The preparation of starch from the Coontie root was taught by

143

Great White Heron prized by the "plumers" and first described and painted by Audubon in 1832 is shown with the city of Key West in the distance.

Of Plumes and Poachers

The large scale slaughter of birds for their feathers prompted the founding of the Florida Audubon Society in 1900. Less than a year later, the Florida legislature was persuaded to pass a bill forbidding the killing of some species of plumage birds. "Plumers" suddenly became poachers. The Audubon Society hired a warden. Guy Bradley was sent out to protect the most vulnerable rookeries in the area of Florida Bay. While trying to protect a rookery in 1905, Mr. Bradley was shot and killed by plume hunters. Mr. Bradley's shocking death dramatized the plight of the birds. Plume poaching continued for a number of years, but passage of a national plumage law finally destroyed the U.S. market for plumes. A marker was placed on Cape Sable in memory of the man who died to defend the birds.

GUY M. BRADLEY
1870 – 1905
FAITHFUL UNTO DEATH
AS GAME WARDEN OF MONROE
COUNTY HE GAVE HIS LIFE FOR
THE CAUSE TO WHICH HE WAS
PLEDGED
ERECTED BY THE FLORIDA AUDUBON SOCIETY

the Indians, who also could tell the best times and places for hunting wild-life in the region. Some of the children of white traders came to speak the language of the Seminole quite well, and absorbed their lore and skill at hunting and tracking across the Everglades. Some say there was little antagonism between whites and Indians in frontier Florida at the turn of the century, although later friction occurred as the wildlife began to disappear, and competition was keen for the remaining pelts and hides. Good will, built up over a long period of time, saved the Seminole Indians from a harsh fate when they had to find other ways to make a living. Then their white friends took the lead in having federal and state reservations established in Florida as a permanent home for their Indian neighbors—quite different from the western United States where the Indian tribes had been driven to vast tracts of useless land and had become almost prisoners on the reservations.

In 1906 the State of Florida, under the leadership of Governor Napoleon Bonaparte Broward, began a program to drain the Everglades and use the land for farming. Little thought was given to the effect this would have on the native plants and animals of this unique region in the United States, and even less to the disastrous impact it would have on the hunting-trapping economy of the Seminoles. As the water table dropped over the next few years the game diminished. Both white and Indian hunters found it difficult to survive. Other factors combined with the drainage of the Everglades to bring the profitable trading period to a close.

Beginning in 1900, a succession of federal and state laws effectively ended the plume trade as a legal enterprise; although there was a thriving "blackmarket" until fashions changed and women no longer wore feathered outfits. A near collapse of the market for alligator hides occurred prior to World War I. When it recovered somewhat during the "Roaring Twenties"

Roseate Spoonbills were common in South Florida when this painting was made by Audubon nearly one hundred and fifty years ago. Cold weather keeps Spoonbills near the Keys although some fly halfway up the state during summer months. Audubon noted that their feathers were traded even then: "The feathers of the wings and tail . . . are manufactured into fans by the Indians and Negroes of Florida; and at St. Augustine these ornaments form in some degree a regular article of trade."

the Indians were in no position to recapture their share of the profits. An Indian poling his canoe and hunting with a torch had difficulty competing with white men using motorboats, high powered rifles, and searchlights. The same was true with otter and raccoon pelts. By the early 1900s the Seminole Indians had become a minor factor in the Florida pelt and hide trade.

And what became of the trading posts which handled the pelts, plumes and hides? Some simply became general stores catering to local citizens and Indians of the area. The Raulerson Department Store and Meserve's Hardware still operate out of Okeechobee City. In the Ten Thousand Islands the Smallwood Store on Chokoloskee Island is a designated historical site, and the original Storter home at Everglades City is part of the world famous Rod and Gun Club. The Brickell homestead, the scene of most Miami trading before the coming of the railroad, is gone but the street name survives. Farther north in Fort Lauderdale the Pioneer House stands sentinel over the New River just as it has since the Stranahans built it in 1900 as their home and trading post. Today, winter visitors dine in a restaurant on the ground floor of the old building, surrounded by artifacts of the Seminole trading days. Some of the original trading post sites have, of course, been abandoned and no evidence remains. The site of W.H. Brown's "Boat Landing," the only trading post that was exclusively devoted to the Seminole trade, is a two-hour journey west of Fort Lauderdale in the Big Cypress Seminole Indian Reservation. There, residents who are descendants of Indian hunters can point out an unobtrusive marker for the most isolated of the trading posts. Today the site is high and dry as the result of drainage programs, and is next to a lush cattle pasture of the modern Seminole people. It remains a poignant reminder of a colorful past and a vibrant era in Florida history.

—HARRY A. KERSEY, JR.

Pensive Seminole boy is a reminder of colorful Florida past.

145

ENERGY: THE DYNAMO WORD

Energy is the requirement for all things and the basis for human existence. The energy of the sun working over the seas separates fresh water from the salts of the sea, bringing the rains to Florida. Fresh water is not often thought of as energy, until it must be made in a desalination process, but pure water does have a high energy content. The energy flow in water is an important indirect energy flow from the sun.

Some energies like solar energy, although abundant, are dilute and of low quality. These energies serve men only after they have been concentrated by plants, and much of the energy is used in the process. Water, however, is a concentrated energy. The weather systems transform dilute solar energy to the concentrated energy of the rain. Because Florida is blessed with much rain, it receives more of the energy of the sun in

upgraded form as water than it receives directly from the sun. Little wonder that water is the precious, controlling resource in Florida, for the chemical energy of pure water supports the Florida economies, past, present, and future.

In Indian times energy from the sun, growing the plants and indirectly the animals, supported humans as hunters, fishermen, gatherers of shellfish, and growers of corn on a small scale. The Indian economy was a solar energy economy, and the population which could be supported in this way was small. The environmental systems for maintaining luxuriant life were, however, self maintaining. The swamps were a natural means for holding water in any season and for keeping water quality high.

Another energy principle helps explain, in energy terms, how the colonists displaced the Indians and how the English colonies eventually displaced the Spanish influence in Florida. A culture which develops a system with more energy flow takes over from one with less flow of energy. The colonists were able to control more energy in developing their cultural system than the Indians, partly because they could draw initially on the very high quality energy of their weapons. Concentrated energies doing work miles away in Europe were directed into more firepower and more concentrated social organization in Florida. The diseases of the colonists, in addition, apparently hurt the Indians more than Indian diseases hurt the colonists.

The imported colonial cultures also used the capital stored in the Indian system—the virgin forests, the virgin soils, and the wildlife—as temporary energy sources to establish their new pattern. In depleting

Sun atop the peak of a house is symbolic as Floridians are again turning to this basic energy source. The shape and size of a pyramid form also is touted by some as a primary energy source. As fossil fuels disappear life styles change and new mechanical energy devices appear.

Florida Indians living in villages draw on the resources of the land and the sun.

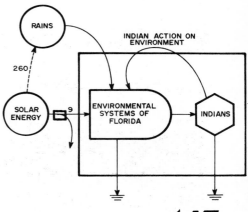

147

Rain shower sweeps across a Florida landscape

these resources, they took energy away from the Indian system. By the time these special stores were exhausted, the colonists had another energy source going, their more extensive agriculture and, later, fuels.

The Spaniards exchanged search and shipments of gold and other products back to Spain for their energy needs. The English colonies, however, emphasized the development of assets in this country, especially agriculture. They drew on a broad source of energies from the new continent. As a result, economically and militarily, dominance went to the English colonies, and their independence from the mother country developed early. This influence ultimately displaced the Indian system.

Fortunately for the American colonists (or unfortunately, depending on the time scale of your view), new sources of energy were found as the colonists were running out of virgin soils and timbers. Instead of leveling off, the economy, energy use, and populations could continue to grow as coal came into general use and then oil and natural gas. These new fuel resources were available in local areas, like Texas and Appalachia. States like Florida had to purchase them. To attract an income with which to buy the fossil fuels, and the goods and services made in distant cities with fossil fuels, Florida began to export remaining cypress timbers, winter agricultural products, range cattle, oysters, phosphate fertilizers, naval stores from natural pine flatwoods, and other rural resources. New energy directly and indirectly began to flow into Florida due to energy discoveries miles away. These new ways carried more energy flow and thus displaced or added to the older ways.

Growth continued as the twentieth century opened. Some industries began to develop in Florida, using the fossil fuels within the state and selling the products for money to buy the fuels. Fuels were priced cheaply because they were close to the surface and cost little to pump and transport. Even agriculture and forestry shifted. A pattern based only on sun, wind, rains, and the geological input of the rocks to form soil changed. A more intensive role developed for men. Fossil fuels were used directly and indirectly to provide planting, weeding, fertilizing, insecticiding, harvesting, and special care for high yielding but delicate plant varieties. Fossil fuel agriculture emerged, along with pine forest plantations to supply paper for a business world in bustling new cities based on fossil fuels.

As the rich fossil fuels poured into industrialized areas to the north, there were great energy excesses compared to less developed countries elsewhere in the world. The United States led the world in tapping this energy excess and connecting it to useful work through technology. Unparalleled levels of energy per person developed a high standard of living that included the energy to travel, to be a tourist, and to retire from work before death. Florida became one of the places where this energy was used, for tourism, for retirees, and for the expenditure of the luxury energies of the northern cities. The attraction in Florida for the luxury energies was the sun and, based on the sun and water, the beautiful Florida ecosystems—the beaches, the palms and cypress greenery, the swamps, the springs, fishing, the feeling of green panorama and the mild climate. Soon special facilities and man-made tourist attractions were added, making Florida the vacation image and retirement center.

New incomes, from tourists, retirees, and developers anticipating incomes from these sources, poured into the state, in some places dominat-

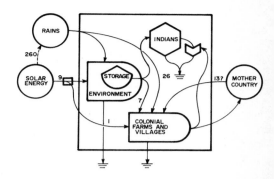

Spanish and, especially, English colonists deplete stockpiles of natural products and wildlife, and energy flow changes.

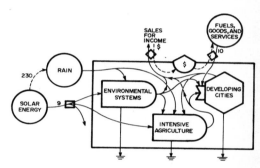

World turns to fossil fuels as major energy source. Florida sells native products and its sunshine attracts money from other areas so the needed fuels can be purchased.

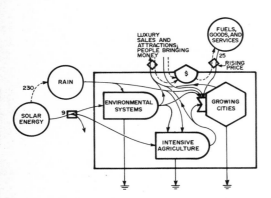

Florida becomes the luxury state as cheap fuels create energy surplus and people spend money on food and vacations and retire from work early.

Lights of large electric power plant reflect across waters that are an indirect energy source from the sun. New ways to make electricity are now sought as fossil fuel and nuclear plants become more expensive.

ing everything else. These monies bought more fossil fuel, and fossil fuel developed goods and services that Florida used to accelerate its growth. In a sense, the large money inflow for military bases and the space program was another consequence of general energy richness in the United States as a whole. These funds were focussed in Florida because of the good weather and solar energy. Agriculture shifted to luxury products, a greater percentage of high quality beef, heavier emphasis on citrus and winter vegetables for northern luxury markets, and more pine trees for luxury packaging and advertising.

As the United States and other western countries accelerated their growth on the rich fossil fuels, they began to exhaust their own easily reached resources, leaving themselves with fuels only deep in the ground, far at sea, or dilute in their distribution in the rocks. The only rich, easily tapped fuels remaining were in other countries, especially the Near East. As the energy spent in getting energy increased everywhere, the cost of energy began to rise. Then those with the richer sources found they had a monopoly on cheap fuel and could jump the price.

Florida was buying much of its energy incomes based on other activities, and the four-fold rise in fuel prices in the fall of 1973 suddenly reduced the energy basis for Florida. It had to send out more goods and services per unit of energy obtained than before. The excess energy inflow that had been generating rapid growth was stopped. Furthermore, the luxury part of the Florida income began to decline as the fuel pinch affected northern monies for vacations, retirement funds, and the purchase of luxury products from Florida. Reduction of energy is a reduction of the work a dollar does, a reduction of its buying power. Energy reduction generated inflation and reduced the real income to Florida from savings and retirement funds. So finally in 1974 the energy budget turned down and with it the flow of real money. There was high unemployment in those industries related to growth, like construction, and luxury, like tourism.

Many thoughtful people had worried about running out of fuel before, and nuclear energy was developed at great cost to supply a substitute. The hidden energy subsidies, however, from the fossil fuels that made nuclear energy look economical, began to disappear. The fossil fuels and everything they supported became more expensive. Nuclear energy was analyzed and found to barely supply more energy than it takes to process it. It is not as rich an energy source as it was originally thought. Huge capital is required to build a nuclear energy plant, and the ultimate resources run out as soon as fossil fuels do. Nuclear energy is not easily usable in the flexible ways that fossil fuel is used—for transportation, heating, and industry—because much energy is lost in the extra step of converting to and distributing electricity.

As soon as there was a fossil fuel shortage and the fossil fuels and everything they supported became more expensive, it became difficult to make the new nuclear plants pay for construction costs, let alone the unknown costs for the waste disposal and safety protection often discussed in public forum. The use of electricity by consumers often had been for luxuries, and the demand for electricity decreased as energies became more expensive.

Although many people could not believe growth had stopped for good, the energy situation suggested that a new pattern was ahead. Leaders would admit it in private but not mention it in public, fearing public backlash. The situation was a little like the time before the Civil War when shifting energies from agrarian sunlight to fossil fuels for industries was tipping power to the North; this reality was outside the experience of Southern people and it took a terrible war to bring home the energy reality, and still they did not understand. Now again, at this bicentennial time, there are changing realities of energy in Florida.

If the fuels continue to be more and more costly as the oil rich countries go deeper and deeper, and if the far-out propositions for energy are not very rich in their contribution of net energy (energy beyond what is used in the process), then Floridians must face a long range future of once again running on renewable resources: the sun, the waters, some fuels, and small amounts of minerals that are moved upward each year by the slow turn of the geological cycles. There is no reason why a fine cultural pattern for humanity cannot be built in balance with the energy flow that is available, but it will not be one of explosive growth and expanding luxury. For Florida, the luxury state, this may eventually mean drastic changes.

A regime of men on renewable resources will have some of the features of the earlier Indian system, but man will have a larger role in interaction and use of all the resources. Ultimately, there may be more people dispersed and working on the land again, and cities may be less concentrated. The steady state which may come later is fascinating, but the reality of need is now, the time of transition.

Toward whatever comes, uphill and downhill, Americans have always faced challenges with enthusiasm and enterprise. Floridians are called upon to do this again, but in a new way and with a new energy ethic. It is an opportunity for the next 200 years.   —HOWARD T. ODUM
                                                                —SANDRA BROWN

KEY WEST

Key West Harbor at sunrise.

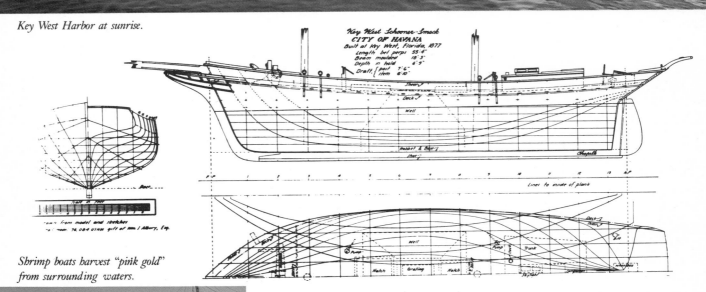

Key West Schooner-Smack
CITY OF HAVANA
Built at Key West, Florida, 1877
Length bet perps 55'4"
Beam moulded 18'3"
Depth in hold 6'9"
Draft {post 7'6" / stem 6'10"

Shrimp boats harvest "pink gold" from surrounding waters.

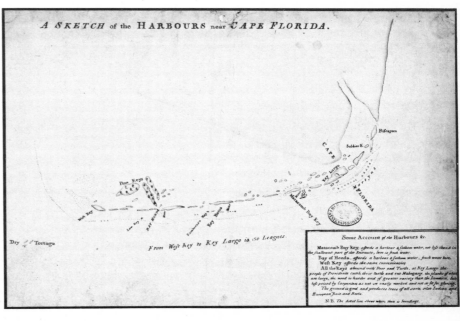

A SKETCH of the HARBOURS near CAPE FLORIDA.

Old fort, Martello Towers, houses a museum.

Sailors of Maine *are honored by monument in Key West cemetery.*

Tortugas

"To the west of these islands is a great channel, which no pilot dares go through with a large vessel; because, as I have said, of some islands that are on the opposite side towards the west, which are without trees, and formed of sand. At some time they have been the foundations of cays, and must have been eaten away by the currents of the sea, which have left them thus bare, plain sand. They are seven leagues in circumference, and are called the Islands of the Tortugas; for turtles are there, and many come at night to lay their eggs in the sand. The animal is of the size of a shield, and has as much flesh as a cow; it is like all kinds of meat, and yet is fish."
—*Hernando D'Escalante Fontaneda, circa* 1575

Loggerhead Turtle: "so excellente a fishe."

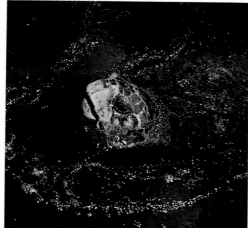

Spanish Lace House.

Water turns to gold under a Florida Keys sunset.

Carved and joined by ships carpenters, "conch houses" still line Key West streets.

The big mouthed brown pelican, bane of many a Florida fisherman, is shown by Audubon on the branch of a red mangrove tree.

Recently Floridians responded to a plea from Louisiana where the brown pelican population had gone down to zero. Today Florida pelicans have begun a new colony in Louisiana.

"Scarcely an hour of daylight passed without our having Pelicans all around us, all engaged at their ordinary occupations, some fishing, some slumbering as it were on the bosom of the ocean, or on the branches of the mangroves."
—John James Audubon

Dr. Benjamin Strobel who sojourned as a physician in Key West and began the first newspaper, wrote observations of visitors (below). Dr. Strobel himself, it is said, remained in Key West only briefly, involving himself in a matter of some consequence over a lady, being challenged to a duel, and migrating, like the birds, swiftly home to Carolina.

An Early Sketch: John J. Audubon

Every thing relating to this gentleman, is calculated to excite a lively interest. I therefore deem no apology necessary for introducing his name into my Sketches. In the months of March and April, 1832, he visited the Florida Reef, and touched and remained three or four weeks, off and on, at Key West, where I had a good opportunity of becoming acquainted with him. By a friend (from whom he bore a letter of introduction) I had been apprised of his expected arrival in the Revenue Cutter Marion, Capt. Day. It being intimated that he was coming ashore in one of the boats, I walked down about sun set with a number of persons to see him land. On his landing, I was introduced to him by Capt. Day. He immediately took me aside, in-

formed me that he had letters for me from my friend Mr. B. and that he was anxious to have some conversation with me. I invited him to my house, where we sat down; Mr. Audubon at once proceeded to business, making a number of enquiries respecting birds and other objects of his pursuit. After a long conversation, we parted for the night. I saw him again on the following day, and almost every day when he came ashore during his stay. Mr. Audubon is a very extraordinary man. An acquaintance of half an hour enabled me to enter at once into his character and feelings. Divested of every thing like pedantry, he is frank, free and amiable in his dispositions, and affable and polite in manners. His engaging manner and mild deportment, united to a perfect possession of what the french term "Savior [sic] faire," enables him to accomplish many things, which to another person would be unattainable; every one appears to enlist at once in his

service, and to be disposed to promote his views. In addition to the possession of these qualities, Mr. Audubon is the most enthusiastic and indefatigable man I ever knew. It is impossible to associate with him without catching some portion of his spirit; he is surrounded with an atmosphere which infects all who come within it, with a mania for bird-killing, and bird-stuffing. For my own part, I must confess that I have become an incurable victim to the disease.

When we examine Mr. Audubon's celebrated drawings and plates, we can not but yield him our warmest approbation and applause; but how few of us can estimate the danger and toil which they have cost him, or through what "untried scenes and changes" he has passed in procuring his specimens. In our admiration of the Artist we are too apt to forget the labor and privations of the man. In order to give some faint idea of Mr. Audubon's exertions, I will briefly relate the oc-

The Florida Cormorant is well-known as a catcher of fish.

"The Keys were separated by narrow and tortuous channels, from the surface of the clear waters. . .were reflected the dark mangroves . . . .large colonies of cormorants had already built their nests, and were sitting on their eggs. There were many thousands of these birds and each tree bore their nests. . .some five or six, others perhaps as many as ten."
—John James Audubon

Throughout the history of the world, ibis have been held sacred, symbols of nobility. The Florida coastal regions and marshes have long been blessed with these remarkable birds of antiquity, and Audubon painted species recognizable to ancient Egyptians and modern Floridians. A major university in Florida honors the sacred ibis as its mascot and symbol.

currences of one day's excursion, on which I accompanied him. At half past two o'clock, A.M. our party assembled at a given place, we were provided with two good boats, a number of hands and all the necessary apparatus. At three o'clock we started, and steered for 2 or 3 small Mangrove Keys lying to the Northward of Key West; we made a circuit around them, but saw nothing worthy of note.—Previous to our getting clear of these Keys, we got ashore upon a long bank making out from one of them, which rendered it necessary for all hands to get overboard, Mr. Audubon being among the foremost. We hauled the boat over the bank, and bore away for a narrow opening between Key West and Stock Island, through which we proposed passing. There we again got into shoal water, and were again compelled to get overboard. Our boats were hauled over a flat nearly a mile in length before we could get them afloat.—Having passed through

the cut, we landed on a long sandbank on the Eastern extremity of Key West. An hour or more was spent here in collecting shells; after which, we footed it around to Key West while the boats were rowed along the beach by the hands. Not a pond, lake or bog, did we leave unexplored, often ·did we wade through mud up to our knees, and as often were we obliged to scramble over the roots of the Mangrove trees which happened in our

course. About 8 o'clock, the sun came out intensely hot; we occasionally penetrated the woods to escape his scorching beams, and as often were driven from the woods by myriads of Musquetoes and Sandflies. One of our party gave out about this time and took to a boat. Most gladly would I have followed his lead, but was deterred by pride. Onward we went, baking and broiling, and what was more discouraging still, we could discover

155

not a single bird worthy of note. Mr. Audubon went on neither dispirited by heat, fatigue, nor bad luck, whilst we began to lag, and occasionally would dodge under some tree, to catch a breath, or sit down to blow. We toiled along in this way for several miles, and finally reached the Light House, tolerably well broken down. I gladly accepted of the use of a horse, whilst the rest of the party returned to town in a boat. I arrived at home about 11 o'clock, A.M. having made the circuit of Key West. I went to bed immediately and slept soundly for several hours, when I got up and took some refreshment, pretty well satisfied with the jaunt, and no ways ambitious of repeating it. To Mr. Audubon this was an every day affair; he rose every morning at 3 o'clock and went out in a boat, and cruized in search of birds, etc. until 12 or 1 o'clock, at which time he usually returned to dinner. During these expeditions he took no refreshments but biscuit and molasses and water, proving by his example that ardent spirits are never necessary to health even under the greatest exposure and fatigue. Before and after dinner, as soon as he returned from the morning jaunt, Mr. Audubon employed himself in drawing such

birds as he might have procured during the morning, and in the evening he was on the hunt again. Thus has Mr. Audubon been employed day after day, for weeks and months on the Florida Reef, exploring Mangrove Keys, swamps and other places, into which I question much, if any animal two legged or four legged, had ever before penetrated, unless it was the Pelican or Cormorant.

Not soon will the recollection of this surprising man pass from my memory, and often as I call him to mind will I admire his unquenchable ardor in the pursuit of science, and his amiable deportment as a gentleman; nay more, the recollection will always be associated with a warm sensation of gratitude, for his kindness and friendship to one, from whom he had reason to expect but little in return.

–Sketches of Florida

DR. BENJAMIN B. STROBEL
1833

Recollections of Mark Twain

Traveling by steamer from California to New York by way of Nicaragua, Mark Twain made the following observations in his journal about his stopover in Key West, in 1867: "I attended Episcopal service. Heap of style–fashionably-dressed women, 350 of them and children and 25 men.

"Don't see where so much dress comes from in a town made altogether of one and two-story frame houses, some crazy, unpainted, and with only thick board shutters for windows—no carpets, no mats—bare floors—cheap prints on the walls.

"Only about ten or twelve houses with any pretention of style, and one half of these are military officer's quarters. . . .

"Men stylishly dressed with yellow ribbon cravats. Town full of cocoanuts of the many-leaf, low-branching pattern, very pretty. Girls singing in most houses.

"This is really a big town, big enough to hold over 2,000, though many houses seem deserted. Business mostly gin mills—that is, for soldiers."

"To the west of these islands is a great channel, which no pilot dares go through with a large vessel; because, as I have said, "These Indians have no gold, less of some islands that are on the opposite side towards the west, which are without trees, and formed of sand. At some time they have been the foundations of cays, and must have been eaten away by the currents of the sea, which have left them thus bare, plain sand. They are seven leagues in circumference, and are called the Islands of the Tortugas; for turtles are there, and many come at night to lay their eggs in the sand. The animal is of the size of a shield, and has as much flesh as a cow; it is like all kinds of meat, and yet is fish."
—HERNANDO D'ESCALANTE FONTANEDA,
circa 1575

The Keys - Raccoon

"On these islands are many deer, and a certain animal that looks like a fox, yet is not, but a different thing from it. It is fat and good to eat. On other islands are very large bears; and, as the islands run from west to east, and the land of Florida passes eastwardly towards these islands, that must be the reason of bears being on them: for the mainland is near, and they can cross from island to island. But what was a great wonder to the captives who were there, and to those of us in other places, was the existence of deer on the Islands of Cuchiyaga."
—HERNANDO D'ESCALANTE FONTANEDA,
circa 1575

Geiger House, where Audubon stayed during his visit to Key West. Once neglected the old Key West home, now known as Audubon House, is restored and boasts folios of the original Audubon paintings.

157

Key West, 1837.

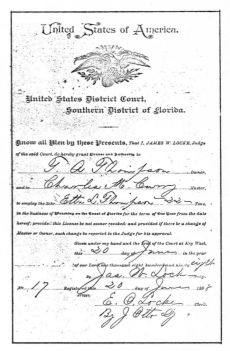

Pirates and Wreckers

When people talk about the long wars in which the United States has been engaged, the longest conflict of all is likely to be overlooked—the war against piracy. The United States inherited the "piracy war" from the British following the Revolution, and, in 1801, fought at Tripoli rather than pay tribute to Barbary pirates. But, for half a century, West Indian pirates and Bahamian wrecker-pirates gave this country a worse headache than the Mediterranean corsairs. Florida played a role in this conflict, and, when the offspring of the pirates turned to the more acceptable occupation of legalized wrecking—today we call it salvage—they left another colorful page in Florida history.

By the time the Revolution ended, pirates had been looting, raping, murdering, and burning in the West Indies for two centuries, beginning with the licensed forays by English and French buccaneers. John Hawkins and Francis Drake were knighted by Queen Elizabeth I for plundering Spanish shipping and enriching the English treasury with the Queen's share of captured gold and silver. The French corsair Pierre le Grand captured a Spanish warship with a handful of men, while Jean David Nau's greatest pleasure was discovering new and more painful ways of putting captives to death. Henry Morgan was much later, in the middle 1600s. In 1671 he looted and destroyed key Spanish cities in Panama.

After monarchs stopped licensing pirates to attack enemy ships, the pirates became "free agents," attacking ships of all countries, including their own. By the late 1600s, pirates were so bold they entered colonial ports to sell their loot and to carouse. Although the British navy waged continuous war against them, the colonists welcomed the pirates because of their free spending. William Teach, known as Blackbeard, was slain in 1718 in a fight with a British warship off the coast of Virginia. His head was severed and exhibited as a warning to colonists who dealt with the pirates.

Florida, with no important settlements but St. Augustine and Pensacola, offered little enticement to the early pirates. Robert Davis did sack and burn St. Augustine in 1668, killing a fourth of the 250 civilian residents, but after construction of San Marcos, the Spanish stronghold was no longer vulnerable. The Bahamas was a more popular headquarters for pirates than Florida, but at the same time shallow Florida harbors, with changeable, treacherous inlets, frequently were used as hiding places from British and Spanish gunboats.

At one time most of the residents of the Bahamas appeared to make their living from piracy. When Woodes Rogers became governor, he found more than 2000 pirates working out of New Providence. Unable to hang them all without decimating the population, he gave them pardons in 1718 in exchange for their "retirement." Those who broke the contract went to the gallows—when caught.

Florida was the headquarters of one notable pirate, Black Caesar, who, according to tradition, used Caesar's Rock in south Biscayne Bay as his stronghold. Upon sighting sail off the Florida Reef, he would emerge from the winding channel of Caesar's Creek to make his attacks. When chased by American gunboats, he would flee through the swash channels of Biscayne Bay to hide in one of the winding creeks among the mangroves, removing the masts from his vessels so they could not be detected. The huge, black man eventually was captured and hanged—again according to tradition.

The most colorful Florida period came as the piracy era was coming to a close. Thomas Jefferson purchased Louisiana Territory from Napoleon in 1803, opening the development of the Gulf Coast. For more than half a century, until the development of steamships and the building of cross-country railroads, the Florida Straits was one of the busiest water thoroughfares in the world. Not only were thousands of sailing craft rounding the tip of Florida between the East Coast and Gulf Coast, but the Straits was a popular route for ships sailing between the East Coast and Central and South America, as well as ships traveling between Europe and the Gulf Coast. Holds were filled with choice silks and other fine fabrics, silver and china, wines and liquors, fine furniture and oriental rugs, men's and women's apparel of the latest styles.

While bold piracy had been discouraged in the Bahamas and the Florida Straits by the hangman's noose, a new profession arose that drew a fine line between the legal and illegal—"wrecking." Bahamian seamen, most of them former New Englanders who fled the colonies during the Revolution, set up camp in the Florida Keys and lay in wait to pounce on vessels wrecked on the unmarked Florida Reef.

Florida was then owned by Spain, but Spain was too weak to police its wide do-

158

WRECKERS AT WORK.

Gasparilla Takes Tampa

An island in Charlotte Harbor gained notoriety as the headquarters of José Gaspar, a bloodthirsty buccaneer who gave the island his nickname, Gasparilla.

On December 21, 1821, Gasparilla reached his self-appointed age of retirement. He gathered his men on the island to dig up $30 million in buried gold and have a few drinks before disbanding the crew. During the party, Gasparilla spied a British merchantman on the horizon, and all hands set off for one last fling, leaving only a few diggers behind.

Too late, Gasparilla realized the ship was a U.S. Navy vessel, the *Enterprise*. A battle ensued. When it turned for the worse the pirate leader, preferring death to capture, wrapped himself in an anchor chain and plunged overboard. All his crewmen were killed except ten who were taken to New Orleans and hanged. Only the diggers escaped—and memories which are recreated each year in the lavish Gasparilla Day celebration at Tampa.

The only problem with this magnificent tale is that it apparently is untrue. The *Enterprise* was far to the south in the Caribbean on the date of its alleged battle with Gasparilla, and the island probably was named a century earlier after Father Gaspar, a Spanish missionary.   —G.L.

Lighthearted Currier and Ives view of problems and rewards of shipwreck and salvage.

main. The Spanish governor at St. Augustine approved the outfitting of an expedition by Captain John (Don Juan) McQueen, Revolutionary War veteran, to drive out the Bahamians and take over the "wrecking" for the governor and himself. On the eve of his departure, McQueen died and the Bahamians continued to occupy the keys, mainly Cape Florida, Indian Key, and Key West. These vultures—eagles if you prefer—were only a cut above pirates.

After Florida became a United States possession in 1821, a federal court was set up at Key West and the wreckers were made subject to federal law. The establishment of a navy base at Key West in 1822 by Captain David Porter was as much a move to deter the wrecker-pirates in the Florida Straits as it was to bring a halt to rampant piracy in the West Indies after the decline of Spanish power.

Under federal maritime law, whenever a ship went aground on the reef the wrecker who got there first automatically became wrecking master, and the wrecking master got a major percentage of any cargo salvaged. Fierce competition developed, and these hardy mariners went all out to build fast boats that would get them there first when twenty or thirty craft unfurled all the sail

they could carry and started out for a "wrack on the reef."

Some especially colorful characters emerged, best known of which was Captain Bradish (Hog) Johnson, a New Englander, who won the title of "King of the Wreckers." But the one who made the most money off wrecking was not himself a seaman or a wrecker. He was William Curry, who came over from Green Turtle Cay in the Bahamas in the 1820s at fourteen. Starting out as a tradesman, Curry built a major business of supplying the wreckers. He is reputed to have been the first Florida millionaire. At least he became wealthy enough to have Tiffany make him a gold table service costing $100,000.

The marking of the Florida Reef with lights reduced the number of wrecks, but, also, the numerous smaller vessels were replaced by larger, steel-hulled steamships, which not only offered better control in storms, but were operated by better trained pilots. Rail transportation developed after the Civil War and cut the volume of maritime shipping through the Florida Straits. But, for several decades, and particularly during the 1820–1840s, Key West enjoyed a prosperous and colorful era the like of which will not be seen again.   —NIXON SMILEY

ANY PORT IN A STORM.

EXPLORING THE SPIRIT

Seminole Wheel of Life.

Church spire, St. Augustine.

BELIEFS AND BELONGING

Spaniards were the first to show their sails off the coastline of Florida. The first westerners to hold hands of benediction over the land that Juan Ponce de León called *Pascua Florida*, or Flowery Easter, were priests of the Iberian religious faith, Roman Catholicism. Today the peninsula and panhandle that carry the ancient name of Florida are predominantly Protestant in religion. By contrast, the New England states where Protestantism was first established by the Puritans are today of equal measure, and in some places predominantly, Roman Catholic. Thus the vicissitudes of history.

A church, the first permanent Christian church in North America, was founded at St. Augustine by the parish priests who accompanied Pedro Menéndez de Avilés in 1565. Soon afterwards, an effort began to convert the Florida Indians, who had their own remarkable religious structures, to the religion practiced by the explorers. Franciscan priests constructed a mission network that extended first northward along the Georgia coastal islands, then westward, through present-day Palatka and Gainesville, to the juncture of the Suwannee and Sante Fe rivers, and on to the fertile Apalachee country around what is now Tallahassee. By the middle of the seventeenth century, some 30,000 Indians lived around the missions, and were learning not only the Christian catechism but also the rudiments of European arts and crafts. Many had learned to read and write, and studied books in their own language provided by the friars.

A mission with a resident friar was called a *doctrina*. A mission where the friar visited on Sundays and holy days was known as a *visita*. Buildings were simple, even primitive. Pine tree trunks held up the roof and walls, and between the rough-hewn pillars, small posts were inter-woven with horizontal wattles tied with leather thongs. Clay was then daubed on the latticework and, once dry, whitewashed on the interior. Palmetto thatching served as roofing, and wide eaves provided outside shade from the sun. This wattle-and-daub type of construction charac-terized the Florida mission compounds throughout most of their history. Ultimately all the buildings would be destroyed by English marauders in the first decade of the eighteenth century, but the meaning of western religious ideas was implanted for future generations.

The missionaries carried a mighty faith, demonstrating the kind of selfless service that reflected the fervency of their particular beliefs. These were men, scores of them, who divested themselves of everything to live their entire lives in service to their faith. The records only hint at the hardships: Voluntarily, these men ministered, often under jungle condi-tions, including constant hunger, long and exhausting treks overland, the searing heat, the ceaseless torment from mosquitoes by night, as well as the physical dangers of wilderness living.

The missionaries came not to expropriate Indian lands or to push the people back along an ever-receding frontier, as happened later in Indian lands to the north. They came to teach religion. They also taught cattle-raising, carpentry, weaving. They taught reading and writing. And they did this not for two or three years, but for twenty years, thirty or forty years, risking uprisings and inter-tribal conflicts. Their effort is regarded by some as one of the more heroic humanitarian efforts recorded in American history. In this Bicentennial year, as present needs of the disadvantaged come to mind—in the ghettos, in the migrant farmer huts, in the pockets of rural poverty—the story that the Spanish friars wrote in Florida is one to ponder.

Social justice is one frame of reference suggested by the Spanish experience. Today peoples around the world are raising basic questions: What is man or woman? What is the significance of human life? What are natural, social, political, and religious rights? Almost the same questions were asked in Spanish colonial times about the Indians: What is the Indian? Is he a complete human being like the Spaniard? Are his human and civil rights of the same order as those enjoyed by Spaniards?

Ideals of social justice are not new. They were articulated here in Spanish Florida 400 years ago. A spirited defense of Indian civil rights was made by the missionaries during the governorship of Diego de Rebolledo in the 1650s when the Indians of Apalachee had been impressed as slave laborers to carry corn and other supplies between various points in the province.

Another example of social justice was demonstrated when England took direction of Florida during a twenty-year period, 1763–1783, the time of the American Revolution. Spanish justice did not grant religious liberty, and the Anglican tradition of the Church of England gains credit for the introduction into Florida of the concept and practice of freedom of reli-gion. That freedom extended to all Spaniards who might wish to remain in Florida under English rule: "His Britannic Majesty agrees on his part to

FIRST LANDING OF COLUMBUS ON THE SHORES OF THE NEW WORLD
AT SAN SALVADOR, W. I. OCT 12TH 1492.

"I liked revival meetings particularly. Dur-ing these meetings the preacher let himself go. God was called by all of His praise-giving names. The scenery of heaven was described in detail. . .Hallelujah Avenue ran north and south across heaven, and was tuned to sound alto and bass. Amen Street ran east and west and was tuned to 'treble' and tenor. These streets crossed each other right in front of the throne and made har-mony all the time.

—ZORA NEALE HURSTON
Dust Tracks on a Road

Charming chapel at Mandarin, where Harriet Beecher Stowe worshiped.

Indian rattle made of turtle shells, used in the Green Corn Dance.

Magic in the Glades
First Written Description of the Green Corn Dance

"After supper in the various camps the signal was given, and all repaired to the dance circle. A fire of lightwood was blazing in the center around which the dancers moved on the hard ground, in a perfect circle. The males had a rendez-vous on one side, and on the opposite side the females had their place of assembling, far enough back to be invisible. At a signal from a kind of whistle, or rude musical instrument, the men and youths, decked out in new hunting shirts of various colors, and some in white, all with picturesque turbans, plumes and streamers moved first into the circle, the leader giving forth a strain, the others answering in a corresponding refrain. The women fell in later, and from the opposite side. They looked very solemn and moved along behind the men with short, mincing steps, the yuck-chop-a-lund-kies, which are invisible, but are fastened on their limbs, keeping time with the step. These gopher shells, filled, as they are, with a kind of hard round seed, can scarcely be held in the hand without giving forth a rattling sound; and yet, as soon as the dance is over, the females step out of the ring on their side and not a sound is heard as they glide away to their quarters. In only two of the dances did the men ever touch the women, and then it was only to swing them around as they clasped the hand. In all the movements which were modest and graceful, I did not see, on the part of male or female, any movement inconsistent with the strictest modesty.

"Soon after eleven o'clock the closing dance was called for and immediately after the whole space around the fire-light was cleared as by magic."

—BISHOP'S DIARY, 1900

allow the inhabitants of the country above ceded the liberty of the Catholic religion and that in consequence his Britannic Majesty will give the most exact and effectual orders that his new Roman Catholic subjects may profess the worship of their religion according to the rites of the Roman Church, so far as the laws of Great Britain permit." Although the Spanish population of the peninsula left Florida, Roman Catholic Minorcans, with some Italians and Greeks, were freed from servile bondage to a plantation developer at New Smyrna and brought to St. Augustine in 1777. Under their pastor, Father Pedro Camps, the refugees were treated with respect and fairness and allowed to hold their religious services freely.

The Reverend John Forbes, M.A., was the first Anglican rector in St. Augustine. The English took over the old Spanish parish church of La Soledad, renamed it St. Peter's and added a wooden spire, clock, and bells. Although Englishmen aboard the vessels of John Hawkins, visiting in the St. Johns River off French Fort Caroline in 1565, had formally read the Anglican service, St. Augustine was the first formally established Anglican Episcopal Church in East Florida. Regular services were conducted in Pensacola and West Florida during the period of English rule.

When Spain returned to take possession of East and West Florida following the close of the American Revolution in 1784, and following the ceding of Florida to the United States in 1821, histories begin for all the various formally organized congregations of Protestant Christianity and Judaism in Florida.

The Anglicans were the first to organize a congregation in Florida in American times, under the Reverend Andrew Fowler at St. Augustine in October, 1821. The name Trinity Church was adopted in 1825, the cornerstone laid, and the building substantially completed in 1831 as the first Episcopal church building in Florida. In 1829 at Pensacola, the Episcopalians numbered twelve, Methodists ten, Presbyterians two, and Baptists two. St. Paul's Episcopal Church was organized at Key West in 1833, the third oldest in Florida. Subsequent congregations were formed at Apalachicola, Jacksonville, and Tallahassee.

December 1821 marks the official beginnings of the Methodist Church in Florida, when the Reverend Alexander Tally was appointed to a circuit that included Pensacola. Two months later, in February, 1822, the Reverend Elijah Sinclair was assigned to a circuit that included Fernandina on the east boundary of Florida. The first Methodist preacher assigned exclusively to a Florida appointment was the Reverend Joshua N. Glenn, of South Carolina, who came to St. Augustine in April, 1823. Although Glenn found only one Methodist in the town at the time of his arrival, within a year he had ten members in his congregation. Methodist ministers used court chambers, homes, barns, stables, and brush arbors as places of worship on their wandering circuits. St. Augustine, Tallahassee and Pensacola had the first permanent buildings.

The Baptist Churches furnished Territorial Florida with many pioneer preachers and became a strong Protestant denomination by the time of the Civil War. The Reverend Wilson Connor entered Florida as far as St. Augustine with the United States Army in 1812 as the first Baptist preacher on Florida soil. The first organized church was founded at Bethlehem on March 12, 1825. Newnansville, near Gainesville, was the site of the second, founded in 1828. Others followed soon after, in Bellville, New Hope, New Prospect, Fayetteville, Hatch Bend, Midway, Sand Hill, Macedonia, Rose Mary and Fort Clark with mighty congregations numbering from fifteen to fifty persons. In the beginning decades of United States rule, Florida Baptists were mainly in rural districts; it was years before St. Augustine and Pensacola attracted preachers.

St. Augustine was an early center of Presbyterianism. A church with thirteen members was organized on June 10, 1824, under the Reverend William McPhir, with a church building erected in 1830. One church was built in Pensacola of logs in 1828 by Scottish travellers from North Carolina. This simple structure was a center for pioneer Florida presbyterianism. Other Protestant bodies were formed, but those named were numerically the largest. As the Territory became the twenty-seventh State in 1845, passed through the Civil War and Reconstruction, and entered the present century, and now the Bicentennial, many religions emerged.

Chronologically, the Jews were the last of the now prominent Florida religious groups to organize formally. The first recorded Florida Jews were Alexander Salomon, a money broker in Pensacola during the 1760s, and David Moses, a store owner who in 1783 was listed on the Spanish census at St. Augustine. After transfer of the Floridas to the United States in 1821, the Jewish heritage really began in Florida, according to St. Augustine and Pensacola records. Moses Elias Levy, whose son, David Levy Yulee, later became the first United States senator from Florida and the first Jew elected to the U.S. Senate, were prominent citizens. After the Civil War most Jewish families in the state were located in Micanopy, Gainesville, Newnansville, DeLand, Palatka, Tampa, and Jacksonville. It was in Pensacola, however, where the first synagogue, Temple Beth-El, was established in 1874. The second, Temple Ahavath Chesed, was chartered at Jacksonville in 1882. The Jewish population remained relatively small until the 1880s: one survey, conducted in 1881, showed 772 Jews in Florida, of whom 130 lived in Jacksonville. By 1900 an estimated 2,500–3,000 Jews were residents, and some were moving into the southern counties.

Isidor Cohen moved to Fort Pierce, West Palm Beach and, finally, in 1896, to Miami. Arriving three months before Henry Flagler's Florida East Coast Railroad reached that point, Cohen, with twenty-five other Jews in newly incorporated Miami, founded a congregation to observe that city's first Rosh-Ha-Shanah. It was said of Cohen ". . .that no American Jew played a comparable role in fixing the foundations of an evolving metropolis. . . ." The contemporary Jewish community of Greater Miami dates from 1913, when seventy-five residents founded Congregation B'nai Zion, later renamed Beth David, and allocated a section in the city cemetery for Jewish burials. Only forty-three years later, in 1956, that seventy-five had grown to 75,000!

Today there are many religions, denominations, and cults in Florida. Few states in the nation have a religious scene so rich and diversified—and none has a western religious history so old.

—MICHAEL V. GANNON

The Koreshans

The early Koreshans came to Estero from Chicago in 1893 to practice their faith and build New Jerusalem, a planned city for eight million people. Koreshanity originated with Dr. Cyrus Reed Teed, a physician, surgeon, and brain specialist who experienced a "divine illumination" in 1869 and took the Biblical name, Koresh. Teed's research in metaphysics and electromagnetism led him to conclude that the earth is a hollow globe—a "macrocosmic egg"—about 8000 miles in diameter, with people, the sun, moon, planets, and stars on the inside. These elements, he said, constitute the whole of the universe.

Along with this principle of "cellular cosmogony," Teed formulated a detailed constitution for a new society, which included a celibate order of church leaders, a marital order of cooperating families, and an external order of members at large in the church. The basic principles of the society were communal: love and service to one's neighbors and denial of monetary gain.

Teed exhorted his followers to abjure profanity, tobacco, intoxicants, and licentiousness. He was an early exponent of ecology and outdoor education, consumerism, economic development of underdeveloped nations, racial and sexual equality, and other causes still considered "liberal" today.

At its peak this community of about 200 people boasted a tropical flower garden, art gallery, printing house, university, and the first symphony orchestra in Florida.

Despite these achievements, the new society suffered from internal dissension. Some reports say a sore point was the celibacy rule, from which Koresh and his aide, Miss Victoria Gratia, were exempt because they had attained earthly perfection.

Neighbor troubles also plagued the Koreshans in Florida. Equal treatment of Blacks and women by the sect provoked much hostility. In 1908, at age 69, Koresh died of injuries suffered when he was stoned while speaking in Fort Myers. —G.L.

"Religion as a sense of the whole is the most individualized of all things, the most spontaneous, undefinable, and varied."
—JOHN DEWEY

COLONIAL FEVERS AND FLUXES

Dr. John Lorimer

"To a putrid bilious fever succeeded an epidemic of flux, which, from want of a regular Hospital, and the crowded situation of the sick, in the dirty, despicable, confined huts of the garrison, was followed by the Jail or Hospital fever which became universal."

—ROBERT R. REA,
Graveyard for Britons
WEST FLORIDA, 1763

"East Florida, as regards sickliness, has often been judged with the same disfavor which experience attaches to the southern parts of North America generally; but without reason. Augustine itself is widely known to be a healthy place, so that weaklings and consumptives from the northern provinces resort hither, and always to their advantage."

—JOHANN DAVID SCHOEPT
Travels in the Confederation,
1783–1784

The first quotation describes the unhealthy conditions in West Florid[a] contrasting strongly to the healthy report of East Florida in the sar[ne] period. This was the British Period, 1763–1783, when East Flori[da] remained relatively healthy and West Florida became the "graveyard f[or] Britons."

Dr. John Lorimer, the military surgeon at Pensacola, 1765 to 178[ ] and a physician of extraordinary ability, describes the sequence of diseas[es] that plagued the province: "The bilious remitting and intermitting feve[rs] that set in, and continued by repeated relapses throughout the months [of] July, August, and September. . . At the approach of the cold weather, t[he] fevers abated, and they then fell into fluxes, dropsias, and cachexie[s.] Other diseases in Florida included consumption (tuberculosis), asthm[a,] pleurisy, scurvy, worm fever, lockjaw, smallpox, hydrophobia, sunstro[ke] and veneral disease. Some deaths resulted from accidents; occasior[al] suicides are recorded, as well as homocides and starvation, but far a[nd] away the leading killers were the fevers and the fluxes.

The intermittent fevers were probably malaria; bilious remittir[g] fever and putrid bilious fever are typical of yellow fever. In his writings [on] *Diseases Incidental to Europeans in Hot Climates, with the Method of Preventir[g]*

The first record we have of a hospital in St. Augustine is a letter from Governor Gonzalo Méndez de Canzo to the Crown dated Feb. 23, 1958, in which he states that when he arrived in 1597 a hospital was being formed in conjunction with the Hermita de Nuestra Señor de La Soledad (the Church of Our Lady of Solitude). Canzo states that had the hospital not been in operation during the summer of 1597 many soldiers, Indians and Negro royal slaves would have died of the epidemic fever.

In 1659 epidemic measles killed 10,000 Indians and many soldiers of the garrison at St. Augustine.

their Fatal Consequences, James Lind, a British Naval physician of this period, mentioned Mobile as a place, "where intermitting fevers prevail in the months of July, August and September." The Dutch cartographer, Bernard Romans, who travelled in Florida, 1771 and 1772, reported these fevers in, ". . .most of the settlements on the St. Johns, in East-Florida, at Campbelltown, near the mouth of the Escambe and at Mobile in West-Florida. . ." The bilious remitting fever is reported to have been epidemic at Pensacola in 1764 and 1765, but is not mentioned thereafter during the British Period.

The fluxes were diarrheas and dysenteries caused by dysentery, typhoid, or cholera bacilli and probably amoebae. Dropsias produced an accumulation of fluid in the body cavities and tissues and followed the fevers.

Jail or hospital fever was a disease ". . .incident to every place ill-aired and kept dirty, that is, filled with animal steams from foul or diseased bodies," according to Sir John Pringle. It probably is murine typhus which is transmitted by the rat flea. Rat infested ships that brought soldiers, settlers, and supplies also brought typhus.

Only meager details of the treatments administered to Britons in Florida are available. The medications requested for the troops probably were chosen from the "supply table" of the British Army. Medical supplies were at times lacking or had been damaged on the long sea voyage or in the heat of West Florida.

Fevers of all types were attacked by more or less vigorous blood letting. Removal of blood was then thought to reduce or break the fever. This treatment was followed by a purge such as tartar emetic powdered with "crab eyes." Crab eyes were not literally the eye of a crab but a concretion of calcium carbonate found in the stomach of European crawfish. The sovereign remedy for the intermittents was "the Bark" of the quina-quina also called Peruvian Bark and Jesuit's Bark which contained quinine. For the fever headache, the application of leeches or a blister to the temple was the proper treatment.

For the jail or hospital fever (typhus) first the patient must be removed from the foul air or the air must be purified with steams of vinegar. Bloodletting by use of three leeches on each temple or from a vein in the arm might be helpful if the patient became delirious but must be used cautiously for it was occasionally followed by death. Rhenish or "a small French" wine in quantities of "near a quart a day" was also helpful.

Preventive medicine and public health measures of the day were based on the miasmic theory of disease: the concept that particles, atoms or animalcules, ". . .arise from distempered, putrefying or poisonous bodies,

In January 1600 Governor Canzo "Founded at my expense a house of boards for use as a hospital . . . with its rooms in the attic and having beds with their mattresses, blankets, sheets, and pillows for the stated purpose that all poor and sick people may seek shelter by going to it." This palmetto-thatched hospital of six beds (so arranged about an altar in the center of the room that the patients might observe mass without leaving their beds) was dedicated to "The Lady Santa Barbara." —W.M.S.

The accounts of Florida in the 16th and 17th Centuries are glowing in the best Chamber of Commerce tradition. A geography book of 1688 states, "The area of Florida and Carolina is so temperate that men live to the age of 250 years, while the children of five generations are all alive at the same time."

A list from the "supply table" of the British Army compiled in August, 1764, detailed by Laura D. Harrell in the original spelling:

Camphora.
Cera flava.
Cortex Cinnamon.
Elixer Paregoric.
Flor. Chamomel.
_____ Sulphur.
Magnesia alba.
Manna.
Olea Chum.
Pulvis Cortic. Peruvian.
_____ Jallap.
_____ Radic. Ipecacuan.
_____ Rhabarb.
Radex Gentian.
Sal carthartic. amar.
_____ Glauber. Miral.
semen Lini.
spiritus Vini retificat.
Tinctura Thebaic.
Unguent. Basilic.
_____ dialth.
_____ Mercurial fort.
_____ alb.
Virtum ceret antimon.

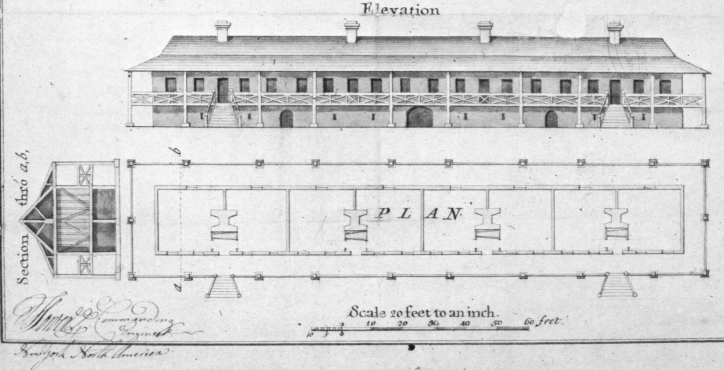

PLAN, ELEVATION and SECTION of the new defign'd BARRACKS to be buil[t] for lodging the Officers of four Company's at the RED CLIFFS at PENSACOLA. N.B. The framing of this building is to be the same as shewn in the Section of Officers Barracks, which are to be built in the Town of Pensacola for the Officers and Staff, with a Kitchen &c.

Elevation

Section thro' a,b,

P L A N

Scale 20 feet to an inch.

10   20   30   40   50   60 feet

Plan for new British barracks at
Pensacola, prepared as Britons take over
rule of Florida from Spanish.

Dr. Odette Phillippe

and affect people at a distance." Brigadier General Frederick Haldiman[d] began a program of improvements at Pensacola soon after his arrival i[n] March, 1767, which included moving the high pallisades of the fort furthe[r] from the barracks to permit a freer circulation of air. He also ordered th[e] construction of privies, the draining of the swamp behind the town and th[e] provision of a better water supply.

Dr. Lorimer advised the construction of a two-story barracks (I[t] was thought safer to sleep on the second floor as the damp exhalations o[f] the ground were thought to cause dysenteries and fevers.) with "piazzas" t[o] protect the men from the sun and provide ventilation. He emphasized th[e] need for cleanliness and in particular that relating to the "common neces-sarys." In the British Army in Florida, just as is true in modern day armie[s] afield, there were problems in getting the men to avail themselves of th[e] "common necessarys." Pringle comments: "In order therefore to preserve [a] purity of air in the dysenteric season, let there be some slight penalty, bu[t] strictly inflicted, upon every man that shall ease himself anywhere abou[t] the camp, but in the privies."

Lorimer also insisted upon boiling the drinking water "in vessels o[f] tin or iron, for copper will not do in this climate." He suggested assignin[g] fishermen to provide food from the sea and trading the regulation issue o[f] salt meat to the Indians for wild fowl and venison. "But as the soldier[s] must live upon salt meat after all, mustard (?) veniger or sour-crout ough[t]

MEDICINAL HERBS MOST COMMONLY USED BY THE MICCOSUKEE SEMINOLE:

Bay leaves	Persea borbonia	25 times
Cedar	Juniperus cilicicola	11 times
Sassafras	Sassafras albidum	10 times
Southern willow	Salix amphibia	8 times
Ginseng	Panax Quinquefolium	6 times
Lizard's tail	Saururus cernuus	6 times
Button snakeroot	Eryngium synchaetum	5 times
Common buttonbush	Cephalanthus occidentalis	5 times
Downy milk pea	Galactia volubilis	4 times
Royal fern	Osmunda regalis	4 times
Beard fern	Vittaria lineata	4 times
Serpent fern	Phlebodium aureum	4 times
Frost-weed	Verbesina virginica	4 times
Gopher-apple	Chrysobalanus oblongifolius	4 times
Huckleberry	Vaccinium myrsinites	4 times
Spike-sedge	Eleocharis caribaea	4 times

This list of medicinal herbs used by the Seminole Indians
was compiled by William C. Sturtevant of the Smithsonian Institute
and is arranged in the order of most frequent use.

The wonder drug of the day was sassafras which was found in Florida. It was given to the Huguenots at Fort Caroline by the Indians and the knowledge of it conveyed to the Spanish by survivors of the Huguenot massacre. —W.M.S.

Another remedy to be found in Florida was tobacco. This was useful for many things including headaches, shortness of breath and the treatment of chronic ulcers. The cough and expectoration produced by the tobacco smoke was thought to clear out the lungs and thus help shortness of breath. This remedy, it is said, was learned from the Indians and, indeed, LeMoyne, the Huguenot artist, in one of his drawings shows the Indians inhaling tobacco smoke. —W.M.S.

Seminole beliefs include the soul wandering concept and the theory that if a soul faces due east it will walk the Milky Way to the west and the body will die. For this reason a sick Indian must always lie with his head to the east, for if he lies with his head to the west, he may well die. When the Seminole lies down to sleep at night, but not necessarily during the day, he is careful to lie with his head to the east. At death, Seminoles, by custom, are buried with their heads to the west. —W.S.

to be procured & serv'd to the messes and soup provided for the sick and convalescent." Both mustard and sauerkraut were used to prevent scurvy, an ever-present disease in West Florida. Lorimer recommended that troop ships be dispatched so that they would arrive: ". . .about the last of October, when the Climate is healthiest & the heat is most supportable to an English Constitution. . ."

Quarantine of a sort was practiced. When new troops with illness among them arrived at Pensacola, they were landed on Santa Rosa Island and detained until their health returned. Again in May, 1769, when smallpox became epidemic at Pensacola the Lieutenant Governor issued a proclamation that all poor persons might apply to be taken to Santa Rosa Island and there be nursed back to health at the expense of the government.

If things were hard for the military in British West Florida, the situation was worse for the civilians. The civilians in November, 1766, petitioned the "Right Honorable the Lords Commissioners of Trade and Plantations" to construct hospitals for civilians at Mobile and Pensacola. The petitioners note: "It is needless to remark to your Lordships. . . that there are so many Diseases incident to the first clearing of a Country, and so many Diseases incident to such Labour, as well as to the changes of Climate, that the first Settlers have in general proved a Sacrifice to the prosperity of their Successors. . ." —WILLIAM M. STRAIGHT

Dr. Benjamin Strobel

TERRITORIAL TREMORS
AND TREATMENTS

The Franklin Stove
And the Gorrie Ice Machine

Was the genius of Benjamin Franklin matched by an inventor from Apalachicola? Indeed Dr. John Gorrie, M.D., searching for a malaria cure manufactured what only nature had previously made: ice. In turn, he invented the first air conditioner, a discovery that was to southerners what the Franklin Stove was to northerners.

Few inventions, other than screens for windows and mosquito repellent, have so radically affected life in Florida.

Dr. James C. Bronaugh

Frontier conditions faced the doctors who tried to solve health problems during territorial days in Florida. Yellow fever was a particular problem—partly because no one yet suspected that the cause was the pesty mosquito. When *Aedes aegypti* was found to be the carrier of yellow fever, some doctors noted that Florida physicians had been engaged in a hopeless struggle against the disease throughout the century.

Although the people of the Florida Territory suffered the ailments common to all America—pulmonary diseases (consumption in particular), dysentery, cancer, childbed fever, broken bones—here the most relentless enemies were typhoid, malaria, yellow fever and other intermittent fevers, prevalent diseases known to flourish in tropical and subtropical lands made worse by poor drainage and indifferent sanitation. Here mosquitos and flies thrived.

To complicate matters,commercial and military vessels plying the waters of the Caribbean and the Gulf of Mexico usually made Pensacola, Key West and St. Augustine their ports of call. Frequently they brought their ailing fever victims into these ports, often abandoning them to the mercies of the townspeople.

Within weeks after the American flags were raised, both Pensacola and St. Augustine established boards of health. The board of health of St. Augustine announced its members on July 16, 1821: in addition to the mayor, an alderman, a merchant and a Roman Catholic priest, there was an Irish physician, Dr. Richard Murray, who had been in the town since 1816. The next year, Dr. Micah Stone was added as "resident physician of the City."

Medical officers on military detachments were expected to participate in public health programs. When Governor Andrew Jackson issued commissions creating a temporary government for the town of Pensacola in 1821, Dr. James C. Bronaugh, an army surgeon in the War of 1812 and personal physician of General Jackson, was named "resident physician and president of the board of health."

In the summer of 1822 the Legislative Council of the Florida Territory met in Pensacola where Dr. Bronaugh presided. Its work was scarcely begun when yellow fever broke out. In near-panic the entire body fled sixteen miles to the safety of a plantation owned by Don Manuel Gonzalez. It was only a brief escape: Dr. Bronaugh was next on the fever

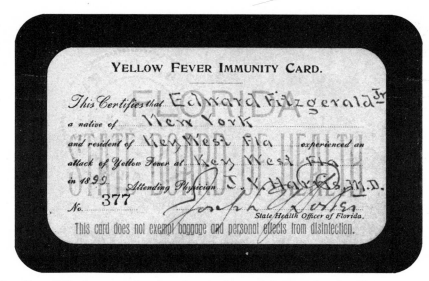

YELLOW FEVER IMMUNITY CARD.

This Certifies that Edward Fitzgerald Jr

a native of New York

and resident of Key West Fla experienced an

attack of Yellow Fever at Key West Fla

in 1899. Attending Physician J X Hayes, M.D.

No. 377

State Health Officer of Florida.

This card does not exempt baggage and personal effects from disinfection.

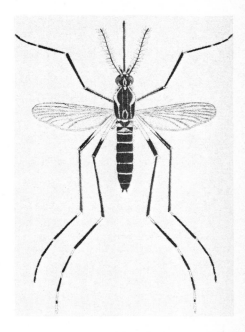

The yellow fever mosquito, Aedes aegypti, is still prevalent but the disease has come and gone somewhat mysteriously. Moreover since World War II a one hundred percent effective vaccine has been available and not surprisingly the doctor who discovered it was a recipient of a Nobel prize.

victim list. His last professional words, published in the Pensacola *Floridian*, were dire warnings concerning the deadliness of the disease. On September 2, 1822 the first legislative act establishing the Board of Health in the cities of Pensacola and St. Augustine was signed by Governor Duval, the very day of Dr. Bronaugh's death from the fever.

Florida health hazards continued through the next two decades (1822–32); yet the population increased. Hundreds of settlers from Georgia, Alabama and the Carolinas poured into north Florida. The first official Florida census, taken in 1825, did not include the Indians but found 13,554 others in the territory. By 1830 the number had grown to 34,730. In spite of fevers and the waging of the Second Seminole War by 1840, settlers numbered 54,477.

Physicians came into Florida in unexpected numbers. Like Dr. Bronaugh, some were victims of the fevers they were trying to treat, but those who survived the hazards and hardships played important roles in their communities. Their literacy and professional education projected them into leadership roles in political, religious, educational, and economic matters.

The migration of physicians to Florida during this period defies explanation. Of course there was the lure of cheap land. Also a surplus of diploma-holding practitioners who graduated from some colleges of dubious standards found the frontier appealing with its lack of medical regulation and remoteness. So there were some charlatans and some adventurers, along with honest conscientious practitioners on the Florida scene.

Was the quality of medical practice in the Territory of Florida any better or worse than in any other part of rural America? Probably not, but the necessities and privations of Florida frontier practice demanded an inventiveness and adaptability. Dr. David L. White of Gadsden County, a gentle and cultivated practitioner, summed it up in the following words: ". . . in the treatment of the diseases of our climate, we are perhaps not as deficient as many suppose. . . .those who toil in the medical profession among us command few of the ordinary advantages enjoyed in large and populous cities and are hence driven mainly upon their own resources. . . we are, I hope, open to the reception of new impressions and eliciting new lights. It is important that we watch, interrogate, and scrutinize nature."
—E. ASHBY HAMMOND

Physician Printers

The Wells Print Shop was opened in the eighteenth century in St. Augustine where Dr. John Wells, Jr. practiced two arts, as a doctor from England, and as the publisher of the *East Florida Gazette*. This newspaper, the first printed in Florida, was issued in 1783. In Key West in the early 1830s, another doctor with ink on his stethoscope, Dr. Benjamin B. Strobel, put out the *Key West Gazette* in a printing shop which was as short-lived as the doctor's stay in Florida .

DOLLARS AND DREAMS

Japanese Floridians

Joseph Sakai, an American educated expatriate dreamed of establishing agricultural colonies of his countrymen in America. He came to Florida in 1903 to select lands for a Japanese colony. Land purchase arrangements were coordinated by Henry M. Flagler's Florida East Coast Railway, and a year later the first immigrants arrived and settled on a several thousand acre site just north of present day Boca Raton.

Christening their own new community "Yamato," the ancient name for Japan itself, the Japanese experimented with growing silk, tea, tobacco, rice, and pineapples. By 1907 with two hundred settlers Yamato was given over almost entirely to the raising of pineapple, and as clear signs of prosperity, received a station on the Florida East Coast Railway and an official branch of the United States Post Office. The Japanese produced some of the largest and most productive pineapple fields in South Florida, but eventually were pushed out of the market by plant disease and competition from Cuban pineapple plantations.

When pineapples no longer turned a profit, most of the Japanese gradually drifted to other communities along the coast or returned to their homeland. Today only one of the original settlers survives, Mr. George Morikami of Delray. Yet, his donation of forty acres of choice land to the State of Florida for an Agricultural Experiment Station and an additional forty acres to Palm Beach County for a recreational park insures a lasting memorial to the role of Japanese settlers in Florida.

—GEORGE E. POZZETTA

Russians

Several small Russian colonies existed in southern Florida at the turn of the century. A typical undertaking encompassed 11,000 acres of land and had large plantings of vegetables and general farm crops. One experiment that generated public attention featured communal living arrangements.

—GEORGE E. POZZETTA

BERTHA PALMER

Most developers who have left a mark on Florida had several things in common: they found great satisfaction in transforming swamp and tidal mud flats into salable real estate, and, once they contracted the development fever they remained stricken until broke or until death intervened. Many died broke. An exception was a woman, Bertha Honore Palmer, the "Queen of Chicago" and "Boss of Sarasota."

In 1870, beautiful Bertha Honore, 21, was married to Potter Palmer, 23 years her elder. His gift to his bride was the Palmer House, the best hotel in Chicago. After it burned in the Chicago fire, he replaced it with a new Palmer House, a sumptuous tower. The proud, confident, and glamorous Bertha Potter set the social pace in Chicago for a quarter century and, by the time of her husband's death in 1902 at 76, she was one of the best known women in America and probably the best known American woman in Europe. Her appreciative husband did not forget. He left her every cent he had—$8 million.

In 1911, during a blizzard, a Sarasota real estate ad in a Chicago newspaper attracted Mrs. Palmer. Almost as soon as the blizzard was over she was heading toward Florida. She wound up buying 140,000 acres and, with her name, Sarasota bloomed. Her efforts at farming were a failure, but she went into the cattle business and showed the Crackers that what they could do she could do better. Upon her death in 1918, at 69, she left an estate of $20 million, much of it made in Florida.

CARL FISHER

Carl Fisher, at fifty, could look back and say he had made an average of a million dollars a year since the day he was born in Greensburg, Indiana, in 1874. His fabulous career included the creation of the Lincoln and Dixie highways, the building of the Indianapolis Speedway, and making of millions of dollars off a French invention, Prest-O-Lite, a carbide light for automobiles.

In 1913, while vacationing in Miami, Fisher lent John Collins $50,000 to complete a bridge across Biscayne Bay to Miami Beach. In return, Collins gave Fisher a 600-foot wide strip of Miami, mostly worthless, because Miami Beach at that time was only a sand spit separating the ocean from a mosquito-breeding mangrove swamp. Fisher also met the Lummus brothers, J.E. and J.N., who were attempting to fill the southern part of the Miami Beach swamp with adjacent bay bottom sand.

The result: with Fisher's money, Fisher, Collins, and the Lummus brothers filled over a thousand acres of mangrove swamp. With more knowledge about promotion than any other developer in Florida history, Fisher launched a campaign to make Miami Beach a national household word, based on a steady flow of public release photographs of bathing beauties and a baby elephant that caddied for President Harding when he played golf at Miami Beach.

Worth $50 million in 1924, Fisher moved to Long Island to develop Montauk Beach as the "Miami Beach of the North." But the boom blew up and a hurricane followed. Fisher died broke in 1939.   —N.S.

George Merrick, Creator

George E. Merrick, dreamer, poet, was the only Florida developer who grew up to turn the vegetable farm on which he was reared into one of the most successful real estate ventures. The family home, "Coral Gables," still stands in the city of Coral Gables that Merrick created.

Merrick was still in his twenties when he dreamed of creating the most beautiful city in America. He began buying property adjacent to the original 160-acre Merrick farm, but his goal was so great that he could only direct. He employed architects, artists, surveyors, salesmen. By the time the land boom was under way, Merrick had a sales force of 3000.

Merrick sold $150 million worth of lots, but spent $100 million in the development of his dream city—in construction, in streets and sidewalks, parks and parkways. He erected the Miami Biltmore Hotel, gave land for the University of Miami. Then the bottom fell out and Merrick went broke. He and his wife, Eunice, returned to the Florida Keys and established a fishing camp on property she had inherited. Merrick became postmaster of Miami in 1940, but died in 1942 at 56, not broke but far from the multi-millionaire he once had been.

—N.S.

Dutch

Small settlements of Hollanders dotted Florida. One 1883 colony counted twenty-five immigrants who landed at Fernandina and migrated to a location near Tallahassee. These people were drawn to Florida by a promotional pamphlet translated into Dutch and distributed throughout Holland.

Slovaks

Slovaks settled in Florida at Slavia and Masaryktown. The town of Slavia, was established by the Slavia Colony Company, a stock company formed by the Holy Trinity Slovak Church of Cleveland, Ohio. An initial group of eighty-two people began work on 1200 acres of land in Seminole County in 1911. The community specialized in growing celery on rich "muck" lands. The harvests reaped by Slavia residents clearly showed that celery was an excellent cash crop for this part of Florida. Masaryktown was not settled till 1925. Located in north Hernando County, this community attempted to act as a source of investment and employment opportunities for older Slovaks who could not readily find acceptance in the general marketplace.

VIEW OF
MONTICELLO, FLA.
COUNTY-SEAT OF JEFFERSON CY.
1885.

Spanish

Spanish workers in post-Civil War Florida tended to concentrate in the tobacco industries, first in Key West and then Tampa. It is less well known that they constituted twenty to twenty-five percent of the entire work force that built the famous Key West Extension of the Florida East Coast Railway. Railroad officials described Spaniards as unusually "efficient and industrious" and sought them above all other laborers.

—G.E.P.

Plucked Petals

Yankee money was spent to attract more Yankees and their money by a series of books written about Florida by well known people who came to the state both as visitors and residents.

Harriet Beecher Stowe, the most famous woman writer in the North, settled with her husband at Mandarin on the St. Johns and wrote *Palmetto Leaves*. Her sister-in-law, Mrs. Henry Ward Beecher, wrote *Letters from Florida* published in New York. Sidney Lanier, already well-known as a Southern poet, living, for his health, in Tampa, was paid to write, beautifully, *Florida, Its Scenery, Climate and History*. Perhaps the best writer of all was an intrepid young newspaper woman, Abby M. Brooks, who ventured everywhere inland and along the West coast in a schooner to write, as "Sylvia Sunshine" a good book with the incredible title of *Petals Plucked from Sunny Climes*. Frederick Ober as "Fred Beverly" wrote "Life in Florida" for the magazine, *Field and Stream*, and was one of the first white men to reach and describe the unknown Lake Okeechobee.

All this writing followed the romantic tradition; no one mentioned hardships, mosquitoes, bitter struggles, hurricanes, dirt-floored cabins, lack of schools, libraries, adequate doctors or hospitals or roads. Yellow fever, hookworm, malaria. No one said anything about the violence and injustice by which the newly enfranchised slaves were stripped of their civil liberties and reduced to serfdom. The dreadful conditions of convict labor in the turpentine camps, some owned by northerners is revealed in only one book, plainly written, revealing conditions similar to *Crime and Punishment* and called *An American Siberia or Fourteen Years Experience in a Southern Convict Camp* by a man who had been in charge of one, J.C. Powell.

—M.S.D.

Danes

Dozens of advertisements for Florida land circulated in Danish language publications in the early 1890s. One enterprising land agent, Mr. Louis Pio, responded to these inducements and brought several hundred Danes to White City in 1893. The death of Mr. Pio and the dishonesty and thievery of the colony's financial manager threatened the settlement but, with the help of the Florida East Coast Railway, it survived. By 1900 it was sufficiently affluent for the young men of White City to advertise for "young marriageable ladies" to come to the colony. Another settlement, Modelo, languished until 1901 when Mr. A.C. Frost was appointed land agent by the Florida East Coast Railway. Frost was an experienced colonizer who actively recruited Danish settlers and guided the community, rechristened Dania, to permanent stability. Tomatoes proved to be the mainstay of the colony economy and by 1908 one thousand Dania residents produced an impressive three hundred sixty-five train car loads of this savory vegetable, along with fifty car loads of pineapples.

Swedes

Swedes made their first large scale appearance in Florida during the early 1870s when Floridians imported several groups of Swedish agricultural laborers to work on plantations and in citrus groves. The largest experiment of this type was carried out by Henry Sanford. In 1871 Sanford and other businessmen of the area contracted for more than one hundred Swedes to work in the Sanford Groves and other ventures. Events combined to thwart the high hopes of the planners and a heavy stream of Swedish immigration never developed.

A few families began the community of New Upsala which was fed by a trickle of newcomers over the years. Descendants of these people live there still. A land development scheme organized by the Florida East Coast Railway was based on Swedish language appeals, and carried out by promoter Olof Zetterlund. In response, a group of Swedish Lutherans purchased land in south Florida and began the vegetable community of Hallandale in 1897.

—GEORGE E. POZZETTA

172

Harvesting tomatoes near Homestead, 1922

SEA MYSTERY

For a feeling of the kind of person a Florida developer during the 1920s real estate boom must have been, there's no better name than that of D.P. Davis, a little man and a braggart. Davis was born in Green Cove Springs, which turned out another entrepreneur, Charles Merrill, founder of Merrill Lynch, Pierce, Fenner & Smith. After growing up in Tampa, Davis dropped out of school—a common practice of future millionaires—and went into construction work. He wound up in the real estate business in Miami.

While Davis made money, he observed that more money was made by dredging up shallow bay bottom and selling waterfront lots. He returned to Tampa, where there was more bay bottom than in Miami. Paying $10,000 down for several hundred acres of mudflats near the mouth of the Hillsborough River, he brought in dredges, and, against considerable opposition, built a sea wall and began filling in behind it. Presto, Davis Islands were created.

By October, 1925, Davis had sold all lots for $18 million—or at least the buyers had made downpayments. He hastened to St. Augustine and began developing Davis Shores. But before Davis realized what had hit him, the Florida land boom had "busted." People who had bought lots on Davis Islands stopped making payments, and Davis lost the islands to creditors.

In 1926 he sailed for France. On the first night out he plunged through the porthole in his stateroom and the sea swallowed him. Glamorous Lucille Zehring, a Mack Sennett bathing beauty, said she was in the room with him when he jumped. She said he suffered a fit of jealousy after another male on board ship, an old acquaintance of hers, paid her some attention. "You don't think I'll do it, do you?" she quoted him as he climbed into the porthole. Then he was gone. Another story is that Davis was a daredevil at walking the rail on ships—that he tried it one time too many, and fell off the wrong side. Although Davis died broke, he had experienced sufficient foreboding before departure to take out an insurance policy for $300,000.

—N.S.

Sponge divers, Tarpon Springs.

LAND MAGIC

For crustiness and willingness to spend, none present or past surpass Arthur Vining Davis, Pittsburgh tycoon who helped to build the Aluminum Company of America. Davis was in his middle eighties when in the 1950s he began buying Florida properties. He seemed to want everything—and people sold him plant nurseries, construction companies, dairies, farms, groves, limestone escavating firms, hotels and thousands upon thousands of acres of land.

Like D.P. Davis, who created Davis Islands at Tampa, A.V. Davis was a small man, and he was crusty, too, but no braggart like D.P. And, while D.P. was a grade school dropout, A.V. had a degree from Amherst. He began working for the firm that became the Aluminum Company of America for $50 a month. By the time he was elected chairman of the board, he had parlayed that measly income into a stock fortune worth in excess of $100 million. "I never retired," he told a newspaperman when he was 88. "I'm working as hard as ever—sixteen hours a day."

He was spending money, too, fantastic amounts of it. He bought and bought in Dade County until he owned a twelfth of the county. He bought thousands of acres at the Isle of Pines, which Castro took, and thousands of acres in the Bahamas. Sir Harold Christy, Bahamas broker, took Davis in a boat to show him land at Eleuthera he was considering buying. "How much of this were you thinking of buying, Mr. Davis?" asked Sir Harold. "I want all of that," replied Davis with a wave of his hand. "All as far as I can see." The land Davis referred to was a swinging shoreline that disappeared in the horizon, ten miles distant.

Davis died in 1962 at 95. Much of his original wealth had been squandered in efforts to resurrect decadent businesses he had purchased. Yet, the worth of his estate was some $60 million, which after gifts to relatives and to his secretary, whom he left a million, went into Arthur Vining Davis Foundations, to further education and the arts.   —N.S.

Greeks

The magnet that drew Greeks to Tarpon Springs was the sponge industry. Near the turn of the century, John Cocoris, a traveling sponge wholesaler, saw the possibilities that existed for deep water sponging. He purchased mechanical diving equipment and imported a crew of experienced Greek divers from his homeland. From their arrival in 1905 to the present day, the sponge industry, staffed heavily by Greeks, has remained the mainstay of Tarpon Springs. Greek culture and customs are still very much in evidence; the annual Epiphany celebration draws thousands of visitors to witness this unique cultural event. Indeed, many observers claim that Tarpon Springs is "more Greek than Hellas itself."

Poles Come to Florida

A Florida land agent, Mr. S.C. Wood, organized and promoted the first Polish settlement near present day Bayard, Florida. A Polish banker and labor agent from Brooklyn, New York, Mr. Burt Mikulski, actually settled the colony by bringing fifty Polish families to Florida in September, 1910, to engage in truck farming. Most of the immigrants came from the capital city of Poland, and they named their new settlement, Warsaw. Crops of fruits and vegetables were marketed throughout the surrounding area, often shipped to Jacksonville by horse and wagon. Poor, sandy soil, unfamiliar climatic conditions, and low cash reserves, however, forced most of the settlers out of the colony and into neighboring communities.

Polish immigrants also formed the colony of Korona in Flagler county. Established in 1912, the first residents were recently arrived Polish immigrants who migrated south from Chicago. They chose the name Korona (a Polish word meaning crown) after one of the titles of the Blessed Virgin Mary, Queen of the Crown of Poland. A landmark, St. Mary's Catholic Church was built on the Dixie Highway, four miles south of Bunnell. The colony flourished during its early years by raising potatoes and garden vegetables for market, but frosts and floods during the twenties and thirties, and the gradual deterioration of its canal systems led to a gradual decline.

—GEORGE E. POZZETTA

IN CONGRESS, JULY 4, 1776.

The unanimous Declaration of the thirteen united States of America.

When in the Course of human events, it becomes necessary for one people to dissolve the political bands which have connected them with another, and to assume among the powers of the earth, the separate and equal station to which the Laws of Nature and of Nature's God entitle them, a decent respect to the opinions of mankind requires that they should declare the causes which impel them to the separation. _____ We hold these truths to be self-evident, that all men are created equal, that they are endowed by their Creator with certain unalienable Rights, that among these are Life, Liberty and the pursuit of Happiness. — That to secure these rights, Governments are instituted among Men, deriving their just powers from the consent of the governed, — That whenever any Form of Government becomes destructive of these ends, it is the Right of the People to alter or to abolish it, and to institute new Government, laying its foundation on such principles and organizing its powers in such form, as to them shall seem most likely to effect their Safety and Happiness. Prudence, indeed, will dictate that Governments long established should not be changed for light and transient causes; and accordingly all experience hath shewn, that mankind are more disposed to suffer, while evils are sufferable, than to right themselves by abolishing the forms to which they are accustomed. But when a long train of abuses and usurpations, pursuing invariably the same Object evinces a design to reduce them under absolute Despotism, it is their right, it is their duty, to throw off such Government, and to provide new Guards for their future security. — Such has been the patient sufferance of these Colonies; and such is now the necessity which constrains them to alter their former Systems of Government. The history of the present King of Great Britain is a history of repeated injuries and usurpations, all having in direct object the establishment of an absolute Tyranny over these States. To prove this, let Facts be submitted to a candid world. _____

He has refused his Assent to Laws, the most wholesome and necessary for the public good.
He has forbidden his Governors to pass Laws of immediate and pressing importance, unless suspended in their operation till his Assent should be obtained; and when so suspended, he has utterly neglected to attend to them.
He has refused to pass other Laws for the accommodation of large districts of people, unless those people would relinquish the right of Representation in the Legislature, a right inestimable to them and formidable to tyrants only.
He has called together legislative bodies at places unusual, uncomfortable, and distant from the depository of their public Records, for the sole purpose of fatiguing them into compliance with his measures.
He has dissolved Representative Houses repeatedly, for opposing with manly firmness his invasions on the rights of the people.
He has refused for a long time, after such dissolutions, to cause others to be elected; whereby the Legislative powers, incapable of Annihilation, have returned to the People at large for their exercise; the State remaining in the mean time exposed to all the dangers of invasion from without, and convulsions within.
He has endeavoured to prevent the population of these States; for that purpose obstructing the Laws for Naturalization of Foreigners; refusing to pass others to encourage their migrations hither, and raising the conditions of new Appropriations of Lands.
He has obstructed the Administration of Justice, by refusing his Assent to Laws for establishing Judiciary powers.
He has made Judges dependent on his Will alone, for the tenure of their offices, and the amount and payment of their salaries.
He has erected a multitude of New Offices, and sent hither swarms of Officers to harrass our people, and eat out their substance.
He has kept among us, in times of peace, Standing Armies without the Consent of our legislatures.
He has affected to render the Military independent of and superior to the Civil power.
He has combined with others to subject us to a jurisdiction foreign to our constitution, and unacknowledged by our laws; giving his Assent to their Acts of pretended Legislation:
For Quartering large bodies of armed troops among us:
For protecting them, by a mock Trial, from punishment for any Murders which they should commit on the Inhabitants of these States:
For cutting off our Trade with all parts of the world:
For imposing Taxes on us without our Consent:
For depriving us in many cases, of the benefits of Trial by jury:
For transporting us beyond Seas to be tried for pretended offences:
For abolishing the free System of English Laws in a neighbouring Province, establishing therein an Arbitrary government, and enlarging its Boundaries so as to render it at once an example and fit instrument for introducing the same absolute rule into these Colonies:
For taking away our Charters, abolishing our most valuable Laws, and altering fundamentally the Forms of our Governments:
For suspending our own Legislatures, and declaring themselves invested with power to legislate for us in all cases whatsoever.
He has abdicated Government here, by declaring us out of his Protection and waging War against us.
He has plundered our seas, ravaged our Coasts, burnt our towns, and destroyed the lives of our people.
He is at this time transporting large Armies of foreign Mercenaries to compleat the works of death, desolation and tyranny, already begun with circumstances of Cruelty & perfidy scarcely paralleled in the most barbarous ages, and totally unworthy the Head of a civilized nation.
He has constrained our fellow Citizens taken Captive on the high Seas to bear Arms against their Country, to become the executioners of their friends and Brethren, or to fall themselves by their Hands.
He has excited domestic insurrections amongst us, and has endeavoured to bring on the inhabitants of our frontiers, the merciless Indian Savages, whose known rule of warfare, is an undistinguished destruction of all ages, sexes and conditions.
In every stage of these Oppressions We have Petitioned for Redress in the most humble terms: Our repeated Petitions have been answered only by repeated injury. A Prince, whose character is thus marked by every act which may define a Tyrant, is unfit to be the ruler of a free people.
Nor have We been wanting in attentions to our British brethren. We have warned them from time to time of attempts by their legislature to extend an unwarrantable jurisdiction over us. We have reminded them of the circumstances of our emigration and settlement here. We have appealed to their native justice and magnanimity, and we have conjured them by the ties of our common kindred to disavow these usurpations, which, would inevitably interrupt our connections and correspondence. They too have been deaf to the voice of justice and of consanguinity. We must, therefore, acquiesce in the necessity, which denounces our Separation, and hold them, as we hold the rest of mankind, Enemies in War, in Peace Friends. _____

We, therefore, the Representatives of the united States of America, in General Congress, Assembled, appealing to the Supreme Judge of the world for the rectitude of our intentions, do, in the Name, and by Authority of the good People of these Colonies, solemnly publish and declare, That these United Colonies are, and of Right ought to be Free and Independent States; that they are Absolved from all Allegiance to the British Crown, and that all political connection between them and the State of Great Britain, is and ought to be totally dissolved; and that as Free and Independent States, they have full Power to levy War, conclude Peace, contract Alliances, establish Commerce, and to do all other Acts and Things which Independent States may of right do. _____ And for the support of this Declaration, with a firm reliance on the protection of Divine Providence, we mutually pledge to each other our Lives, our Fortunes and our sacred Honor.

Button Gwinnett
Lyman Hall
Geo Walton.

Wm Hooper
Joseph Hewes,
John Penn

Edward Rutledge.

Thos Heyward Junr.
Thomas Lynch Junr.
Arthur Middleton

John Hancock

Samuel Chase
Wm Paca
Thos Stone
Charles Carroll of Carrollton

George Wythe
Richard Henry Lee
Th Jefferson
Benja Harrison
Thos Nelson jr.
Francis Lightfoot Lee
Carter Braxton

Robt Morris
Benjamin Rush
Benja Franklin
John Morton
Geo Clymer
Jas Smith
Geo Taylor
James Wilson
Geo. Ross
Caesar Rodney
Geo Read
Tho M:Kean

Wm Floyd
Phil Livingston
Frans Lewis
Lewis Morris

Richd Stockton
Jno Witherspoon
Fras Hopkinson
John Hart
Abra Clark

Josiah Bartlett
Wm Whipple
Saml Adams
John Adams
Robt Treat Paine
Elbridge Gerry
Step Hopkins
William Ellery
Roger Sherman
Sam el Huntington
Wm Williams
Oliver Wolcott
Matthew Thornton

THIS IS OUR HERITAGE HOW DO WE PRESERVE IT?

WE HOLD THESE TRUTHS

FLORIDA AND THE DECLARATION OF INDEPENDENCE

The Continental Congress officially adopted the Declaration of Independence on July 4, 1776, but it was not signed until August 2nd. Broadside copies of the document could not have reached British St. Augustine by slow sailing boats from Charleston or Savannah until much later. Rumors of shots at Lexington and Concord and rebellious gatherings everywhere must have been seeping in to the Governor and the military authorities at the great once-Spanish Fortress long before. The cheers, speeches, bells, and bonfires of the Fourth of July to the north in time prompted hanging effigies of John Hancock and Sam Adams, loyal toasts to the King at official dinners, the clash of increased bayonet drills, and drumbeats and marching soldiers in the streets of St. Augustine.

If any of the educated gentlemen among the upper class of plantation owners in East Florida secretly agreed with the Declaration of Independence, there is no record of it. No one seems to have spoken out for the rebellious thirteen colonies, even among the group of Freemasons gathered about the first British governor, Scottish James Grant, those whom the second governor, Patrick Tonyn sneered at for their liberalism. He called them "Americans," and even went so far as to jail Andrew Turnbull. In Florida there was no hardworking, tough-minded, middle class of farmers, artisans, fishermen, shopkeepers, and traders, writing with energy and hope of great opportunity—the people who in the north, formed the strong body of the Revolution. Below the small group of land owners there was only a large mixed class of slaves and indentured servants; Blacks, Christianized Indians, Minorcans, a few Italians and Greeks, and especially lower class Englishmen from the jails and gutters of London who had no official voice at all. There was no one else in East Florida to speak out, or in weakened West Florida and Pensacola where the trading house of Panton, Leslie dealt only with the free Indian tribes between the Mississippi and the eastern colonies. Successful revolutions are rarely initiated by the completely down-trodden, only by those already free enough, but still brimming with a sense of old oppression, to take armed and divisive action.

Here in Florida, the King still could do no wrong. Taxes, trade restrictions, remote control, the overwhelming pressure of a standing army, were prices cheerfully paid by the land owners for the Royal benefits of protection and their superior positions. The loyal Florida

General James Grant of Ballindalloch, Governor of British East Florida, 1764–1771, began representative government in the colony and settled differences with the Indians by conference.

"The spirit of rebellion can exist only in a society where a theoretical equality conceals great factual inequalities."
—ALBERT CAMUS

175

colonies so recently established in 1763, were politically and socially about at the same point the thirteen original American colonies had been a century before. If anyone in Florida, other than the British officials, took time to read the Declaration of Independence, the protest over the arrogance and injustice of British rule must have horrified them and overshadowed the great words of the first two paragraphs.

The following war years only increased the loyalty of British Florida. More British troops occupied the city of St. Augustine, which was enlarged and excited by a stream of loyalist refugees from the war in the north. The city hummed with the gaiety of a British garrison town in war-time, constant parades and drills, official banquets, halls with regimental bands, amateur dramatics, gambling, prostitutes, and every opportunity for riotous enjoyment.

The triumphant progress of Lord Cornwallis and his army through the Southern colonies toward Yorktown added to the general sense of victory. Even the pressure in St. Augustine of groups of young American officers, sent down to the Fortress as prisoners but allowed to take lodgings in the city and enjoy the general high living, was tolerated. It did not matter that late at night, half-drunken after some wild party, the Americans marched through the moonlit streets howling, "Long Live the Thirteen States," to the tune of "God Save the King." After all, it was probably argued, they were of sound English stock and, now that the war was almost over, would soon come to their senses.

It was an incredible shock when word came that Cornwallis had surrendered at Yorktown. Even more disastrous for the refugees and residents who had been sure of safety under the British Crown was the news that East and West Florida were to be turned back to the enfeebled American ally, Spain.

By 1822, Florida was an American territory, entirely controlled from Washington. Its western boundary was drawn in from the Mississippi to the Perdido. Its newly established northern borders were long since overrun by Americans, mostly from Southern states, goaded and excited by the ancient myth of unlimited riches from unlimited cheap land, especially the fine prairies and coasts long held by the Indians by right and title from the Spanish and British kings.

There is no indication that Floridians had the slightest conception of the meaning of the words of the first two paragraphs of the Declaration of Independence, not the British ruefully moving out of Florida, not the Spanish re-occupying and holding it with a weakened grasp from 1783 to 1822, not the incoming horde of American frontiersmen. They knew as little of the Constitution of the United States which was the practical first working out of the principles set forth forever in the Declaration of 1776. Without the principles of the Declaration of Independence the Constitution could not have been written. Without the Constitution and all its subsequent changes, developed not by any one man but by the extraordinary consensus of a group of thinking people, the Declaration never could have found life.

The Floridians who became Americans under those two majestic documents included land owners and slave holders. Alongside was a larger mass of citizens too poor to own slaves. These were not town-dwellers,

The truth is that all men having power should be distrusted.

—JAMES MADISON

176

Currier and Ives lithograph of signing of the Declaration of Independence.

artisans, or shopkeepers so much as hunters and fishermen—the true American border types, each with his remote log cabin, hound dogs in the breezeway, a cow, a mule, some half-wild hogs, a few chickens, and patches of sweet potatoes, corn, and sugar cane. They were implacable Indian fighters and their fierce pride was that they were free White Americans and not Blacks. In between was another great division, maintained by those whose religion led them to believe that men must remain "in that state of life where it has pleased God to call them."

"We hold these truths to be self-evident that all men are created equal." Even today people often misunderstand the fact that this great sentence from the Declaration of Independence was the triumph of six hundred years of developing English law and the logical progression of French philosophy. It was the result of the Magna Carta and the whole basis of "The Rights of Man." To Jefferson it meant what it can only mean, individual equality under the law. Nothing more, or less. Without it, democracy would never work. For mankind there would be no safety, no freedom, no justice, and no hope.

At the time of the Declaration, for men largely trained in the law, this was a more powerful principle than the idea of democracy. "Demos" to

Those who have once got an ascendancy and possessed themselves of all the resources of the nations . . . have immense means for retaining their advantage.

—THOMAS JEFFERSON

177

American Eagle
Mark Catesby, 1731

"Experience declares that man is the only animal which devours his own kind, for I can apply no milder term . . . to the general prey of the rich on the poor."
—THOMAS JEFFERSON, 1787

"Whatever the apparent cause of any riots may be, the real one is always want of happiness. It shows that something is wrong in the system of government that injures the felicity by which society is to be preserved."
—THOMAS PAINE, 1792

"The logic of the rebel is to want to serve justice so as not to add to the injustice of the human condition, to insist on plain language so as not to increase the universal falsehood, and to wager, in spite of human misery, for happiness."
—ALBERT CAMUS
The Rebel

many leaders meant "the mob" and the rule of mob passion was feared as the rule of a single despot. It had not yet been shown that the powerful and richest class cannot be trusted to set aside its own advantage and deal justly and love mercy. There was no proof yet the consensus of the whole people would supply a slow, almost unconscious, balancing force against the constant unrelenting encroachment of special interests.

It was typical of the times that Floridians would have little sympathy or concern for the principle of equality under the law. They were not alone. Within the territory and the state the Indian wars were fought, denying to the red men their rights, not only as human beings, but as legal holders of land under titles given and recognized, and immediately repudiated. The greater war involving the whole nation only thirty-five years after Florida became a territory and twenty-three after it had been admitted to the Union of States, tested not only the statement that all men must be considered equal under the law but also the strength of the contract called "The Constitution." That war also put to dreadful test the sentences of the second paragraph of the Declaration which pledges to all people that they are endowed by their Creator with certain "unalienable" rights; that among these are "Life, Liberty and the Pursuit of Happiness."

When Thomas Jefferson first put pen to the rough draft of the Declaration, he wrote, "Life, Liberty and Property." This was an old phrase in the French philosophy of law. But Jefferson must have stopped short there to think about the word "Property," and of himself, a property owner who would see the beginning of its loss, and a slave holder who believed that no man should be held in slavery. He crossed out the word "Property" and put in the words "Pursuit of Happiness." It is to this day, new concept of the possibilities of human life.

Jefferson could not, in all honesty, say that mankind could be given happiness by law. No man, no law, no human hope can guarantee that. But mankind has the right, and since those words were written no one has been able to refute them. It is safe to believe that Jefferson meant also "so long as it is not at the expense of others." No other set of laws has ever included the possibility, the hope, of happiness as a natural right. It added a new dimension to the human concept of law.

The Declaration moves forward, in a great upwelling of meaning as profound as music, "That to secure these rights, governments are instituted among men, deriving their just powers from the consent of the governed." Where is the slave, the captive, the prisoner in that?

Floridians found, in time, it was more difficult to be loyal to the Constitution than to their state. They came back, in time, to resume their loyalties, not only to the Constitution but to the great principles of the Declaration of Independence, to the new ideas of equality and justice.

The sayings of Thomas Jefferson were proved right and true; the forms of government could be changed as the people chose to change them. As a result of that Civil War the forms of government and of the Constitution were indeed changed and clarified, making them more work able. We are still slowly changing the Constitution, to meet the needs of changing times and always toward a better application of the unchanging principles of the Declaration.

We are only too aware that we have not yet succeeded in establishing completely the great principles of 1776. The Pledge of Allegiance to the Flag is repeated daily all over the United States and we are still struggling to make these words come true, "with liberty and justice for all." It is an undying hope. But we do see, more clearly now than when the Declaration of Independence was signed, that if we cannot make that hope more true with every year of our lives, then we have failed, and the great design of our founding and our future is in doubt.

We have recently lived through a crisis in our government that Thomas Jefferson would not have believed possible. By the sheer weight and balance of the Constitution, by a kind of unmoving almost inarticulate slow working of the concept of what is true and what is not true, we have seen an attempt to take over the control of our government, not by force, but by guile and trickery, suddenly dissolve into dust. The mounting tale of the deceptions practiced on the nation, so that its acts were concealed and mishandled to the point of vast tragedy, shocked the whole people. The deceptions were revealed as so false, so shifting, so complex that when they became known, it was like the lifting of a dark cloud of apathy and ignorance. At other times in world history these deceptions would have been called treasons. The attempt failed, as an ill-woven cloak is unravelled by pulling a single thread. The Constitution worked. The principles of our government were not overthrown. We learned, as never so clearly before, that the principles in which we believe will work. Unprincipled men, singly or in groups, may still work to adopt the systems of the Republic for their own ends, but the judgment of the people is still the ultimate rule.

It is now two hundred years after the Declaration of Independence was signed by those men who well knew their own peril and the peril of immediate and overwhelming war to the infant republic only then being born. Facing the future which we, like them, have no way of knowing, not knowing how long or how well this nation will endure, we can do no better than to subscribe again as they did, to the pertinent sentences of the last great paragraph of the Declaration of Independence where the name of our country appears for the first time.

"We therefore, the representatives of the United States of America in General Congress assembled, appealing to the Supreme Judge of the World for the rectitude of our intentions do, in the name and by authority of the good People of these colonies, solemnly publish, that these United States, are, and of right ought to be, Free and Independent States. . . . And for the support of this Declaration, with a firm reliance on the protection of Divine Providence, we mutually pledge to each other our lives, our Fortunes and our sacred Honor."

—MARJORY STONEMAN DOUGLAS

"No point is of more importance than that the right of impeachment should be continued. Shall any man be above justice? Above all, should that man be above it who can commit the most injustice?"
—GEORGE MASON, 1787

"Control is the crux of our freedom. Without it, we are pushed from behind. With it we walk in the light." —JOHN DEWEY

EAGLE

179

GOVERNMENT

Old Capitol

Government

The United States of America was founded on the belief that the people could be trusted to govern themselves. The new country could become a reality only if its citizens accepted the rights and the responsibilities that would be required of them. The interest and participation of citizens in government was encouraged and was based on their right to know and their right to act.

Citizens in a representative government can use their rights and responsibilities only if they know and understand how their government works. Action and participation by the people of Florida in their government can assure that they and their descendants will in the future have a place in the sun.

HOW DOES FLORIDA GOVERNMENT WORK?

Government in the United States is organized as a republic, and operates through representatives elected by the people. A similar system of government exists at both the state and the federal level. The powers of Florida state government are separated into three branches, the executive, the legislative, and the judicial. This is similar to government on the national level, but the structure of Florida state government in several areas is unique in the United States.

WHO RUNS FLORIDA GOVERNMENT?

In most states the chief executive, the governor, has a cabinet which is appointed by him and helps him administer his duties and programs. This is similar to the national president and his cabinet. In Florida, however, a large part of state government is controlled by the State Cabinet, which is a group executive composed of the governor, the secretary of state, the attorney general, the treasurer, the comptroller, the commissioner of agriculture, and the commissioner of education. Cabinet members are all independently elected officials, and the Cabinet functions like a board of directors. All decisions are reached by majority vote, and several Cabinet members have independent authority.

The governor has direct control over the departments of commerce, health and rehabilitative services (prisons, public health, mental health, and welfare), community affairs and business regulation (land sales, alchoholic beverages, and parimutuel wagering). He has the power to fill vacancies in state and county offices or suspend any state or county officer for cause, subject to review by the Senate. The same power extends to municipal officers without review of the Senate. The governor may veto acts of the legislature subject to an overriding vote. He may call the legislature into special session and is commander-in-chief of the military forces of the state.

The heads of the departments directly under the control of the governor, along with the governor's senior executive assistant, have come to be known informally as the "Little Cabinet." The top aids to Cabinet officers meet in advance to review subjects scheduled for cabinet meetings, and are called the "mini-cabinet."

The governor and members of the Cabinet are elected to four-year terms in even numbered years between presidential elections. The governor may serve two terms; other Cabinet members may serve any number of terms. The lieutenant governor is elected on the same ticket with the governor and assumes the office of governor should it become vacant.

The secretary of state runs the public records office, regulates all elections, publishes rules and regulations of state agencies, charters corporations, records trademarks, contracts, commissions notaries public, licenses employment agencies and private detectives, registers all organizations and charities, handles library services through the State Library, oversees the Division of Archives, History and Records Management, and coordinates cultural activities.

The attorney general appears on behalf of the State in all suits in the courts of appeal in which the State is in any manner interested, heads the Department of Legal Affairs, and answers inquiries concerning law by most public agencies, state, county, district, city. The attorney general does not answer questions of law from private persons.

The comptroller is the "watchdog of the public treasury," heads the Department of Banking and Finance, serves as Commissioner of Banking, and approves county budgets as to form.

The treasurer is insurance commissioner and treasurer, serves as state fire marshal, enforces laws covering liquified petroleum gas, and administers the funds for retirement of policemen and firemen.

The commissioner of agriculture oversees eleven divisions: standards, marketing, dairy industry, fruit and vegetable inspection, animal industry, inspection, forestry, chemistry, plant industry, consumer services, and administration.

The commissioner of education supervises the entire system of public education in Florida, from the kindergarten through graduate school.

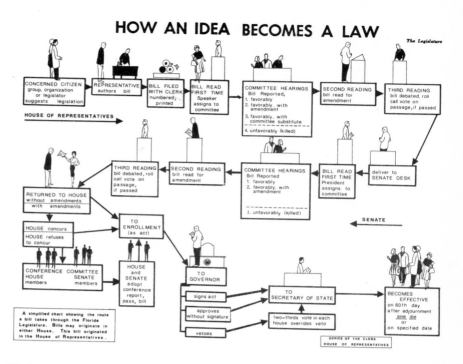

HOW AN IDEA BECOMES A LAW

The Legislature

HOUSE OF REPRESENTATIVES

CONCERNED CITIZEN group, organization or legislator suggests legislation

REPRESENTATIVE authors bill

BILL FILED WITH CLERK numbered; printed

BILL READ FIRST TIME Speaker assigns to committee

COMMITTEE HEARINGS Bill Reported,
1. favorably
2. favorably, with amendment
3. favorably, with committee substitute
4. unfavorably (killed)

SECOND READING bill read for amendment

THIRD READING bill debated, roll call vote on passage, if passed

THIRD READING bill debated, roll call vote on passage, if passed

SECOND READING bill read for amendment

COMMITTEE HEARINGS
1. favorably
2. favorably, with amendment
3. unfavorably (killed)

BILL READ FIRST TIME President assigns to committee

deliver to SENATE DESK

SENATE

RETURNED TO HOUSE without amendments with amendments

HOUSE concurs / HOUSE refuses to concur

TO ENROLLMENT (as act)

CONFERENCE COMMITTEE HOUSE members / SENATE members

HOUSE and SENATE adopt conference report, pass, bill

TO GOVERNOR — signs act / approves without signature / vetoes

TO SECRETARY OF STATE — two-thirds vote in each house overrides veto

BECOMES EFFECTIVE on 60th day after adjournment sine die or on specified date

A simplified chart showing the route a bill takes through the Florida Legislature. Bills may originate in either House. This bill originated in the House of Representatives.

OFFICE OF THE CLERK HOUSE OF REPRESENTATIVES

WHO REPRESENTS THE PEOPLE?

The state legislature is a two-house body composed of the Senate and the House of Representatives. It meets once a year for a minimum of 60 days and is apportioned on a one-man one-vote basis. Both houses of the legislature have equal power, and legislation on any subject may be introduced into either house. Half of the 40 members of the State Senate are elected every two years to a four-year term providing staggered terms. Senate districts are based on a population ratio of approximately 170,000 residents. The 120 members of the House of Representatives are elected to two-year terms during general elections in even numbered years. House districts represent approximately 55,000 residents. Two senators are elected to staggered six-year terms in the national Senate from Florida. Representatives from the districts are elected every two years to the national House of Representatives.

WHO ENFORCES THE LAWS?

After an idea becomes a law by vote of the Legislature and signature of the governor, it is up to public officers or regulatory commissions or boards to see that the law is observed. Violations of the law or arguments about the law are brought before the courts of the judicial branch. The judge or jury becomes the arbiter in the case to administer justice. State laws may not be passed by the Legislature which are contrary to federal law. Controversies over state or municipal laws are heard in these courts; controversies over federal law are heard in federal courts. The Supreme Court of the United States is the final court of appeal.

FROM WHERE DOES THE MONEY COME?

Most of the money needed to run the government of the state of Florida comes from taxes on things that people buy and use. These are called use taxes. Most of the money for county and city government comes from taxes on things people own, like land and buildings. These are called ad valorem taxes on real estate and tangible personal property. Money may be borrowed, through bonded indebtedness backed by tax revenues, by the state or by counties and cities for capital projects like roads, buildings, or land.

WHAT HAPPENS IN THE NEIGHBORHOOD?

Counties were created as administrative subdivisions of the state so that governmental matters could be handled on a decentralized basis. Cities are designed to provide additional services desired by the residents. Special districts are created for a single purpose, like area street lighting, and can cross municipal or county boundaries. As the state has become more urbanized counties have often assumed city responsibilities and the distinctions between these governmental divisions have become blurred. Charter counties are under the jurisdiction of the state legislature. Non-charter counties have the power of self-government.

THE COURTS OF FLORIDA

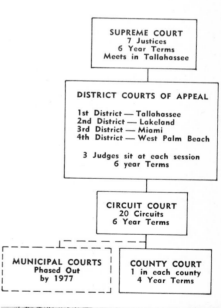

SUPREME COURT
7 Justices
6 Year Terms
Meets in Tallahassee

DISTRICT COURTS OF APPEAL
1st District — Tallahassee
2nd District — Lakeland
3rd District — Miami
4th District — West Palm Beach

3 Judges sit at each session
6 year Terms

CIRCUIT COURT
20 Circuits
6 Year Terms

MUNICIPAL COURTS
Phased Out
by 1977

COUNTY COURT
1 in each county
4 Year Terms

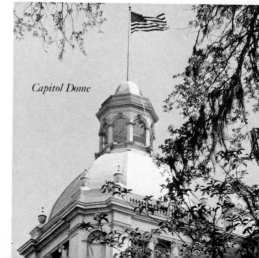

Capitol Dome

Young Tallahassee residents hitch a ride aboard a column headed for the new Governor's Mansion.

Old engraving of Tallahassee vista

TALLAHASSEE

Who Takes Consumer Complaints?

DEPARTMENT OF AGRICULTURE AND CONSUMER SERVICES, Division of Consumer Services, Mayo Building, Tallahassee, 32304. 904-488-2221; Toll-free: 800-342-2176.

DEPARTMENT OF BUSINESS REGULATION, Carlton Building, Tallahassee, 32304. 904-488-2645.

DEPARTMENT OF COMMERCE, Caldwell Building, Tallahassee, 32304. 904-488-3104.

DEPARTMENT OF COMMUNITY AFFAIRS, 2571 Executive Center Circle East, Tallahassee, 32301. 904-488-8466.

COMPTROLLER, Department of Banking and Finance, Carlton Building, Tallahassee, 32304. 904-488-5275; Toll-free: 800-342-3557.

DEPARTMENT OF EDUCATION, Knott Building, Tallahassee, 32304. 904-488-3115.

DEPARTMENT OF HEALTH AND REHABILITATIVE SERVICES, 1323 Winewood Blvd., Tallahassee, 32304. 904-488-7721.

DEPARTMENT OF HIGHWAY SAFETY AND MOTOR VEHICLES, Neil Kirkman Building, Appalachee Parkway, Tallahassee, 32304. 904-488-2276.

DEPARTMENT OF INSURANCE, Larson Building, Tallahassee, 32304. 904-488-5314.

DEPARTMENT OF LEGAL AFFAIRS, FAIR TRADE PRACTICES DIVISION, Bloxham Building, Tallahassee, 32304. 904-488-4481.

DEPARTMENT OF NATURAL RESOURCES, Larson Building, Tallahassee, 32304. 904-488-7150.

DEPARTMENT OF POLLUTION CONTROL, 2562 Executive Center Circle East, Montgomery Building, Tallahassee, 32304. 904-488-4807.

DEPARTMENT OF PROFESSIONAL AND OCCUPATIONAL REGULATIONS, Suite 820, 315 Calhoun St., Tallahassee, 32302. 904-488-6602.

PUBLIC SERVICE COMMISSION, 700 S. Adams St., Tallahassee, 32304. 904-488-7238; Toll-free: 800-342-3552.

DEPARTMENT OF REVENUE, 104 Carlton Building, Tallahassee, 32304. 904-488-3052.

DEPARTMENT OF STATE, The Capitol, Tallahassee, 32304. 904-488-7735.

DEPARTMENT OF TRANSPORTATION, Burns Building, Tallahassee, 32304. 904-488-8772.

State Symbols

State Seal: "of the size of the American silver dollar having in the center thereof a view of the sun's rays over a highland in the distance, a cocoa tree, a steamboat on water, and an Indian female scattering flowers in the foreground, encircled by the words, 'Great Seal of the State of Florida: In God We Trust.'"

State Flag: the state seal centered over red diagonals on a white background.

State Tree: the Sabal Palm.

State Flower: the orange blossom.

State Song: "Old Folks at Home."

State Shell: the horse conch or *Pleuroplaca giganta.*.

State Nickname: "Sunshine State."

State Gem: moonstone.

State Bird: mockingbird

State Beverage: orange juice.

State Theatre: the Asolo Theatre, Sarasota.

State Fish: fresh water: the largemouth bass; salt water: the Atlantic sailfish.

State Symphony and Opera: Florida State University School of Music.

State Day: Pascua Florida Week (March 27–*April* 2).

Poet Laureate: Mrs. Vivian Laramore Rader.

State Play: "Cross and Sword" by Paul Green.

The Grove, Tallahassee

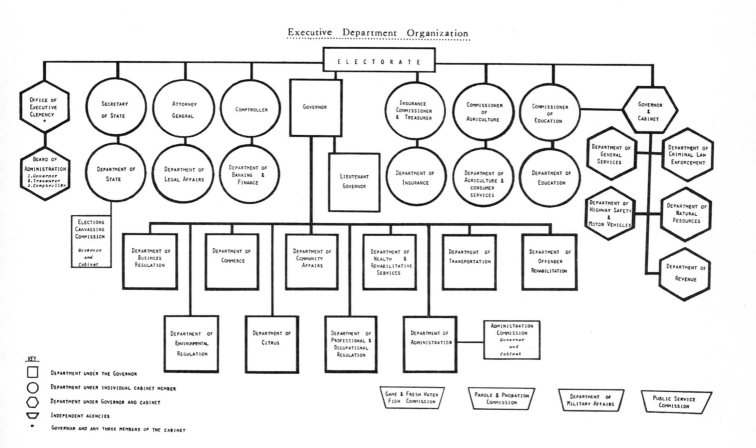

Executive Department Organization

ELECTORATE

OFFICE OF EXECUTIVE CLEMENCY •

BOARD OF ADMINISTRATION
1. Governor
2. Treasurer
3. Comptroller

SECRETARY OF STATE

ATTORNEY GENERAL

COMPTROLLER

GOVERNOR

INSURANCE COMMISSIONER & TREASURER

COMMISSIONER OF AGRICULTURE

COMMISSIONER OF EDUCATION

GOVERNOR & CABINET

DEPARTMENT OF STATE

DEPARTMENT OF LEGAL AFFAIRS

DEPARTMENT OF BANKING & FINANCE

LIEUTENANT GOVERNOR

DEPARTMENT OF INSURANCE

DEPARTMENT OF AGRICULTURE & CONSUMER SERVICES

DEPARTMENT OF EDUCATION

DEPARTMENT OF GENERAL SERVICES

DEPARTMENT OF CRIMINAL LAW ENFORCEMENT

DEPARTMENT OF HIGHWAY SAFETY & MOTOR VEHICLES

DEPARTMENT OF NATURAL RESOURCES

ELECTIONS CANVASSING COMMISSION
Governor and Cabinet

DEPARTMENT OF BUSINESS REGULATION

DEPARTMENT OF COMMERCE

DEPARTMENT OF COMMUNITY AFFAIRS

DEPARTMENT OF HEALTH & REHABILITATIVE SERVICES

DEPARTMENT OF TRANSPORTATION

DEPARTMENT OF OFFENDER REHABILITATION

DEPARTMENT OF REVENUE

DEPARTMENT OF ENVIRONMENTAL REGULATION

DEPARTMENT OF CITRUS

DEPARTMENT OF PROFESSIONAL & OCCUPATIONAL REGULATION

DEPARTMENT OF ADMINISTRATION

ADMINISTRATION COMMISSION
Governor and Cabinet

GAME & FRESH WATER FISH COMMISSION

PAROLE & PROBATION COMMISSION

DEPARTMENT OF MILITARY AFFAIRS

PUBLIC SERVICE COMMISSION

KEY

☐ DEPARTMENT UNDER THE GOVERNOR

◯ DEPARTMENT UNDER INDIVIDUAL CABINET MEMBER

⬡ DEPARTMENT UNDER GOVERNOR AND CABINET

▽ INDEPENDENT AGENCIES

• GOVERNOR AND ANY THREE MEMBERS OF THE CABINET

BARBER'S HOUSE AT THE FORD ON BIG CREEK, COLONEL BARTON'S HEADQUARTERS.

HISTORIC MARKERS

Alachua County.
   County Seat: Gainesville
Alachua County Courthouse
City of Gainesville
Dickison and His Men;
   Jefferson Davis' Baggage
East Florida Seminary
First Gainesville Skirmish;
   Battle of Gainesville
Newnansville
Spanish Cattle Ranching
William Bartram (1739–1823)
Baker County.
   County Seat: Macclenny
Camp at Sanderson
Bay County.
   County Seat: Panama City
Confederate Salt Works
Panama City Airport
St. Andrews Bay Skirmish
Bradford County.
   County Seat: Starke
Captain Richard G. Bradford
Broward County.
   County Seat: Fort Lauderdale
Calhoun County.
   County Seat: Blountstown
Blunt Reservation and Fields
Charlotte County.
   County Seat: Punta Gorda
Albert Waller Gilchrist
City of Punta Gorda
Ponce de León at Charlotte Harbor
Southernmost Railroad Terminal
Citrus County.
   County Seat: Inverness
Cottonwood
Clay County.
   County Seat: Green Cove Springs
Fort Heilman
Fort St. Francis de Pupa
Collier County.
   County Seat: East Naples
Big Cypress Swamp
Naples Pier
Sunniland Oil Field

Columbia County.
   County Seat: Lake City
Alligator
Town of Leno
Dade County.
   County Seat: Miami
Cape Florida Lighthouse
Tuttle Home
DeSoto County.
   County Seat: Arcadia
DeSoto County
Dixie County.
   County Seat: Cross City
Old Town
Duval County.
   County Seat: Jacksonville
Church of Our Savior (Episcopal)
Duval County's First Court
Harriet Beecher Stowe Home
The Huguenot Memorial Site
Site of Cow Ford
Site of the Mission of
   San Juan del Puerto
The Beginning
Escambia County.
   County Seat: Pensacola
Alger Railroad, Century, Florida
Cannons of Ft. Pickens
Captain Richard G. Bradford
Christ Church
Indian Village Site (ES-2)
Indian Village Site (ES-5)
Pensacola Navy Yard Established in 1825
Flager County.
   County Seat: Bunnell
King's Road
Washington Oaks Gardens
Franklin County.
   County Seat: Apalachicola
Chestnut Street Cemetery
   of Early Apalachicola
Fort Gadsden
Franklin County
Trinity Episcopal Church
When the River was King!

Gadsden County.
   County Seat: Quincy
Rocky Comfort Plantation
The Quincy State Bank
United States Arsenal (1832–1861)
Gilchrist County.
   County Seat: Trenton
Glades County.
   County Seat: Moore Haven
Gulf County.
   County Seat: Port St. Joe
Florida's First Railroad
Fort Crevecour;
   Fort Crevecour Abandoned
Fort Place—St. Joseph & Iola
   Railroad
Old St. Joseph Cemetery
St. Joseph Cemetery
St. Joseph Confederate Saltworks
Shipyard Cove
Hamilton County.
   County Seat: Jasper
White Springs
Hardee County.
   County Seat: Wauchula
Hendry County.
   County Seat: LaBelle
Hernando County.
   County Seat: Brooksville
Hernando County
Highlands County.
   County Seat: Sebring
Fort Basinger
Hillsborough County.
   County Seat: Tampa
Celi's Exploration and Survey:
   Hillsborough River—April 24–27, 1757
Founding of the Cigar Industry in Tampa
Tampa as Port of Embarkation:
   Spanish-American War
Tampa Bay Hotel
Holmes County.
   County Seat: Bonifay
Holmes County
Indian River County.
   County Seat: Vero Beach
Sebastian
Jackson County.
   County Seat: Marianna
Battle of Marianna
Sylvania Plantation
Jefferson County.
   County Seat: Monticello
Monticello Cotton Mill
Site of the Pensacola-St. Augustine Road
LaFayette County.
   County Seat: Mayo
Lake County.
   County Seat: Tavares
Fort Butler
Lee County.
   County Seat: Fort Myers
Billy Bowlegs
Fort Myers

LEGAL HOLIDAYS IN FLORIDA

New Year's Day: January 1.
Robert E. Lee's Birthday: January 19.
George Washington's Birthday: third Monday in February.
Shrove Tuesday or Mardi Gras (in counties where carnival associations are organized for the purpose of celebrating this day).
Good Friday.
Confederate Memorial Day: April 26.
Memorial Day for Veterans of all Wars: last Monday in May.
Jefferson Davis' Birthday: June 3.
Independence Day: July 4.
Labor Day: first Monday in September.
Columbus Day-Farmers' Day: second Monday in October.
General Election Day: first Tuesday after first Monday in November of even-numbered years.
Veterans' Day: fourth Monday in October.
Thanksgiving Day: fourth Thursday in November.
Christmas Day: December 25.
All Sundays.
Gasparilla Day: Hillsborough County.
DeSoto Day: Manatee County.
Parade Day: Hillsborough County; designated day of the Hillsborough County Fair and Plant City Strawberry Festival.

CEREMONIAL DAYS

Arbor Day: third Friday in January.
Pascua Florida (or State) Day: April 2.
Pascua Florida Week: March 27–April 2.
Pan American Day: April 14.
Grandmother's Day: second Sunday in October.

BICENTENNIAL COMMISSION OF FLORIDA

STATUTORY MEMBERS

The Honorable Reubin O'D. Askew
Governor
Tallahassee, Florida

The Honorable J. H. Williams
Lieutenant Governor
Tallahassee, Florida

The Honorable Bruce A. Smathers
Secretary of State
Tallahassee, Florida

The Honorable Ralph D. Turlington
Commissioner of Education
Tallahassee, Florida

The Honorable Robert Williams
Director, Division of Archives,
  History, and Records Management
Tallahassee, Florida

Mr. James J. Gardener
Fort Lauderdale, Florida

Mr. Ney C. Landrum, Director
Division of Recreation and Parks
Tallahassee, Florida

The Honorable Edward J. Trombetta
Secretary of Commerce
Tallahassee, Florida

STATE SENATORS

The Honorable Jim Glisson
Tavares, Florida

The Honorable Mattox Hair
Jacksonville, Florida

The Honorable Richard R. Renick
Coral Gables, Florida

The Honorable Alan Trask
Fort Meade, Florida

The Honorable Lori Wilson
Merritt Island, Florida

Executive Director:
  Mr. William R. Adams
  Tallahassee, Florida

PUBLIC MEMBERS

Dr. Johnnie Ruth Clarke
St. Petersburg Jr. College
St. Petersburg, Florida

Mrs. Raymond Mason
Jacksonville, Florida

Mr. Carl C. Mertins, President
Barnett Bank of Pensacola
Pensacola, Florida

Dr. Charles E. Perry, President
Florida International University
Miami, Florida

General W.E. Potter
Walt Disney World
Orlando, Florida

Professor F. Blair Reeves
Department of Architecture
University of Florida
Gainesville, Florida

Mr. George E. Saunders
Orlando, Florida

Mr. Don Shoemaker, Editor
The Miami Herald
Miami, Florida

Mr. Harold W. Stayman, Jr.
Executive Vice President
Palm Beach County Economic Council
West Palm Beach, Florida

Mrs. Robert L. Shevin
Tallahassee, Florida

STATE REPRESENTATIVES

The Honorable Dick J. Batchelor
Orlando, Florida

The Honorable A. H. "Gus" Craig
St. Augustine, Florida

The Honorable Thomas L. Hazouri
Jacksonville, FLorida

The Honorable Jane W. Robinson
Cocoa, Florida

The Honorable Mary L. Singleton
Jacksonville, Florida

King George III Pays Loyalists

By the treaty of peace concluded at Paris in 1763, East Florida was ceded to Great Britain as an equivalent for the island of Cuba. In consequences of this cession many British subjects settled there, obtained grants of land and cultivated estates. During, the troubles in North America prior to the Declaration of Independence by the United States of America, East Florida remained faithful to the English Crown. In 1776 the people rejected the invitation to join in the great confederation, raised a militia and repulsed the Georgians in 1777, and East Florida became a rallying point and refuge for loyalists, from the revolted provinces. In 1780 a legislature was formed, which, granted in perpetuity to the Crown of England an irrevocable duty of 2½ percent on certain imports.

By the 5th article of the Treaty of Peace concluded at Versailles, 1783, this colony was delivered up to the King of Spain. A commission was constituted and two commissioners were appointed to inquire into the respective losses of the sufferers by the cession of the above province. A time was limited for the reception of claims, viz.: in the Bahamas, where many East Floridians had taken refuge, March 1, 1787, and in Great Britain, January 1, 1787. A further act was passed entitled "an Act for giving relief to such persons as have suffered in their rights and properties during the late unhappy dissensions in America in consequence of their loyalty to the British government and for making compensation to such persons as have suffered in their properties is consequence of the cession of East Florida to the King of Spain." By the second section of this act the East Florida Commissioners were required to make report to the Treasury, prior to January 1, 1789 and by the third section the Lords of the Treasury were empowered to make provisions for payment to claiments entitled to compensations."

In the British Colonial Office eight reports, 1787–1789, from Col. Nisbet Balfour and John Spranger Esq., Commissioners on East Florida Claims, record the number of claims as 369, the total amount claimed L647,405 6s. 9d, and the amount actually allowed, L169,818 18s. 5½d.

–Guide to the materials for American History to 1783. In the Public Record Office of Great Britain. Vol. I, The State Paper, Charles M. Andrews.

At the Council Chamber Whitehall
The 21st of May 1764
By the Right Honourable the Lords of the Committee of Council for Plantation Affairs

His Majesty having been pleased by His Order in Council of the 10th of this Instant to refer unto this Committee a Representation from the Lords Commissioners for Trade and Plantations, proposing that an Instruction should be given to the Governor of the Province of East Florida to restrain him from granting to any person whatever, without His Majestys' particular Orders and directions, those parts of the Coast of the said Province frequented by the Animals called the Manati or Sea Cow, where they have their Shores or Landing Places. The Lords of the Committee this day took the said Representation into their consideration, and agreeing in Opinion with what is proposed by the said Lords Commission for Trade and Plantations, do therefore hereby order that the said Lords Commissioners do prepare a Draught of an Instruction conformable to what is proposed by the said Representation and lay the same before this Committee.

Public Record Office, London.

In the early days, some families moved to seaside cottages along the Atlantic or the Gulf believing the clean salt air acted as a disinfectant against disease.

"Our neighbor to the north, who had built a pretentious sea wall, upbraided me one day for not building one too, and was unable to understand what I could see that was beautiful in our tiny beach. I had not the language with which to fend off his torrent of words, but later the argument was given me by that grand old landscape gardener John McLaren, the builder of the Golden Gate Park in San Francisco. Said he: 'The most beautiful sound I know is the lapping of the waves on the shore. Build a sea wall and you have stopped the music forever.'"

—DAVID FAIRCHILD

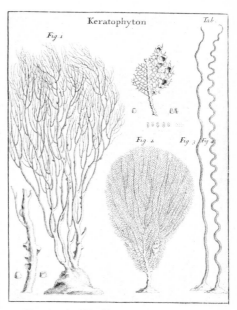

Keratophyton

Research Challenges

Advances in science, including medicine and nutrition as well as cosmetics, have often been stimulated by the accessibility of special Florida products from land and sea. Climatic and geologic conditions offer researchers rich and diversified land and marine harvests including those from citrus, palms, aloes, sea fans, seaweed. A surprising number of unexpected creatures are being used in studies and products.

A Salubrious Climate

When he first settled in Fort Myers, Thomas Edison was 38 years old, a widower with three children, in such poor health that his physician told him to settle in a tropical climate or risk death within a year. The Florida sunshine was just what the doctor ordered; Edison lived to the age of 84.

—G.L.

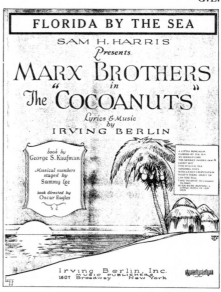

Wild Turkey takes wing as it is flushed from undergrowth by hunters. Common in North America when the European colonists arrived, turkey is a traditional food for American feast days and has been domesticated for food production. The Wild Turkey is now extinct in nearly half of the states where it once flourished but still is at home in Florida woodlands. Benjamin Franklin wanted the Wild Turkey to be the national emblem, but it lost out in that competition to the Bald Eagle.

Florida Feast

Colonial recipes compiled for the Bicentennial by the Florida Department of Agriculture include Florida game and products harvested by the month. The November menu is appropriate for the great American feast day, Thanksgiving, first celebrated in America in 1564 by the Huguenots in Florida. Menu calls for stuffing the traditional bird in a typically Florida fashion.

Haunch of Venison	Roast Pork
Roasted Turkey with	
Johnnycake Stuffing	
Baked Acorn Squash	
Scalloped Potatoes	
Cauliflower	Celery Sticks
Pumpkin Pie	Pecan Pie
Plum Pudding	Spicy Carrot Cake
Hot Spiced Cider	

Newcomers to Florida may need this Old Florida recipe for Johnnycake:

1 cup sifted all purpose flour
¼ cup sugar
1 teaspoon baking powder
¾ teaspoon salt
½ teaspoon baking soda
1 cup corn meal
1 egg, well beaten
1 cup buttermilk
2 Tablespoons butter, melted
2 Tablespoons molasses

Sift first five ingredients together in a bowl; stir in corn meal. Make a well in center of mixture. Mix together last 4 ingredients, and add to dry ingredients. Beat with electric or rotary beater until just smooth (do not over beat). Pour batter into greased 8-inch square pan, and spread to corners. Bake at 425°F for about 20 minutes, or until bread shrinks from sides of pan and is light brown on top. Use crumbled in Johnnycake stuffing.

The white mangrove honey is held to be a gourmet's delight better known to aficianados a century ago than now. There is a venerable tradition among discriminating beekeepers, and honey lovers, in Florida where the industry is burgeoning today: From special exotic and indigenous trees like Tupelo in the north of Florida and mangrove in the south the bees make honeys with special flavors. Those who believe in the digestive, medicinal and cosmetic magics of honey are seeking it as another kind of Florida gold: nectar for the gods, it once was called.

Cane Syrup
The Sweetener of the Past

It's used today for watering pigs. That old broad brimmed iron kettle of the syrup maker may not even be recognized for what it was. The cane crusher lies, as it has for fifteen years, in the weeds where it slowly rusts, unneeded, unwanted and maybe forgotten.

Time was when the farmers of Old Florida depended upon their patch of cane and the kettle and the crusher which converted a crop to what might have been their sole source of sweetener and something for sale besides. For some honey might have augmented syrup and, upon occasion, "store boughten" sugar. But the patch of cane, of whatever variety the farmer judged best for his soil and taste, was a part of almost every "Cracker" farm. Today there are few who carry on in this tradition of the past. Others relive a cherished part of that past through the syrup they may purchase—with considerable difficulty—or better yet, in socializing at the syrup making of a friend.

The cane, carefully cut and trimmed to provide the most desired balance of sugar and glucose, was crushed in an upright roller "mill," typically mule or, less often, horse powered. Hitched to a long pole sweep, around and around went the mule while cane stalks were fed, one by one. This was work for which many a boy was assigned. Crushing time brought friends and neighbors, however, so the work was rotated with everyone enjoying participating.

The juice, after filtering, went to the open kettle which held sixty or eighty gallons. The more efficient evaporater was rare. A wood fire, closely tended, supplied heat to boil off excess water. Skimming was continuous and carefully done. Judgment gained from long experience provided the syrup maker with the time to draw the fire and remove the syrup. The rich, golden syrup went into glass bottles, perhaps cans as well, to be used at home, given to friends or sold. The amounts made today in the few typical operations average thirty to forty gallons. This probably represents what would have been produced by an Old Florida farmer.

A patch of cane, maybe a quarter acre in extent, is the obvious clue today to this industry so largely of the past. That patch tells of a crusher and a kettle nearby. Look again around November —if in North and Central Florida—for the activities of syrup making. They are scarcer each passing year and may soon be gone leaving only the kettles and the crusher to attest to their having ever been a part of the Florida scene.

—CLARK I. CROSS

Grits, Greens and Gravy: Cracker Cooking

Food preferences are hard to change and the Florida Cracker diet with its few items in almost daily use has been strongly held. This is not surprising because those items could be tasty, nourishing, and acceptable by the stomach even if appearing on the table at almost every meal.

Grits are Cracker fare. So are collard greens. The prominence given cornmeal is another dietary clue to the Cracker region. Poverty and isolation may have conspired to give a significant place in the local diet to lesser known foods as well.

Heart of palm is one example. Usually prepared as a vegetable, sometimes in a salad, it was a gift of the wetlands. If relatively unknown now, this is due to the removal of the terminal bud—heart of palm—which kills the tree and their conservation dictates a policy of limited production.

The gopher turtle, really a land tortoise, contributed to the table, too, usually in a stew. The gopher frequented the higher, better drained, sandy uplands, whereas the soft shelled turtles were provided by the swamps and open bodies of water. Guinea fowls, those half wild imports from Africa, were noisy but needed little care and were well suited to the Cracker economy. The chickens of virtually every household tended towards toughness but were fine with rice, a pilau ("per-loo" to the Crackers) that could stretch a chicken to satisfy a large family. Still, rice was "store boughten" food and less common than supposed. Actually fresh home ground cornmeal, for cornbread, corn pone or corn cakes, was their staff of life. And, well it might have been for covered with gravy, syrup, honey or jam, eaten alone or with greens, those products of corn are superb fare for the hungry.

The early visitor to the Cracker Florida of not long ago frequently complained of the food. Time was when the cook worked over a fireplace fire, for few possessed a stove. Little wonder then that the cornbread was not always thoroughly baked or maybe burnt. Little wonder, too, that the meal was simple and lacked variety. Even when stoves became common, Crackers had little money, few stores, no refrigerators, or electricity, too, for that matter, nor did they possess a sophisticated appetite that demanded the setting of a complicated table.

One traveler in the 1870s wrote that tough bacon was the only meat, except for game, and that was served for every meal. This was accompanied by grits, the finely ground hominy of the South, covered with gravy. This, he complained, was the only food procurable or thought necessary. Another reported of sweet potatoes, baked and fried in slices, yellow cornbread, fat pork and muddy coffee. He complained but the Crackers thought it fine.

If you had come back later, traveler, you would have observed a more productive farm. There would have been oranges and, maybe, bananas in the warmer south, pecans, peaches and hard pears where frost struck harder. The cane patch for syrup and the garden helped to improve the culinary selection. In that garden collards were widely found in Northern Florida because they could be harvested in winter but also because they were well liked.

Despite the availability of new items, greens, grits and gravy with cornbread, cane syrup and fat pork—or bacon—made up most of the Cracker diet. They are prominent today in many homes of the area where they appear by choice.

—CLARK I. CROSS

"The old house sat in the mossy trees, refusing to lease to ghosts. It was far from dead, not even dying; merely waiting for somebody to come.

"A shutter slapped and a hinge snapped and the wind blew all around easily. Florida stretched out like a puddled prairie, a thumb of palmettoed sand in patient seas.

"The edges of Florida were bright-lighted and frantic but the interior was the soft dark blue, down south."

—JOHN KEASLER
Surrounded on Three Sides

In many old areas of Florida, the weather-worn sidings of old buildings speak of another era. More stately homes like this one in Micanopy are being restored as Floridians attempt to preserve their heritage.

ACKNOWLEDGEMENTS AND OTHER NOTES

The book is designed by Joan Blank and the Editors who thank Ted Winters for mechanical production. The book is set in Janson, a 17th century typeface with display type in Friz Quadrata. For preliminary concept conversations, the editors especially thank the Honorable LeRoy Collins, Marjory Stoneman Douglas, and Hugh L. Popenoe, Maxine Alspach, and Bruce Alspach. The members of Robert W. Williams' staff in the Division of Archives, History and Records Management, Florida Department of State, especially Thomas Baker, James Macbeth, Jerry Butterfield, Barbara Fisher, and Ross Morrell were extremely helpful. Special thanks for the continued support of Joan Morris, who has been generous with her time and pictures at the State Photographic Archives at Strozier Library, Florida State University. We appreciate the interest of Dr. William Sturtevant and those at the Smithsonian Institution who opened archives for Florida related art, especially Paula Richardson in the National Museum of Natural History. We acknowledge the generous use of books from the collection of Harvey Blank. We thank three photographers who have been particularly generous with their Florida collections: Paul Barton, Franke Keating, Therold Lindquist. Thanks also to S. David Webb at the Florida State Museum; Paul Eugen Camp at the Florida State Historical Society; Randolph Nimicht at the Historical Society of Southern Florida. To those in the Public Record Office in London, England, we express our appreciation, and to Dale Williams of the University College of Wales; also to Milton Kaplan and others at the Library of Congress, to John Griffen in St. Augustine, and to Angela Regas. Grateful thanks are given to Pat Gissing, assistant *par excellance*. We want those whose names might have been omitted inadvertently from this list to know their assistance was deeply appreciated. *Born of the Sun* is the result of a cooperative effort that has involved numerous people throughout Florida and far beyond. And finally, thanks are overdue to the publisher, Hal Herman, for his strength and enthusiasm, and without whom this book would not have been possible.

PUBLISHER'S ACKNOWLEDGEMENT

The publisher gratefully acknowledges the encouragement and cooperation of the following persons: the late Pat Dodson, Shelton Kemp, Bruce McDonald, Charles Nichols, Don Pride, Dr. Samuel Proctor, Hal Stayman, Jr., Gene A. Whiddon.

CREDITS

Title, page 7, back cover poem: Copyright 1934 and renewed 1962 by Stephen Spender. Reprinted from *Selected Poems*, by Stephen Spender, by permission of Random House, Inc.
American Banknote Company, 29, 30, 52, 54, 60, 103, 176, 177, 178. Paul Barton, 9, 13, 28, 50, 71, 79, 126, 130, 131, 137, 138, 141, 145, 150, 153. William Bartram, 91, 111. Sean Bollar, 87. Joan Blank Collection, 10, 103, 110, 139, 188. H. Kelly Brooks, 82, 84. Mark Catesby, 9, 111, 179. Century Magazine, 118. Cleveland Museum of Art, 95. Lawrence Donovan, reprinted by permission of Metropolitan Dade County Government, endplates, 90, 93, 108. Herbert J. Doherty, Jr. Collection, 120. Bob Dunn, 152. James Elmore, 65, 66, 129. El Prado Museum, 19. M.C. Escher, courtesy of the Haags Gemeente Museum, Escher Foundation, 15. Florida Department of State, Division of Archives, History, and Record Management, 33, 35, 36, 37, 39, 44, 45, 60, 61, 96, 107, 187. Florida Fruit and Vegetable Association, 134. Florida Medical Journal, 130, 131. Florida State Museum, 10, 34, 35, 46, 47, 84, 85. Florida State Photographic Archives, Florida State University, Strozier Library, 21, 24, 30, 48, 49, 50, 51, 54, 55, 56, 57, 58, 59, 62, 63, 64, 65, 66, 71, 74, 75, 97, 98, 114, 115, 119, 120, 124, 125, 127, 137, 159, 168, 169, 180, 182, 189. Florida State Historical Society, 18, 20, 109. Florida State University, 52, 100, 101. Fred Folger, 91, 93, 138, 139. Harley L. Freeman Collection, 22. Donald C. Gaby Collection, 102. Robin D. Gill, 38. Kent Hagerman, courtesy Pat Gissing Collection, 90, 122, 123, 174, 186. E. Ashby Hammond Collection, 166, 167, 168. Historical Society of Southern Florida, 64, 116, 117. James Hutchinson, the Collection of Paintings on the Seminole Indians of Florida, Courtesy University of Miami, 69, 70, 148, 160. Franke Keating, 76, 77, 86, 88, 92, 96, 134. Key West Public Library, 158. Nina Leen, 9. George Leposky, 149. Eugene Lyon Collection, 107. Library of Congress, 11, 16, 22, 23, 29, 30, 31, 40, 41, 47, 49, 53, 55, 57, 58, 59, 68, 72, 73, 88, 89, 99, 114, 115, 128, 159, 161, 179. Therold Lindquist, 7, 8, 18, 19, 23, 26, 67, 74, 96, 117, 146, 147, 150, 151, 153, 159, 160. National Aeronautics and Space Administration, 8, 78, 83, 85, 136. National Geographic Society, 81. National Portrait Gallery, 17, 177. National Oceanic and Atmospheric Administration, 104, 105, 106. Allen Morris Collection, 181, 183. Museum of the American Indian, 32. New York Public Library, 188. Pioneer Park Museum, 132, 133. George E. Pozzetta Collection, 136. Burt E. Pringle, 14, 113. Public Record Office, London, England, 14, 26, 96, 152, 166. Paul Revere, engraved for Royal American Magazine, Vol. I, 12, 17. Al Satterwhite, 31, 191. Flip Schulke, 82, 83, Patrick and Mary Ann Sebrey, 187. Russ Smiley, 140. Smithsonian Institution, 6, 10, 25, 31, 42, 71, 73, 87, 140, 142, 143. William Straight Collection, 164, 165. Tallahassee Chamber of Commerce, 181, 185. Helen Hornbeck Tanner, 18. University of Miami Press, 44, 46, 175. University of Florida Press, 20. Wolfson Family Foundation, 11, 94, 144, 145, 154, 155, 156, 157, 186.

AUTHORS IN ORDER OF THEIR APPEARANCE.

MELVILLE BELL GROSVENOR, who introduces *Born of the Sun* and its subject to the reader, is editor-in-chief and Chairman of the Board of the National Geographic Society, and has roots deep in the Florida experience.

J. LEITCH WRIGHT, professor of history at Florida State University and a specialist in the history of the Spanish colonial period, has written a sketch of Florida in 1776 for Bicentennial readers.

HELEN HORNBECK TANNER, scholarly authority on eighteenth century East Florida, describes in detail the City of St. Augustine of that era as its residents celebrated a new Spanish king.

JERALD T. MILANICH, assistant curator of the Florida State Museum and assistant professor of anthropology at the University of Florida, details the decline and almost disappearance of native Americans from the land of the sun.

MARJORY STONEMAN DOUGLAS, a distinguished and widely published author, is internationally known for her perceptive writing. She is a historian and author of innumerable works on Florida and brings a unique eye and pen to this Bicentennial book.

WILLIAM C. STURTEVANT, authority on Indian matters and anthropologist of note at the National Museum of Natural History, Smithsonian Institution, writes about an old Florida settlement newly discovered and described in the archives in Seville, Spain.

FRANK G. SLAUGHTER,
best-selling author of more than fifty popular historical novels, has a statement about freedom of thought and speech that has particular relevance for Floridians when viewed in the light of Florida history.

WILLIAM H. SEARS,
professor of anthropology at Florida Atlantic University, tells about the science of discovering the past before the time of written history, and what is known of the lives of the first Floridians.

NIXON SMILEY,
widely-known author and folklorist, reporter and columnist, brings to life romantic personalities with Florida connections.

PETER KLINGMAN,
a professor of history at Daytona Beach Community College, traces the flux of politics and politicians from territorial times to the present.

JERRELL H. SHOFNER,
chairman of the department of history at Florida Technological University, explores a particularly emotional and significant period in Florida history as he describes the aftermath of the Civil War.

H. KELLY BROOKS,
professor of geology at the University of Florida, is active in coastal management programs and tells of the ways in which the land of Florida evolved over eons of time.

ARCHIE CARR,
internationally acclaimed naturalist and professor of zoology at the University of Florida, has authored numerous wildlife books and here takes a look at the past and future for Florida wildlife.

DONALD C. GABY,
manager of the satellite Field Service Station of the National Oceanic and Atmospheric Administration, is a long time Florida history buff and takes a space age view of the Florida heritage.

WILLIAM N. THURSTON,
author, economist and specialist in early transportation systems, details the not so royal roads of colonial Florida.

HERBERT J. DOHERTY,
professor of history and chairman of social sciences at the University of Florida, is a former editor of the *Florida Historical Quarterly* and past president of the Florida Historical Society. A native Floridian, he details the difficulties and triumphs of transportation as the Florida frontier was challenged.

FREDRIC BLAKEY,
assistant professor of social sciences and history at the University of Florida, traces the history and impact of timber and phosphate in Florida.

CLARK I. CROSS,
associate professor and acting chairman of the department of geography at the University of Florida, reads history in a special manner for readers of *Born of the Sun.*

JANOS Z. SHOEMYEN,
author and member of the editorial department of the Institute of Food and Agricultural Sciences at the University of Florida, takes a look at the role of citrus and cattle in the Florida story.

HARRY A. KERSEY, JR.,
a professor in the foundations department at Florida Atlantic University, recounts the days when trade with the Seminoles of South Florida brought high fashion to the cosmopolitan centers of the world.

HOWARD T. ODUM,
professor of environmental sciences at the University of Florida is well-known for new ways of looking at the energy problem and with a co-author, Sandra Brown, puts this view in a historical perspective for a Bicentennial look into the past and the future.

MICHAEL V. GANNON,
professor of religion and history at the University of Florida and recognized by the Spanish government for research in the field of Spanish-Florida history, reviews the development of religious institutions in Florida.

WILLIAM M. STRAIGHT,
physician and medical archivist, recounts the physical difficulties of life in colonial Florida and how the early settlers learned to live with the land.

E. ASHBY HAMMOND,
professor of history and the social sciences at Florida State University and a distinguished scholar in medieval medical history, reviews the role of physicians in the Florida territorial days.

GEORGE E. POZZETTA,
assistant professor of social sciences and history at the University of Florida, recounts the colorful counterpoint of the various distinctive ethnic groups that are encountered throughout Florida history.

CHARLTON W. TEBEAU,
dean of Florida historians and editor of *Tequesta,* professor emeritus and chief archivist of the University of Miami and author of the best selling *History of Florida,* serves as validating historian for *Born of the Sun.*